DEFENDING THE SOCIETY OF STATES

Defending the Society of States

Why America Opposes the International Criminal Court and its Vision of World Society

JASON RALPH

UNIVERSITY PRESS

OXFORD

UNIVERSITY PRESS

Great Clarendon Street, Oxford ox2 6DP

Oxford University Press is a department of the University of Oxford.
It furthers the University's objective of excellence in research, scholarship,
and education by publishing worldwide in

Oxford New York

Auckland Cape Town Dar es Salaam Hong Kong Karachi
Kuala Lumpur Madrid Melbourne Mexico City Nairobi
New Delhi Shanghai Taipei Toronto

With offices in

Argentina Austria Brazil Chile Czech Republic France Greece
Guatemala Hungary Italy Japan Poland Portugal Singapore
South Korea Switzerland Thailand Turkey Ukraine Vietnam

Oxford is a registered trade mark of Oxford University Press
in the UK and in certain other countries

Published in the United States
by Oxford University Press Inc., New York

© Jason Ralph 2007

British Library Cataloguing in Publication Data
Data available

Library of Congress Cataloging in Publication Data
Data available

Typeset by SPI Publisher Services, Pondicherry, India
Printed in Great Britain
on acid-free paper by
Biddles Ltd., King's Lynn, Norfolk

ISBN 978–0–19–921431–0

1 3 5 7 9 10 8 6 4 2

For Katy

Preface and Acknowledgements

The origins of this book can be traced to my undergraduate module PIED3625 Human Rights and International Society, which I taught at the University of Leeds from 1999 onwards. I developed this module partly because I was not particularly interested in teaching cold war history, but mostly because I was fascinated by the moral, political, and legal dilemmas raised by the Kosovo conflict of that year. It is easy to overlook the fact that, at such an early stage of my teaching career, I was given the intellectual freedom to pursue my interests in this way. For that I wish to thank my colleagues at Leeds. I would also like to thank Charlotte Bretherton, who as an external examiner offered some very kind words about the module and has continued to be a source of support and encouragement. It is less easy to forget the role that the students on this module played in encouraging me to develop the module's central ideas and its case studies. Their thoughtful enthusiasm helped make teaching this module a particularly rewarding experience.

The early versions of this module concentrated on theories of international society and explored the dilemmas posed by humanitarian intervention. An examination of international criminal justice came later. I made the decision to start writing in this area for two reasons. First, the reading list was not short of references in the area of the English School and humanitarian intervention but there was clearly a gap when it came to political analyses of international criminal justice. Second, it became obvious that many of the themes highlighted by English School authors were acutely relevant to the question of international criminal justice. Moreover, the framework they offered helped me and the students to understand a practice that was becoming increasingly common. Of course, the year 1999 not only gave us the military campaign in Kosovo, it gave us the indictment of Milosevic and the House of Lords judgments on the possible extradition of Pinochet. In addition, the world was slowly coming to terms with the fact that a year earlier states had agreed to set up the International Criminal Court. It was an exciting time to be introduced to these issues. What made that time particularly stimulating were the conversations I was able to have with Martin Cinnamond, who is just completing a Ph.D. thesis on the dilemmas raised by cosmopolitan law enforcement. Martin's commitment to, and knowledge of, his subject is infectious and having him around to test ideas was a real boost to my initial inquiries. No doubt he has a promising career ahead of him but I hope he looks back as fondly as I do on those initial inquiries. I would also like to thank Michael Denison who I met at Leeds around this time. He too has just completed his Ph.D. thesis and is now firmly established as an expert in the politics of Central Asia. We have sparred together on many political issues and, more importantly, he has become a trusted friend.

Having made a commitment to write in this area I benefited enormously from contacts with the Coalition for the International Criminal Court (CICC). Their website and email service have been an extremely valuable source of information and although they have appeared only as names in my inbox I must thank Esti Tambay, Sally Ebhardt, Wasana Punyasena, and many other members of the icc-info mailing list who have over the past six or so years circulated enormous quantities of information. The Coalition was also kind enough to arrange access for me to the April 2002 PrepCom in New York and the September 2004 meeting of the Assembly of State Parties in The Hague. I would particularly like to thank Joydeep Sengupta for arranging this opportunity. At the former of these meetings I was able to talk to William Pace and John Washburn, which helped enormously to clarify the issues raised by the Court and American opposition to it. Likewise, Heather Hamilton of the American Coalition for the International Criminal Court was helpful in the initial stages of my inquiry. The creation of the International Criminal Court is often held up as an example of the practical impact that NGO advocacy can have. This will be debated because after all that is what we academics do. I know for certain, however, that I and many others would be less knowledgeable of the ICC without the hard work of the CICC and I wish to thank them for that. Of course, the opinions and arguments expressed in this book are entirely my own and I take full responsibility for any errors.

Thanks to the library staff at the University of Leeds I have been able to access the kind of sources that until recently I would not have even considered using. I would particularly like to thank Janet Morton for her advice on this matter and for putting up with my emails about not being able to access material. Invariably the mistake was mine and the solution was hers. I would also like to thank Tess Hornsby-Smith who has helped me to maintain the English School website run by Barry Buzan. I hope this plays a part in the growth of scholarship in this area and while it is only a small contribution I also hope my work on the website pays some of the debt owed to those who have encouraged a new generation of English School writers. I would particularly like to thank Barry Buzan here. His willingness to organize panels at various ISA, BISA, and ECPR conferences has enabled me and many others to test out ideas and to receive vital feedback. I look forward to attending many more English School panels in the future. I would also like to thank William Schabas and those contributing to his summer school on the ICC at the Irish Centre for Human Rights in Galway. I attended in the summer of 2004 and I would strongly recommend the school to anyone interested in this subject.

As my ideas developed I received invitations to speak at conferences. I would particularly like to thank the Robert H. Jackson Center, State University of New York, Fredonia and Bowling Green State University for their conferences commemorating the 60th anniversary of the Nuremberg trials. I also benefited greatly from meeting Tim Sellers at the Rothermere American Institute, University of Oxford in November 2004. We shared a panel at the conference 'The United States and Global Human Rights'. Tim's paper and our subsequent discussion really helped to focus my thoughts. He has been a valuable source of encouragement and support since then and I thank him for that. I would also like to thank the United Nations Association, Wales and the David Davis Memorial Institute for the invitation to speak at the University of Wales, Aberystwyth in November 2004. It was particularly nice to see Ken Booth, Andrew Linklater, and Nick Wheeler in the audience. Anyone familiar with the work of these three authors will no doubt spot their influence on my thinking. Thanks also to Dominic Byatt, Victoria Patton, and Clare Jenkins at OUP and the anonymous reviewers who took the time carefully to read the initial manuscript and offered suggestions on how to improve it.

It is too easy for intellectuals to concentrate on those they are writing for and too easy to forget the people they are writing about. There are probably too many words in academic books (this one included) that are about other academic books and there are too few words about the victims of egregious human rights abuses. It might serve only to compound injustice if one gained a sense of satisfaction in completing such a book. My hope is that this book, along with my teaching, informs a public debate on the connection between international society and the victims of human rights abuse. I then hope that Kant is right and that words are not merely 'academic' and that 'publicity' is the engine of reasonable change.

Finally, it is too easy for academics to concentrate on what they are writing about and too easy to forget those who are living with them when they are writing. I would like therefore to thank my wife Katy. She is my daily reminder that a love of humanity might be complicated by, but it is ultimately realized in, the love of one person. For that reason I dedicate this book to her.

J. R.

Leeds
October 2006

Contents

1

Introduction

How should the International Criminal Court (ICC or Court) change the way we view international society and how should we assess American opposition to the Court? International Relations (IR) is ideally placed to inform the interdisciplinary approach that is required to answer this question. The IR community has, however, been relatively slow in responding. What has been produced has mainly been the work of international lawyers.[1] There are exceptions, of course, but on the whole the ICC is under-researched by IR academics.[2] This situation has not gone unnoticed. Leila Nadya Sadat, for instance, calls the 1998 Rome Conference, which founded the Court, 'a constitutional moment'. It represented 'a sea change in international law-making with which political theory...has not caught up'.[3] It is the first aim of this book to address this situation by interpreting the Court through an approach to IR known as 'the English School'. It is increasingly apparent that a rich source of interdisciplinary research lies at the intersection of International Law and IR.[4] It is suggested here that the normative focus of the English School and the centrality of international law to its conception of international society represent significant interdisciplinary meeting points. More specifically the English School's conceptualization of international society and world society and the role played by law in defining these provides a useful framework for

---

[1] For example, see Roy Lee (ed.), *The International Criminal Court. The Making of the Rome Statute. Issues, Negotiations, Results* (The Hague, the Netherlands: Kluwer Law International, 1999); Antonio Cassese, Paolo Gaeta, and John R. W. D. Jones (eds.), *The Rome Statute of the International Criminal Court. A Commentary Vol. I and II* (Oxford: Oxford University Press, 2002); Leila Nadya Sadat, *The International Criminal Court and the Transformation of International Law. Justice for the New Millennium* (Ardsley, NY: Transnational, 2002).

[2] For an exception, see David Wippman, 'The International Criminal Court', in Christian Reus-Smit (ed.), *The Politics of International Law* (Cambridge: Cambridge University Press, 2004), 151–88; Eric K. Leonard, *The Onset of Global Governance. International Relations Theory and the International Criminal Court* (Aldershot, UK: Ashgate, 2004); Steven C. Roach, *Politicizing the International Criminal Court. The Convergence of Politics, Ethics and Law* (Lanham, MD: Rowman and Littlefield, 2006).

[3] Sadat, *The International Criminal Court*, 109.

[4] See, for instance, Christian Reus-Smit (ed.), *The Politics of International Law* (Cambridge: Cambridge University Press, 2004).

examining the issues surrounding the Court and for assessing its impact on global politics.[5]

Among the legal commentaries, there is a definite sense that the Court does have the potential to revolutionize global politics. Indeed one commentator equates the 1998 Treaty of Rome, which founded the Court, with the 1648 Treaty of Westphalia. Both are seen as pivotal moments in the history of global politics. For instance, Frédéric Mégret writes that the creation of the ICC 'might well one day precipitate a revolution of Westphalian proportions which, although it may not do away with the state system, would certainly rest its legitimacy on an entirely different footing'.[6] Sadat too, captures this sense of a new beginning. Recalling the problems of an international criminal justice system that relied solely on the state to adjudicate and enforce universal laws, she welcomes the creation of a permanent and independent Court and describes it as a revolution. She writes:

through a rather astonishing mutation, jurisdictional principles concerning 'which State' may exercise its authority over particular cases have been transformed into norms establishing the circumstances under which the international community may prescribe the rule of international criminal law and punish those who breach those rules.[7]

Sadat would be the first to add, however, that the revolution, if indeed that is what it is, is far from complete or certain ever to be completed. The efforts to transcend an international society of states through the creation of a permanent International Criminal Court (ICC) have demonstrated 'the tenacity of traditional Westphalian notions of state sovereignty'. Concessions to these traditional ideas have weakened the Court and mitigated its impact on international society. The revolution has been, to use Sadat's phrase, an 'uneasy' one.[8]

In this context, one of the most tenacious advocates of Westphalian notions of state sovereignty has been the US government. A frustration with the American position is implicit in many legal commentaries on the Rome Statute and the ICC. Convincing arguments identifying the inconsistencies in the US legal position have been made. The pervading sense of frustration, however, reveals the limitations of the lawyer's perspective. For example, Bruce Broomhall's book *International Justice and the International Criminal*

---

[5] Richard Little, 'International System, International Society and World Society: A Re-evaluation of the English School', in B. A. Roberson (ed.), *International Society and the Development of International Relations Theory* (London and New York: Continuum, 1998), 59–79.

[6] Frédéric Mégret, 'Epilogue to an Endless Debate: The International Criminal Court's Third Party Jurisdiction and the Looming Revolution in International Law', *European Journal of International Law*, 12 (2001), 258.

[7] Sadat, *The International Criminal Court*, 103.

[8] Sadat, *The International Criminal Court*, 1–19.

Court devotes a specific chapter to the question of American opposition.[9] Broomhall is clearly dissatisfied with the US position but there is little indication of what lies behind the US stance and how to address that. As we see, the United States continues to argue that its position is in fact consistent with international law. It will not, however, be moved by commentaries that argue otherwise. Legal reasoning alone is insufficient to change policy because that policy is driven by deep-rooted cultural and political factors. Indeed Broomhall acknowledges that more interdisciplinary study is needed to understand the environment that presently legitimates anti-ICC policies.[10]

This is the second aim of this book. It is dependent on the first aim because without a theory of international society and its alternatives, one cannot fully understand US policy, nor can one pass judgement on that policy. It was only after Hedley Bull had formulated his understanding of international society and great power responsibility in *The Anarchical Society*, for instance, that he was able then to identify the United States as a 'great irresponsible'.[11] As this example suggests (Bull was of course a major figure in the English School), the English School approach is well placed to provide the building blocs of such a theory. It not only provides a useful interpretive guide to global politics today, it is also rich in normative theorizing that sensitizes us to the dilemmas that confront the advocates of progressive change. The concept of international society, therefore, is seen by English School scholars as a good description of contemporary international relations (IR). Beyond this interpretive function, however, it offers a site for normative discussion, where the rules of global politics are negotiated and then applied in order to pass judgement on the behaviour of individuals, states, and non-state groups.

THE ENGLISH SCHOOL: A FRAMEWORK FOR ANALYSIS

The term 'English School' originates as a reference to members of the British Committee of International Relations, which met in the 1960s and 1970s.[12]

---

[9] Bruce Broomhall, *International Criminal Justice and the International Criminal Court. Between State Consent and the Rule of Law* (Oxford: Oxford University Press, 2003), 163–83. See also Sarah B. Sewall and Carl Kaysen (eds.), *The United States and the International Criminal Court. National Security and International Law* (Lanham, MD, Boulder, CO, New York, Oxford: Rowman and Littlefield, 2000).

[10] Broomhall, *International Criminal Justice*, 68.

[11] Hedley Bull, *The Anarchical Society: A Study of Order in World Politics*, 2nd edn. (London: Macmillan, 1977), 194–222; Hedley Bull, 'The Great Irresponsibles? The United States, the Soviet Union and World Order', *International Journal*, 35 (1979–80), 437–47.

[12] See 'British Institutionalists, or the English School, 20 Years on', *International Relations*, 17 (2003), 253–72; Brunello Vigezzi, *The British Committee on the Theory of International Politics (1954–85)* (Milan, Italy: Edzioni Unicopli, 2005).

Whether the term 'English School' is appropriate and who is considered 'in' the School has been a matter of debate. Those debates are not of concern here.[13] What linked these scholars was a shared interest in the existence of a society of states or international society. This is discussed in detail in the next section. For Chris Brown, however, the concept of international society was not the only, nor indeed the main contribution of the English School.[14] That rested with the idea that world politics could be understood in terms of the interplay of three traditions of thought, what Martin Wight identified as realism, rationalism, and revolutionism and what Hedley Bull called Hobbesian, Grotian, and Kantian.[15] This tripartite scheme is used by contemporary writers who draw parallels between Wight's categories and the concepts of international system, international society, and world society.[16] How these concepts are specifically defined and separated is a matter of continuing debate, and by offering a specific definition of world society this book speaks directly to that issue. Yet the idea that Realists emphasize an international system of competing states, Rationalists an international society of coexisting and sometimes cooperating states, and Revolutionists a world society based on ideologies that transcend statehood, has been generally accepted at least as a pedagogical scheme.

From the English School perspective as it is understood here therefore, neither an anarchic international system nor an international society of states is the starting point for IR theorists. Rather the starting point is the recognition that each of the three traditions says something about global politics. The English School approach subscribes in other words to a pluralistic methodology.[17] The extent to which each tradition helps us understand global politics varies according to historical circumstance. In this regard, the Realist's traditional emphasis on anarchy stems not from an arbitrary attempt to separate the discipline of IR from the study of domestic politics. Rather it stems from an understanding that the international system is a product of, and therefore

[13] See Tim Dunne, *Inventing International Society: A History of the English School* (London: Macmillan, 1998) and the exchange between Dunne, Makinda, Knudsen, and Suganami in *Cooperation and Conflict. Nordic Journal of International Studies*, 36 (2001).

[14] Chris Brown, 'World Society and the English School: An "International Society" Perspective on World Society', *European Journal of International Relations*, 7 (2000), 423–41. See also Richard Little, 'The English School Contribution to the Study of International Relations', *European Journal of International Relations*, 6 (2000), 395–422; Barry Buzan, 'The English School: An Underexploited Resource in IR', *Review of International Studies*, 27 (2001), 471–88.

[15] Wight, *International Theory*; Bull, *The Anarchical Society*, 22–6.

[16] Richard Little, 'International System, International Society and World Society: A Reevaluation of the English School', in B. A. Roberson (ed.), *International Society and the Development of International Relations Theory* (London: Pinter, 1998), 59–79.

[17] Richard Little, 'The English School's Contribution to the Study of International Relations', *European Journal of International Relations*, 6 (2000), 395–422.

contingent on, processes of moral, political, and legal reasoning. Moral, political, and legal communities are, from the Realist's perspective, inevitably unique and separate. Sovereignty bestows freedom and therefore moral accountability on the leaders of such communities, yet Realists have tended to argue that 'a nationalist ideology asserts that this accountability should be to the national group itself'.[18]

The English School, therefore, may reject the methodological (as opposed to legal) positivism that underpins certain approaches to IR theory but it does not reject the interpretive value of realism.[19] Where positivists like Kenneth Waltz simply *assume* the presence of egoistic units in their theory of international politics,[20] the English School approach invites the theorization of the state by noting that the self-help logic of anarchy rests on, and is therefore contingent on, distinct ethical communities. Having done that, however, it does not rule out the possibility that realism can offer a convincing account of international politics at a particular time in history. The English School approach, in other words, recognizes that states are not necessarily other-interested agents and that they may sometimes act in ways that are contrary to the common interest. The balance of power may establish order, but without a common interest in maintaining that order, the balance of power is simply the outcome of a mechanical process and not the consequence of moral or legal obligation. In such times, relations between states have been traditionally described by the English School in terms of an international *system*, the structure of which was constituted by the distribution of material capabilities. In an international system, there is no universal concept of crime and even 'the sacredness of human life is a purely municipal idea of no validity outside the [state's] jurisidiction'.[21]

More recently, however, Barry Buzan has helped to consolidate the methodological difference between English School realism and the Neorealism inspired by Waltz by noting that states have never existed in a systemic or pre-social relationship. Relations between states may at certain times be characterized by power politics but to the extent that states communicate with each other then they exist in some form of society. In this respect, Buzan argues for removing the system/society distinction from the English

---

[18] James Mayall, 'Introduction', in James Mayall (ed.), *The Community of States* (London: Allen and Unwin, 1982), 6.

[19] See Hedley Bull, 'International Theory: The Case for a Classical Approach', *World Politics*, 42 (1966), 361–77. See also Richard Little, 'The English School vs. American Realism: A Meeting of Minds Divided by a Common Language?', *Review of International Studies*, 29 (2003), 443–60.

[20] Kenneth Waltz, *Theory of International Politics* (New York, London: McGraw-Hill, 1979).

[21] O. W. Holmes cited by Bassiouni and Wise, *Aut Dedere, Aut Judicare*, 31.

School framework.[22] To be clear, this does not mean that the English School approach rejects the interpretive value of realism. After all, those communicative processes that create the rules that structure the social relationships of states are often heavily influenced by power. Realism is, therefore, still relevant, albeit in a 'modified' form. It can, to use Tim Dunne's words, help illustrate how power 'creates a normative framework convenient to itself'.[23] Indeed, much of the evidence presented in this book supports the modified Realist's position on international society. For them, the state generally has an 'instrumentalist' view of international society and this stems from the tendency to see itself as 'master of its own fate', a trait that is naturally more common among the powerful. In such states, a Machiavellian sense of *virtu* is often valued by those holding power. This has been defined as the practice of 'cloaking the refusal to limit the state's full freedom of action in the garb of . . . purely nominal declarations of some such submission'.[24] Such practices guarantee that international rules, which nominally define the common values that exist between states, do not have the quality of law as they too easily give way to the particular interests of the powerful. If international society exists, in other words, it does so only at the behest of the powerful.

Realism is then very much part of the English School approach yet because the state is the site of ethical reasoning the English School does not assume that states will automatically be in competition with each other or that human rights are meaningless. From the Rationalist perspective, the power of a national kind of communitarianism, which realism tends to rest on, does not necessarily rule out the need to think about international society. 'On the contrary, . . . the need becomes more urgent. . . . [W]hile cultural diversity remains a necessary support for our identity, the development of community depends . . . on our capacity to join together not to merge our separate identities but to preserve them'.[25] For Rationalists, humankind is guided towards this capacity by law. Thus, 'the sovereignty of states in the international community and the absence of any common superior does not involve pure anarchy,

---

[22] On the distinction of 'international society' from 'international system' see Alan James, 'System or Society?', *Review of International Studies*, 19 (1993), 269–88. On the need to do away with the distinction between 'system' and 'society' see Buzan, *From International to World Society? English School Theory and the Social Structure of Globalisation* (Cambridge: Cambridge University Press, 2004). See also Nicholas Onuf, 'The Constitution of International Society', *European Journal of International Law*, 5 (1994), 8. For a response to Buzan which defends the distinction see Tim Dunne, 'System, State and Society: How Does it all Hang Together', *Millennium: Journal of International Studies*, 34 (2005), 157–70.

[23] Tim Dunne, 'Sociological Investigations: Instrumental, Legitimist and Coercive Interpretations of International Society', *Millennium: Journal of International Studies*, 30 (2001), 81.

[24] Hersch Lauterpacht, 'The Grotian Tradition in International Law', *The British Yearbook of International Law*, 23 (1946), 35.

[25] Mayall, 'Introduction', 10–1.

because prior to political organization there still exists law, based on reason and the nature of man being a social being'.[26] Unlike Realists, who dismiss international law and international solidarity as the 'slogans of those who feel strong enough to impose them on others',[27] Rationalists see 'international society as a customary society'.[28] State practice, including the balance of power, is embedded in the institutions of diplomacy and customary international law, which helps to develop and then to articulate an ethic of coexistence based on sovereign equality and non-intervention. This is, as Bull puts it, 'a response to the fact and implied value of diversity on a global scale'.[29]

Rationalism is strongly associated with the Grotian tradition in political theory.[30] For Hedley Bull at least, the work of Hugo Grotius was central to the idea of an international society in which states 'are bound not only by rules of prudence or expediency but also by the imperatives of morality and law'.[31] While this broad definition defines the Rationalist perspective, those working within this tradition dispute the scope and strength of solidarity across international society. This dispute has provided reason for distinguishing the terms 'international society' and 'international community', which in popular discourse are often used interchangeably. In drawing such a distinction, several authors recall the differentiation between *gemeinschaft* and *gesellschaft* made by the German sociologist Ferdinand Tönnies.[32] Tönnies understood community (*gemeinschaft*) as referring to an organic unity with natural bonds between its members. The term emphasizes subjective feelings of commonality. On the other hand, society (*gesellschaft*) was considered artificially created and merely indicated interdependency between autonomous

[26] Wight, *International Theory*, 234.

[27] E. H. Carr, *The Twenty Years Crisis 1919–39*, 2nd edn. (London: Macmillan, 1946), 86. See also Bassiouni and Wise, *Aut Dedere, Aut Judicare*, 36, who write that 'in the present state of international relations, to speak as if an "international community" actually were in being runs the risk of exciting expectations that are bound to be disappointed and, worse yet, of encouraging use of the rhetoric of universality as a cloak for hegemonic objectives'.

[28] Wight, *International Theory*, 39.   [29] Bull, *The Anarchical Society*, 134.

[30] Wight, *International Theory*, 233–4.   [31] Bull, *The Anarchical Society*, 27.

[32] See Andreas L. Paulus, 'The Influence of the United States on the Concept of the "International Community"', in Michael Byers and Georg Nolte (eds.), *United States Hegemony and the Foundations of International Law* (Cambridge: Cambridge University Press, 2003), 59–60; Bruno Simma and Andreas L. Paulus, 'The "International Community": Facing the Challenge of Globalization. General Conclusions', *European Journal of International Law*, 9 (1998), 266–77; Ove Bring, 'The Westphalian Peace Tradition in International Law. From *Jus ad* Bellum to *Jus Contra* Bellum', in Michael N. Schmitt (ed.), *International Law Across the Spectrum of Conflict: Essays in Honour of Professor L. C. Green* (US Naval War College: International Law Studies Volume 75, 2000), 62. For the use of this distinction by IR scholars, see Chris Brown, 'International Theory and International Society: The Viability of the Middle Way?', *Review of International Studies*, 21 (1995), 183–96; Bruce Cronin, *Community Under Anarchy. Transnational Identity and the Evolution of Cooperation* (New York: Columbia University Press, 1999), 4; Buzan, *From International to World Society?*, 108–18.

agents. As Andreas Paulus helpfully puts it, 'Community is prior to its members; society is subordinate to their interests'.[33]

In the international sphere, 'society' is used to identify an association of sovereign states. Those states have interests that are formulated by processes independent of international society. They join to form a society in order to protect and advance those interests but cooperation is the exception and not the rule. As discussed in detail in Chapter 2, this view is often associated with Emer de Vattel. In Vattel's view, the needs of men were met sufficiently within particular nations. Nature had determined that states were the autonomous agents that Tönnies identified. There was little need, according to contractarians like Vattel, to associate beyond the level of the nation-state. While Vattel envisaged a residual responsibility to universal laws of nature (including limits on the conduct of war and universal jurisdiction to prosecute 'enemies of the whole human race'), it was 'for each nation to decide what its conscience demands of it, what it can or can not do; what it thinks well or does not think well to do'.[34] To expect otherwise, in other words to bind a sovereign state to a law it had not consented to, was to threaten the social contract that protected the freedom of the nation. The liberty created by that contract was best preserved if sovereigns recognized that states had duties only to themselves and could only be bound by a commitment, or by a law, to which they had given their consent. With this qualification, the rules that did develop between states could be considered, under this positivist conception of international law, the rules of international society.

On the other hand the term 'community' signifies a normative structure that is prior to, or at least independent of, that which is created solely by the interaction of states. The term 'international community' is in this regard better suited to the kind of association that is structured by rules that states have not necessarily consented to.[35] This view is associated with the Grotian tradition of international thought. This sees states as bound either by natural law or, in the case of the neo-Grotian tradition, customary international law. As Simma and Paulus remind us, this kind of international communitarianism must be distinguished from the use of the label 'communitarian' by those advocates of a closer national society based on national values. As an example of this, it should be noted that the neo-Grotian emphasis on universal human rights and the responsibility of the international society to guarantee those

---

[33] Paulus, 'The Influence of the United States', 62.

[34] Emer de Vattel, *The Law of Nations or the Principles of Natural Law Applied to the Conduct and to the Affairs of Nations and of Sovereigns* (Washington, DC: Carnegie Institution of Washington, [1758] 1916), 6.

[35] See, for instance, Bardo Fassbender, 'The United Nations Charter as Constitution of the International Community', *Columbia Journal of Transnational Law*, 36 (1998), 564.

rights when states are either unwilling or unable to do so, shows that this kind of international communitarianism is not opposed to the individualism of persons, but to state individualism.[36]

Using Tönnies' distinction therefore, one might suggest that 'international community' is not the same as 'international society'. In the former, states have obligations to a prior community of humankind, while in the latter states are only obliged to observe contracts they have consented to. As the terms are often used interchangeably, however, it is more helpful to use different labels. This book uses the overarching term 'international society' to describe relationships between states that are conditioned by rules and institutions that identify rights and responsibilities. Within that, one can identify a 'pluralist' conception of international society, which is constituted by diverse but coexisting moral communities and by the rules of sovereign equality and sovereign consent. One can also identify a 'solidarist' conception of international society, which notes that states have a responsibility not only to each other but also to a wider concept of the common good, which may include a conception of humanity that is founded on natural or customary international law.[37] Both are distinct from 'world society', which is defined below and in more detail in Chapter 4.

This solidarist and pluralist distinction has been illustrated by reference to the classical work of Grotius and Vattel, respectively. This is particularly apparent in English School research on the issue of humanitarian intervention. Where Vattelian pluralists warned against the idea of intervention, Grotian solidarists have argued that a sense of obligation to a community of humankind does transcend the society of states and a right to humanitarian intervention exists within natural and/or customary international law.[38] This distinction works less well in the area of international criminal justice, however, partly because Vattel's positivism did not cause him to reject Grotian ideas such as restraints on the conduct of war and universal jurisdiction. Both

---

[36] Bruno Simma and Andreas L. Paulus, 'The "International Community": Facing the Challenge of Globalization', *European Journal of International Law*, 9 (1998), 271.

[37] This distinction was first suggested by Bull, 'The Grotian Conception of International Society', in H. Butterfield and M. Wight (eds.), *Diplomatic Investigations* (London: Allen and Unwin, 1966), 35–50. Buzan's reworking of the pluralist–solidarist distinction demonstrates that if these labels are general they are not necessarily redundant. His more specific descriptions of interstate societies will be introduced in due course. See Buzan, *From International to World Society?*, 139–60.

[38] See the framework used by Nicholas J. Wheeler, 'Pluralist or Solidarist Conceptions of International Society—Bull and Vincent on Humanitarian Intervention', *Millennium, Journal of International Studies*, 21 (1992), 463–87. It must be noted that this was a development of Bull's original use of the term solidarism, which was merely to indicate the possibility of law enforcement within the society of states. See Andrew Linklater and Hidemi Suganami, *The English School of International Relations* (Cambridge: Cambridge University Press, 2006), 59–60.

Grotius and Vattel, for instance, grounded in natural law a duty of states either to extradite or punish those individuals who were guilty of committing crimes that in some way offended humanity. Nonetheless, the Vattelian principle of sovereign consent is central to understanding why contemporary pluralists reject the exercise of universal jurisdiction and why they are suspicious of the solidarist emphasis on customary international humanitarian law (IHL), which is considered to evolve independently of state consent. The solidarist view of international law is more progressive to the extent that it considers binding states, even those that withhold their consent, to 'the principles of humanity and the dictates of public conscience'.[39] Thus, pluralists and solidarists are separated by their views on the sources of international law. They are, however, united within the Rationalist tradition by their view that the state plays an exclusive role in the adjudication and the enforcement of international law. In other words, pluralists and solidarists may disagree on the way international law is formed, but they agree that responsibility for its enforcement rests solely with states.

For philosophers in Wight's third tradition—the Revolutionists—the state is part of the problem. Far from being a guarantor of an individual's liberty, the state is often the means used to ensure his or her continuing repression. From this perspective, international society is not a prudent association of states that manages ethical diversity and provides the international stability out of which a universal moral consensus may grow. Rather international society is simply 'a global protection racket', the rules of which protect the privileged position of statist elites.[40] Clearly, the Marxist view of history, where the state advances particular class interests but would eventually wither away to be replaced by a communist utopia, fits neatly into this tradition.[41] Yet the tendency to place Immanuel Kant in this tradition and to link his philosophy to a vision of world society that transcends and replaces the state is difficult to sustain.[42] Certainly, Kant argued that the state and the society of states were insufficient institutions to sustain the moral progress that was required to move towards perpetual peace, but it is clear that Kant sought to work with a reformed conception of international society rather than overthrow it. In fact states organized along republican lines were necessary in order to check the power of leaders who might threaten the rights of individuals. Moreover, because some individuals

---

[39] As articulated by the Martens Clause of The Hague Convention II of 1899. See Adam Roberts and Richard Guelff, *Documents on the Laws of War*, 3rd edn. (Oxford: Oxford University Press, 2003), 8–9.

[40] Ken Booth, 'Military Intervention: Duty and Prudence', in Lawrence Freedman (ed.), *Military Intervention in European Conflicts* (Oxford: Blackwell, 1994).

[41] Buzan, 'The English School', 475.

[42] For a similar view see Linklater and Suganami, *The English School*, 160–9.

found liberty in particular communities, international society was needed to help defend the independence of states. In this regard, Kant argued against the forceful intervention of one state into the affairs of another, even when the latter is 'struggling with its internal ills'. He considered such interference to be a violation of the rights of an independent nation. It would, moreover, 'be an active offence and would make the autonomy of all other states insecure'.[43] If Kant did have a conception of world society, therefore, it was one in which the state and the society of states were necessary components.

Yet Kant also argued that national and international law could not guarantee individuals the right to be treated as ends in themselves because these laws did not apply to those individuals who were part of stateless communities. Extending hospitality to these 'strangers'—what Kant called cosmopolitan law—was thus a necessary 'complement' to national and international law.[44] This conception of cosmopolitan law has been interpreted by some as facilitating a 'spirit of commerce', which is said to give states 'a material incentive' to act peacefully.[45] This interpretation is too narrow. Kant did use the term 'commerce', but only as an example of interaction between peoples. The right not to be treated by foreigners as enemies has a much more profound meaning. For Kant,

[t]his right, *in so far as it affords the prospect that all nations may unite for the purpose of creating certain universal laws to regulate the intercourse they may have with one another,* may be termed *cosmopolitan (ius cosmopoliticum).*[46]

'Hospitality to strangers' therefore goes beyond 'commerce' and even beyond what we might now call 'asylum', which is consistent with the categorical imperative of treating people as ends in themselves. The point Kant makes when he says that peoples have a right not to be treated by foreigners as enemies is that their views should be taken into consideration during the process of 'creating certain universal laws' that regulate all aspects of human relationships. Contemporary audiences might interpret this not only in the negative terms of human rights but also in the more positive terms of

---

[43] Kant, *Perpetual Peace*, 96. He also opposed 'attempts to put into practice overnight revolution, i.e. by forcibly overthrowing a defective constitution ... for there would be an interval of time during which the condition of right would be nullified'. Kant, *The Metaphysics of Morals*, 175.

[44] Kant, *Perpetual Peace*, 108.

[45] Michael W. Doyle, 'Liberalism and World Politics', *The American Political Science Review*, 80 (1986), 1161.

[46] Kant, *The Metaphysics of Morals*, 172, emphasis added; and in *Perpetual Peace*: 'In this way, continents distant from each other can enter into peaceful mutual relations which may eventually be regulated by public laws, thus bringing the human race nearer and nearer to a cosmopolitan constitution', 106.

cosmopolitan democracy.[47] Proof that cosmopolitan law was in Kant's view much broader than the 'spirit of commerce' can be found in Kant's observation that trade may in fact violate that law. He writes for instance of the trading republic's encounter with non-sovereign peoples. '[T]hese visits to foreign shores', he recalls, 'can also occasion evil and violence in one part of the globe with ensuing repercussions which are felt everywhere'.[48] As Daniele Archibugi put it, Kant realized that 'nations which are democratic domestically, do not necessarily behave democratically beyond borders'.[49]

Kant's view that reason was universal, which gave rise to the categorical imperative of treating individuals as ends in themselves, and his criticism of the society of states for failing to respond to that imperative, clearly associates him with the English School's idea that a world society of humankind exists independently of states. Yet as is explained in more detail below, Bull's conception of world society was more demanding than the identification of cosmopolitan consciousness based on humanity and reason. The idea of world society was not limited to the expression of common values or to an ideological attack on the normative foundations of international society. World society in Bull's view was itself constituted by rules and institutions. What Kant did share with Bull, however, was the belief that a cosmopolitan consciousness was, at the time they were writing, insufficiently developed for world society to be able to support anything other than the most basic of global institutions. Bull's concern that such institutions could undermine order between morally diverse states is well known to the English School. Evidence that Kant thought along similar lines can be found in his rejection of criminal justice as an institution that could respond to the violation of cosmopolitan law. Kant feared that the global consciousness was insufficiently defined to be able to maintain a check on the jurist or to prevent him from throwing 'the *sword* into the *scales* if it refuses to sink' (i.e. to maintain impartiality based on reason).[50] Thus, the kind of punishments (including the death penalty) that Kant demanded for certain crimes in other settings could not be applied to violations of cosmopolitan law.[51] The institution that enforced cosmopolitan law was thus the rather limited one of 'publicity'. A court of public opinion would expose unlawful acts in a way that would, at least according to Kant, encourage the wrongdoer to reflect on and to change his practices. Despite this limited

---

[47] See Daniele Archibugi and David Held (eds.), *Cosmopolitan Democracy. An Agenda for a New World Order* (Cambridge: Polity Press, 1995).

[48] Kant, *The Metaphysics of Morals*, 172; also *Perpetual Peace*, 106–7.

[49] Daniele Archibugi, 'Immanuel Kant, Cosmopolitan Law and Peace', *European Journal of International Relations*, 1 (1995), 448.

[50] Kant, *Perpetual Peace*, 115.   [51] Kant, *The Metaphysics of Morals*, 154–9.

conception of cosmopolitan law enforcement, contemporary commentators argue that cosmopolitan criminal justice is in fact a logical extension of Kant's thinking. As Archibugi argues, 'it would not have been excessively foolhardy, upon recognition of the rights of citizens of the world, to propose their protection through the creations of bodies ... independent from states'.[52] Indeed, Archibugi interprets the ICC as just such a body.[53] The point here, however, is that if supranational institutions are created to protect cosmopolitan law, they would, in Kant's view, complement rather than replace the institutions of international and national society.

INTERNATIONAL AND WORLD SOCIETY

Hedley Bull used the terms 'international society' and 'world society' in the context of his inquiry into the nature of order in world politics. He argued that order could exist even in the absence of common values and common interests if a balance of power existed between states. Within a society, however, 'order is the consequence not merely of contingent facts such as this, but a sense of common interests in the elementary goals of social life'.[54] In the international context, Bull believed that states shared a common interest in maintaining order, a point that clearly places him within Wight's Rationalist tradition. This common interest was derived 'from fear of unrestricted violence, of instability of agreements or of the insecurity of their independence or sovereignty'. There are, according to Bull, three 'complexes' of rules that emerged from and articulated this common consciousness. The first is what he called 'fundamental' or 'constitutional' rules. These determine the members of society and distinguish the idea of a society of states from alternative ideas such as 'a universal empire [or] a cosmopolitan community of individual human beings'.[55] Thus

the idea of international society identifies states as members of this society and the units competent to carry out political tasks within it, including the tasks necessary to make its basic rules effective; it thus excludes conceptions which assign this political competence to groups other than the state, such as universal authorities above it or sectional groups within it.[56]

---

[52] Archibugi, 'Immanuel Kant', 451–2. See also Garret Wallace Brown, 'State Sovereignty, Federation and Kantian Cosmopolitanism', *European Journal of International Relations*, 11 (2005), 495–522.

[53] Daniele Archibugi, 'From the United Nations to Cosmopolitan Democracy', in Archibugi and Held (eds.), *Cosmopolitan Democracy*, 121–62.

[54] Bull, *The Anarchical Society*, 63.   [55] Bull, *The Anarchical Society*, 65.

[56] Bull, *The Anarchical Society*, 65.

The second complex of rules prescribes behaviour necessary to sustain the ethic of coexistence between states. Bull is quite clear that such rules are not necessarily the same as international law as they exist as customary practice. For instance, states agree that maintaining a balance of power is necessary to securing the elementary goals of society, even if a practice guided by such a rule (as in the cold war) violates the sovereign independence of smaller states. Yet international law does have a key role in articulating rules of coexistence, most notably the basic rules of *pacta sunt servanda* and the reciprocal respect of sovereignty, including respect of the 'supreme jurisdiction of every other state over its own citizens'.[57] The third complex relates to those rules devised by states to advance goals beyond mere coexistence.

While these *rules* help to constitute international society by identifying its members and the interests they share, *institutions* are those shared practices that make, communicate, administer, interpret, enforce, legitimize, adapt, and protect rules. In the absence of world government, these functions are fulfilled by states as they engage in practices such as the balance of power, diplomacy, and war, to the extent that war seeks to protect order. Thus, international society exists when

a group of states, conscious of certain common interests and common values, form a society in the sense that they conceive themselves to be bound by a common set of rules in their relations with one another, and share in the working of common institutions.[58]

The idea that international society is not merely an ideal but also an empirical reality is thus central to English School inquiry. International society takes on a structural form that helps to constitute an agent's identity and restrains or enables its actions. However, the English School's awareness of history leads it to qualify statements such as this. As Bull put it, there is 'nothing historically inevitable or morally sacrosanct' about the society of states. Yet at the time of writing *The Anarchical Society*, Bull accepted that the society of states was the dominant structure in world politics.

A number of other writers not necessarily associated with the English School approach have written in similar terms about the constitution of international society. For instance, Reus-Smit argues that international society contains 'issue-specific regimes' (e.g. the Non-Proliferation Treaty), which are the product of 'fundamental institutions' (e.g. multilateral diplomacy). These institutions, however, are contingent on 'constitutional structures'. These are

coherent ensembles of intersubjective beliefs, principles, and norms that perform two functions in ordering international societies: they define what constitutes a legitimate actor, entitled to all the rights and privileges of statehood; and they define the basic

---

[57] Bull, *The Anarchical Society*, 67.   [58] Bull, *The Anarchical Society*, 13.

parameters of rightful state action. They are 'constitutional' because they are systems of basic principles that define and shape international polities and they are 'structures' because they 'limit and mold agents and agencies and point them in ways that tend towards a common quality of outcomes even though the efforts and aims of agents and agencies vary'.[59]

Reus-Smit's emphasis on structure is echoed by Nicholas Onuf who recognizes the constitutive role played by state practices but claims that international society 'is a thing *and* a process'.[60] Rules occupy the pivotal point between structure and agency. 'By making, following and talking about rules', Onuf writes, 'people constitute the multiple structures of society; through such rules societies constitute people as agents'.[61] Following Hart's distinction between primary and secondary rules, Onuf argues that there are certain (secondary) rules in international society that act as a constitution by recognizing states as sovereign and by conferring and limiting their powers to make, execute, and adjudicate legal (primary) rules.[62] In international law such rules are considered *jus cogens*, that is 'a peremptory rule of law which may only be superseded by another peremptory rule'. Given this, Onuf draws a parallel between such laws and James Madison's claim that constitutional law cannot be changed by the normal procedures of law-making. Furthermore, Onuf argues that the principle of sovereign equality is *jus cogens* and Chapter I of the UN Charter, where the principle is codified, can thus act as a 'material constitution' of international society. Thus,

If [sovereign equality]...is peremptory, it is hard to see why all of Chapter I [of the UN Charter] is not as well. The parallel between claims on behalf of *jus cogens* and Madison's claim that constitutional law is unalterable by law issued under the constitution further supports the view that Chapter I stands apart from the rest of the Charter and the rest of international law. That Chapter I approximates a model constitution strengthens the case for its status as a material constitution [of international society].[63]

To be certain, universal treaties like the UN Charter merely help to affirm and articulate the constitutive rules of international society, which must exist prior to the creation of treaties because they in fact define the meaning of

---

[59] Christian Reus-Smit, 'The Constitutional Structure of International Society and the Nature of Fundamental Institutions', *International Organization*, 51 (1997), 566. Emphasis in original. Quoting Kenneth N. Waltz, *Theory of International Politics* (New York: Random House, 1979), 74.

[60] Nicholas Onuf, 'The Constitution of International Society', *European Journal of International Law*, 5 (1994), 1.

[61] Nicholas Onuf, 'The Constitution', 6.   [62] Nicholas Onuf, 'The Constitution', 13–4.

[63] Onuf, 'The Constitution', 17. See also Bardo Fassbender, 'The United Nations Charter as Constitution of the International Community', *Columbia Journal of Transnational Law*, 36 (1998), 529–619.

such contracts. The rule of sovereignty for instance determines who can make treaties and the rule of *pacta sunt servanda* determines their binding quality. As Nardin points out,

constitutional treaties like the League of Nations or the UN Charter establish only limited associations within international society, not international society itself. The 'Constitution' of international society as a whole...is the unwritten constitution of customary international law, not the voluntary pacts and charters that certain states may occasionally enter into to establish particular, historic associations within the larger society of states.[64]

Nevertheless Onuf's formulation matches both Bull and Reus-Smit's argument that state sovereignty is recognized by custom and treaty law as the organizing principle of international society. Moreover his arguments that Article 38 of the International Court of Justice Statute supplements the UN Charter by limiting the ways in which the Court can discern international law satisfies Reus-Smit's argument, which notes that constitutional structures must incorporate norms of procedural justice, that is norms indicating a baseline agreement on how rules are formulated.[65] Of course, the interpretation of Article 38 and the emphasis on sovereign consent as the procedure by which law is created is very much disputed and this is discussed in detail in Chapter 2.

Before assessing the implications of these arguments it is worth clarifying what is being claimed here. Firstly, international society is based on *common values* and *common interests*. Such values and interests are hard to find outside the nation-state. What is held in common, however, is an ethic of coexistence that accepts diversity as a value in itself or as a reality to be tolerated for the sake of order. On this moral foundation rest *constitutive* or *jus cogens* rules that identify states as the members of society as well as placing limitations on their actions and their freedom of contract. In order to protect the ethic of coexistence, therefore, international society is constituted by the rules of sovereign equality, non-intervention and sovereign consent. Fundamental *institutions* are, to use Reus-Smit's formulation, 'those rules of practice that states formulate to solve the coordination and collaboration problems associated with coexistence under anarchy'. As noted these institutions do not necessarily have to be understood in legal terms and the balance of power is perhaps the best example of a non-legal (and possibly illegal but legitimate) institution. In more cooperative societies, however, the balance of power might be replaced by the promise and, more importantly, the practice of collective security.

---

[64] Terry Nardin, 'Legal Positivism as a Theory of International Society', in D. R. Mapel and T. Nardin (eds.), *International Society: Diverse Ethical Perspectives* (Princeton, NJ: Princeton University Press, 1998), 22. See Chapter 2 for further discussion.

[65] Reus-Smit, 'The Constitutional Structure'.

Reus-Smit's focus on multilateralism as an example of a fundamental institution mirrors Bull's understanding of the role diplomacy plays in protecting the values of international society and cultivating a thicker consensus, although given its centrality to this book it is also worth noting here the importance of diplomatic immunity to this process.

Breaking international society into common values/common interests, constitutive rules, and fundamental institutions in this way allows us to compare *types* of societies and to address a problem at the centre of the English School's research agenda, which is how can we distinguish international society from world society.[66] Bull helped make this comparison by maintaining symmetry between the constitutional structures of international and world society. In other words, both international and world societies are based on common values and common interests as well as shared rules and institutions. So for instance, Bull understood 'world society' to mean

not merely a degree of interaction linking all the parts of human community to one another, but a sense of common interest and common values, on the basis of which common rules and institutions may be built.[67]

What distinguishes international society from world society is the kind of values that are held in common. Where moral *diversity* underpins international society, world society rests on a common conception of *humanity*. As noted above, however, Bull's definition also suggests that world society is more than just the existence of a common or cosmopolitan consciousness. A society develops only when that consciousness can articulate and sustain common rules and it is at the level of rules where the English School's confusion on the difference between international and world society starts. For on the one hand, English School scholarship has tended to equate the idea of world society with Wight's revolutionary tradition where relations between individual human beings are not 'mediated' by states.[68] In this revolutionary conception of world society the state, in Marxian terms, simply 'withers away'. Constitutive rules in this kind of society would simply indicate that human beings are the members of a global society and that supranational institutions would form the structure that mediated their relations. Yet on the other hand, authors like John Vincent have seen the state as an institution of world society.[69] Presumably, the common value in this second conception of world society is

[66] See Buzan, 'The English School'; Dunne, 'Sociological Investigations', 89.

[67] Bull, *The Anarchical Society*, 269.

[68] This term is taken from Evan Luard who argued that states *'mediate* between their own people and those of other countries; that is they can, to a large extent determine what kind of relations they can enjoy', *International Society* (Basingstoke, UK: Macmillan, 1990), 6.

[69] Vincent, J., *Human Rights and International Relations* (Cambridge: Cambridge University Press, 1986).

still humanity, but crucially there is still a role for states as agents of humanity. Yet to distinguish this conception of world society from international society and to make sure that states work to protect different common values (i.e. humanity and not diversity), the constitutive rule in this conception of world society can no longer be state sovereignty or sovereign consent. Instead, one might suggest that the organizing principle in this kind of world society is complementarity. In other words, states are not only expected to be agents of humanity, they are also expected to give up their sovereignty to supranational or world institutions charged with the same function. These two visions of world society have been implicit in the English School framework. They are referred to in this book as a *revolutionary conception of world society* where the state no longer mediates human relationships and, keeping in mind the discussion in the previous section, a *Kantian conception of world society*, where the state complements the work of other supranational institutions.

While this distinction might help the English School better define the idea of world society, it does not by itself address the question driving part of the contemporary research agenda. That question is this: how can we distinguish between solidarist conceptions of international society and world society? The distinction between a solidarist international society, where states are the agents of humanity, and the revolutionary conception of world society where states no longer mediate human relations, is self-explanatory. However, the distinction between solidarist international society and the Kantian conception of world society is less clear cut and at first sight non-existent. However, Barry Buzan's answer to this question is helpful here. In *From International to World Society?*, Buzan makes significant and somewhat radical revisions to the English School framework, many of which are addressed in more detail in Chapter 4. The revision that is adopted here, at least partially, is the decision to refine pluralist and solidarist conceptions of international—or as Buzan prefers—interstate society. Towards (and beyond) the pluralist end of the spectrum Buzan locates what he calls 'Asocial', 'Power Political', and 'Coexistence' interstate societies; and towards (and beyond) the solidarist end of the spectrum Buzan places 'Cooperative', 'Convergence', and 'Confederative' interstate societies.[70] These are to be understood, at least initially, as being distinct from what he calls 'interhuman' and 'transnational' societies. As noted, these categories and the manner in which he ultimately argues that 'world society' should be understood as 'a situation' in which all three domains (i.e. interstate, interhuman, and transnational) are 'in play' together are assessed in Chapter 4. It is useful here, however, to adopt Buzan's categories of 'Convergence' and

---

[70] Buzan, *From International to World Society?*, 139–60.

'Confederative' interstate societies as a means of articulating the difference between solidarist international society and a Kantian world society.

From Buzan's perspective, a Convergence interstate society is characterized by common values other than an ethic of coexistence (e.g. liberal democracy, Islamic theocracy, communist totalitarianism). This inevitably has an impact on the constitutive rule of interstate society, but on this Buzan is somewhat vague. 'Convergence', he writes, 'would almost certainly push non-intervention as a corollary of sovereignty towards obsolescence for many purposes'. One might interpret this to mean that in a society that converges around the value of 'humanity' state practices such as humanitarian intervention and universal jurisdiction are permitted. In a 'Confederative' interstate society, however, states no longer expect (nor indeed welcome) intervention by other states because they have given up their sovereignty to supranational institutions (e.g. the European Union) which function to develop, interpret, and enforce those laws that protect common values and common interests. By serving the moral purpose of the wider society, in other words, the states in a Confederative society are expected to complement the work of supranational institutions. It is proposed here that what Buzan describes as a Confederative interstate society can also be understood as a Kantian world society but only when the Confederation exists on a global scale. In this respect it rejects Buzan's suggestion that 'world' societies can exist at regional levels, for example in Europe. This blurring of distinctions seems out of place in Buzan's work, which does so much to clarify the confusion across English School categories. Clearly, the European Union (EU) might be organized along Kantian lines, but as a regional organization it can be no more than a model for world society to imitate. The implication of this move is that Convergence interstate societies are at the far end of the solidarist spectrum. To go further (i.e. for states give up sovereignty and to complement the function of global supranational institutions) is to move into a Kantian world society.

Before summarizing the argument and chapter outline it is worth saying specifically how criminal justice fits into this framework because it does after all provide the empirical focus for this book. A helpful place to start is Emile Durkheim's perception of the role that criminal justice plays in helping to (re)constitute society. For Durkheim, the identification of a crime and the punishment of the criminal

does not serve, or serves only incidentally, to correct the offender or to scare off any possible imitators. From this dual viewpoint its effectiveness may rightly be questioned; in any case it is mediocre. *Its real function is to maintain inviolate the cohesion of society by sustaining the common consciousness in all its vigour.* If that consciousness were thwarted so categorically, it would necessarily lose some of its power, were an emotional reaction from the community not forthcoming to make good that loss. Thus there would result a relaxation in the bonds of social solidarity. That consciousness must therefore be conspicuously reinforced the moment it meets with opposition. The sole means of doing so is to give voice to the unanimous aversion that the crime continues to evoke, and this by an official act, which can only consist in suffering inflicted on the wrongdoer.[71]

In this sense criminal justice is an institutionalized set of practices that are separate from, but obviously designed to restore faith in, those rules that constitute a society. In this sense, it has a similar sociological function to Kant's conception of publicity and (at the other extreme) Bull's conception of war, where war is considered an institution that enforces international law.[72] Yet the idea that *individuals* can be held criminally responsible for violations of international law is, as Bull noted, 'subversive to the whole principle that mankind should be organized as a society of sovereign states'.[73] This is the case even if the crime that is being tried is a crime against the society of states, for example what the Nuremberg Tribunal called a 'crime against peace' or what is now commonly referred to as the 'crime of aggression'. This is still subversive because in international society only states have responsibilities under international law and to safeguard this it is a fundamental principle that individuals acting on behalf of states—either as Heads of State, as diplomats or as soldiers—are immune from prosecution unless the state has consented to a treaty stating otherwise. Criminal justice is doubly subversive, however, when the act being prosecuted is an act against values other than the coexistence of sovereign states, for example what the Nuremberg Tribunal called 'crimes against humanity'. In this latter sense, the process of criminal justice is, in Durkheim's terms, helping to maintain inviolate the cohesion of a society that is based on humanity rather than sovereignty. It is in other words helping to constitute a society that differs fundamentally from pluralist conceptions of international society. The ultimate subversion, however, is if a process of criminal justice responds to crimes against humanity *when states are unwilling or unable to act*. In this scenario criminal justice is helping to constitute a society that by definition cannot be called international society. It is, in the terms outlined above, helping to constitute world society and, as this book shows, this vision finds expression in the Rome Statute.

---

[71] Emile Durkheim, *The Division of Labour in Society* (Glencoe, IL: Free Press, 1933), 63. Emphasis added.
[72] Bull, *The Anarchical Society*, 181.   [73] Bull, *The Anarchical Society*, 146.

THE ARGUMENT AND CHAPTER OUTLINE

The central claims of this book are as follows: the Rome Statute helps to constitute world society by creating an institution (i.e. criminal justice) and a Court (i.e. the ICC) that respond to a universal interest in prosecuting individuals who commit crimes against universal values (i.e. humanity) even when the society of states is unwilling or unable to do so. The United States opposes this for two reasons: first, the Court can exercise jurisdiction over citizens of states who have not consented to the Rome Treaty and the act of resisting the Court on these terms allows US nationalists to sustain the image of America as *the* example of an independent, self-governing republic that is to be imitated by other states; and second, when criminal justice is exercised through the institutions of international society (e.g. universal jurisdiction exercised by national courts or the limited jurisdiction exercised by UN Security Council courts), the United States can control the constitutive processes in ways that are consistent with its identity and its particular interests. In other words, the United States defends the society of states against the vision of world society articulated in the Rome Statute because the society of states enables nationalists to perpetuate a preferred image of 'America' and it helps Realists advance America's national interests. To develop this argument, the book adopts the following chapter outline.

Chapter 2 begins by explaining the moral purpose of legal positivism. In the Vattelian approach, legal positivism helps to protect individual liberty by maintaining the integrity of the social contract between 'the people' and their sovereign. In this respect, the spread of liberal democracy might signal a shift from a Coexistence international society to one characterized by Convergence but it does not necessarily mean the obsolescence of sovereignty or the principle of sovereign consent. Indeed, if the contractarian notion of accountability underpins constitutional rules such as sovereign consent, then one might expect to see liberal democrats resist moves towards a Kantian world society. The shift between Convergence and Confederative societies requires not merely the spread of common values. It also requires a change in constitutive rules, including a shift away from the positivist notion of sovereign consent to one based on a customary understanding of values that speak for 'international society as a whole'. These rules apply to states and their citizens, even when they withhold their consent, and they are embodied by supranational institutions.

The starting point for this move is found in the critique of post-war solidarists like Lauterpacht, Brierly, and Falk. They demonstrate how positivism itself rests on customary understandings of universal values that cannot be derived from the principle of consent (e.g. *pacta sunt servanda*). This does

not mean that positivist institutions like the state, consent, and *pacta sunt servanda* are necessarily illegitimate. Clearly, they serve important social functions. It does mean, however, that as customary rather than natural institutions their status as constitutional norms is not beyond challenge. Indeed as Chapter 2 demonstrates, the post-war solidarists saw consent as an obstacle to the development of law that can better respond to the growing awareness of universal values and universal interests. The positivist response to this challenge is to emphasize the importance of sovereign consent because it is there that the voice of democratically constituted communities finds expression at the international level. In this respect, by protecting the idea of the social contract between the citizen and the state, positivists stand on strong normative ground. An unspoken consequence of their approach, however, is that it clearly limits the development of a concept of 'the global common good' and as a result, it provides individual states with more freedom than they might otherwise expect. Understanding this helps to explain why positivism is resurgent in parts of US academia and indeed US government. Positivism is not merely a means of defending the social contract; it is a means of defending the privileges that the powerful have in a society organized along what in a domestic context would be called 'individualist' rather than 'communitarian' lines.

Although positivists contest the matter, the question of whether individual human beings have rights and responsibilities as a matter of customary international law is somewhat moot. Since the Second World War, treaties codifying the humane treatment of individuals and non-state groups have received near universal ratification. What remains unsettled, however, is the right of national courts to exercise universal jurisdiction and thereby respond to the common interest in seeing individuals prosecuted for inhumane behaviour. Chapter 3 demonstrates the unsettled nature of this institution by focusing on the questions raised in two cases involving the intended prosecution of public officials for crimes that had no direct connection to the courts in question. In the first case, *ex parte Pinochet*, it is noticeable that the House of Lords agreed to the exercise of jurisdiction but only on grounds that Chile had consented to be bound by the 1984 Convention against Torture. The most significant aspect of the House of Lords' decision, however, was the denial of absolute immunity for a former head of state. In this respect, it challenged a fundamental rule of the society of states. Immunity from prosecution is considered not only an attribute of state sovereignty but also an important institution in facilitating 'comity' or good relations between states. This concern resurfaced in *Yerodia* or the *Arrest Warrant Case* before the International Court of Justice (ICJ) in 2002. Here the ICJ held that as a serving Foreign Minister Yerodia, who had been indicted for war crimes by a court in Belgium, was entitled to immunity. Given that one of the reasons for upholding this principle of the society of states was the need to avoid 'judicial chaos', the judgement stands as an excellent example of what the English School call pluralist conceptions of international society. The dissenting opinion of Judge Van den Wyngaert is offered as an example of the solidarist critique.

The *Arrest Warrant Case* had an important impact on Belgium's decision to reform the legislation that allowed its courts to exercise universal jurisdiction. The pressure it experienced, however, was not merely legal. The Belgian government came under intense political pressure to reform its practices when it became clear that the legislation would be used to target Israeli and US officials. The fact that universal jurisdiction is a threat to good relations between states is a strong normative reason for rethinking the way in which international society responds to the common interest in seeing individuals prosecuted for crimes that offend humanity. An additional reason, one that is clearly demonstrated by Belgium's recent experience, is that universal jurisdiction is highly selective and often contingent on not offending the particular interests of the powerful. This argument is at the centre of Chapter 4's analysis of the Rome Statute. It is argued in this chapter that towards the end of the 1990s, international society experienced what might be termed 'a tipping point'. That is, the common interest in seeing individuals punished for crimes that offended the common value of humanity became so well developed that it was no longer willing to accept the selectivity of a system of criminal justice that was dependent on states exercizing universal jurisdiction or the UN Security Council setting up 'ad hoc' international courts. In other words, in the mid-1990s there was a call for a change in the constitutive rules of global politics so that criminal justice was no longer contingent on the interests of those great powers that sat on the Security Council. The response to that call was the Treaty of Rome, which set up the world's first permanent and independent international criminal court.

Chapter 4 argues that the Rome Statute further clarifies the common values based on the humane treatment of individuals and groups. It specifically defines acts—that is genocide, crimes against humanity, and war crimes—that violate those values. The argument that these are now recognized as *jus cogens* and therefore constitutional rules is evident not merely in the preamble of the Statute, which affirms 'that the most serious crimes of concern to the international community as a whole must not go unpunished'. It is also evident in the fact that the rules designed to protect these values have a higher place in the hierarchy of norms. For instance, the norm of diplomatic and sovereign immunity, which as noted above still governs relations between states, does not apply when the ICC exercises jurisdiction. The Court's independence of the society of states is further articulated in Article 15, which enables the

Prosecutor to pursue a case without prior authorization of either a state or the UN Security Council. The process of criminal justice and the reaffirmation of common values based on humanity can therefore now take place, at least theoretically, without state interference. The Court will no doubt depend on states for material support, yet even this can conceivably be provided by non-state actors and in this respect the Rome Statute does offer a truly revolutionary *vision* of world society. To be certain, the drafters of the Rome Statute created an Independent Prosecutor because they wanted to transcend the political machinations of the Security Council and they did not wish to overthrow the society of states. In fact, it is clear from various compromises made during the Rome negotiations that those drafting the Statute obviously saw international society as part of the solution rather than as part of the problem. In this respect, therefore, it is more fitting to argue that the Rome Statute helps to constitute a Kantian world society where cosmopolitan law and cosmopolitan institutions exist in a complementary relationship with national and international law.

For reasons explained in Chapter 4, the Court can only exercise universal jurisdiction when it receives a referral from the UN Security Council. When the Prosecutor acts independently of states, his jurisdiction is curtailed by Article 12 of the Statute. In this instance, he can only exercise jurisdiction if the accused is the national of a state party or if the crime took place on the territory of a state party. Theoretically then the Court is able to exercise jurisdiction over the citizens of states that have withheld their consent from the Treaty of Rome. This can be justified in two ways. First, one might argue, in a Falkian sense, that the Rome Conference was quasi-legislative (see Chapter 2). In other words, the overwhelming majority of states voting for the Court demonstrated that it did reflect the interests of the 'international community as a whole'. Second, one might argue that Article 12 reflects the customary understanding that states have the right to exercise jurisdiction over their nationals and their territory and that all they are doing by creating an independent court is delegating that right. As Chapter 5 demonstrates, the United States rejects both these arguments and insists that the Court is illegitimate because the Statute violates a constitutional principle of the society of states, which is that the citizens of states cannot be bound by laws their sovereign has not consented to. The specific question addressed in Chapter 5 is why the United States has adopted this policy when many, although by no means all, democratic states have been able to support the Court. The Realist argument that the United States has lost the capacity to determine when and where international criminal justice is done, a capacity it had when international criminal justice was a matter exclusively for states and the Security Council, gives only a partial answer. Chapter 5 argues that while this Realist explanation is clearly relevant,

US policy is contingent on those prior social processes that help construct an image of America as an exceptional state. In fact, the act of opposing the ICC can be considered as one of the many social processes that help construct American national identity.

The influence that the United States wields through the institutions of international society is very much on display in Chapter 6. This chapter examines the success that the United States had in negotiating exemptions from the Court's jurisdiction for its citizens. There were two separate strands to this strategy. The first related to Article 98 of the Statute and so-called 'bilateral non-surrender agreements'. Through these agreements, the United States sought to use the negotiating advantage it has in a bilateral setting to guarantee what it could not secure in a multilateral convention. The second related to Article 16 of the Statute and the authority of the Security Council to postpone the judicial process for twelve months if it identifies that process to be a threat to international peace and security. While these articles were not intended to create indefinite exemptions from the Court's jurisdiction, the United States was able to interpret them in a way that helped it to persuade (and sometimes coerce) certain states to grant US citizens and US peacekeepers exemptions from the Court's jurisdiction. For other states, notably those 'like-minded states' that had been so influential in creating the Court, the US strategy was not consistent with either the letter or the spirit of the Statute. Moreover, to the extent that US strategy posed a threat to international peace and security—the United States implicitly threatened to veto future peacekeeping operations if their demands were not met—these states were presented with the dilemma of having to choose between order and justice. Chapter 6 describes in detail how the European states approached this particular dilemma from different perspectives and it uses this case study to refine the concept of 'good international citizenship'.

When Hedley Bull identified threats to the society of states, his attention was drawn to the activities of sub-state actors as well as supranational actors like the ICC. In this vein, Chapter 7 shifts the focus of the book towards the challenges posed by violent non-state groups like al-Qaeda. Of course, al-Qaeda's ideology of unrestrained violence is an obvious threat to the elementary goals that sustain social life, but that is not the focus of the chapter. Rather Chapter 7 focuses on the threat posed to international society by a willingness to treat violent non-state groups such as the Palestinian Liberation Organization (PLO) and al-Qaeda as 'lawful combatants'. As this chapter demonstrates by examining the negotiations on the 1977 Protocols additional to the Geneva Conventions, this willingness has a political but also a humanitarian impulse. For instance, the PLO saw such designation as an indication of their 'state-like' status and humanitarians who sought to encourage respect for the laws of war argued that it would create an incentive for PLO fighters to think twice before targeting civilians. The key point in this chapter, however, is that the United States resisted such moves in part because it believed the Protocol would lead to a process that Hedley Bull called 'the restoration of private international violence' and that this would undermine international society by changing the constitutive rule that grants states an exclusive right to wage war.[74] In resisting this move, the United States was defending another rule that constituted the society of states and to the extent that it helped a key ally (e.g. Israel) discredit an opponent (e.g. the PLO), the United States was acting as a 'modified Realist'. It was helping to construct, to repeat Dunne's formulation, 'a normative framework convenient to itself'.[75]

This process takes on an alarming dimension following 9/11 when the US government argued that al-Qaeda fighters were not entitled to prisoner of war status because they were fighting on behalf of a non-state actor that had not and indeed could not have consented to the laws of war. The government also argued that these individuals were not protected by US law because they were being held outside the jurisdiction of the US courts. In this respect, the United States was using not merely the state's exclusive right to wage war to further discredit al-Qaeda, it was using other key principles of the society of states (i.e. consent and sovereignty) to manufacture a normative order where its military power and its capacity to conduct aggressive interrogations was unrestrained by law. To be certain, there is no argument that can legitimize al-Qaeda. Its activities were no doubt unlawful and its members who committed terrorist acts could obviously have been prosecuted under national or international law. Rather the point made in Chapter 7 is that the United States has used al-Qaeda's status as a non-state belligerent in the war on terrorism to deny its members the rights they might otherwise have expected as human beings. The fate of those at Guantánamo Bay, in other words, illustrates Kant's point that cosmopolitan law is necessary to address what Lord Steyn called the 'legal black hole' that was created by US national and international law.[76]

Finally, Chapter 8 expands on the modified Realist theme by using E.H. Carr's realism to help summarize US policy on the ICC. Unlike those who use Carr to dismiss the ICC and thereby implicitly justify US policy, this chapter argues that Carr's insights can be used to criticize US policy and justify an alternative approach.[77] When the United States argues the process

---

[74] Bull, *The Anarchical Society*, 258–60.   [75] Dunne, 'Sociological Investigations', 81.

[76] Lord J. Steyn, 'Guantánamo Bay: The Legal Black Hole. 27th F. A. Mann Lecture, 25 November 2003', reprinted in *International and Comparative Law Quarterly*, 53 (2004), 1–15.

[77] For an example of those who attack the Court using Carr, see Jack Goldsmith and Stephen Krasner, 'The Limits of Idealism', *Daedulus*, 132 (2003), 47–63.

of international criminal justice should be confined to either national or to UN courts because these do not threaten international order, it is in effect deploying what Carr described as the 'harmony of interests' argument. This, Carr suggests, is little more than a rhetorical device to disguise the pursuit of selfish interests behind the veil of the common interest. This aspect of great power policy is naively utopian because it fails to see how the defence of an unjust order breeds resentment and revisionism. To sustain international order, great powers should follow the example of those powerful interests in domestic society. In other words, they should forfeit the privileges that the old system offers and respond positively to the demands for just change. This is not unknown within American political culture. Indeed, Carr would no doubt have had the example of the New Deal in his mind when formulating this argument. It is argued in Chapter 8 that US policymakers would do well to recall this kind of internationalism because the policy of opposing the Court is not only harming America's international credibility, it is also exacting unsustainable material costs. In other words, the alternatives proposed by the Bush administration have been shown to be too expensive in political, financial and, most importantly, in human terms. For instance, the Bush administration was politically unable to veto the referral of the situation in Darfur having recognized that genocide was taking place there. Its preferred alternative, that is another ad hoc court, was unconvincing, partly because the Bush administration had previously attacked such courts for being financially inefficient. Finally, support for national courts in failed states is often exceptionally costly because they are invariably part of a broader 'nation-building' agenda. This is clearly demonstrated by the enormous human costs of bringing Saddam Hussein to trial in Iraq.

2

International Society—Consent and Custom as Sources of Law

It was noted in Chapter 1 that international society is made up of a set of constitutive rules. These have been equated to what in international law are known as peremptory, *jus cogens* or general rules of international law. These are the rules that identify states as the members of international society, place non-negotiable limitations on their actions and provide a baseline agreement on how other rules are formulated. This formulation finds expression in Article 53 of the Vienna Convention on the Law of Treaties. It defines the peremptory norm as that which is 'accepted and recognized by the international community of states as a whole'. It is 'a norm from which no derogation is permitted and which can be modified only by a subsequent norm of general international law having the same character.'[1] In this sense there is a duality to international law. At one level, law can be made by consenting states; at another deeper level, law can be made by the 'community of states as a whole'. States cannot object to the second type of law and must observe it when making their own contracts. What exactly passes for this second level of 'general international law' is a matter of dispute. Who exactly speaks for the 'community of states as a whole'? What is clear, however, is that the introduction of 'a new law-making procedure which does not require the consent of individual states for the emergence of peremptory rules . . . would obviously amount to a fundamental change in the constitutional principles of the international legal order relating to law-making.'[2]

Such uncertainty does not mean that international society is non-existent, but it does mean that its constitutive rules are a matter of political dispute. Onuf's claim (see Chapter 1) that sovereign equality is *jus cogens* may be a good place to start. As this chapter demonstrates, however, the corollary of this, that international law can only bind states if they first consent to be so bound, is contested. Indeed, the argument for an alternative to this positivist

---

[1] Vienna Convention on the Law of Treaties (1969) May 23, U.N. Doc. A/Conf. 39/27, at: www.un.org/law/ilc/texts/treaties.htm

[2] Gennady M. Danilenko, 'International Jus Cogens: Issues of Law-Making', *European Journal of International Law*, 2 (1991), 47–8.

approach to law-making is that the principle of sovereign consent is an obstacle to the formation of laws that can respond to a growing cosmopolitan awareness and a thicker consensus on common values and common interests. Hedley Bull called this a 'solidarist' conception of international law.[3] More specifically, contemporary solidarists argue that the positivist conception of law provides certain individuals with the legal space to commit acts which their victims have not consented to and then to escape punishment for those acts. This is because such individuals invariably act on behalf of a sovereign government that has withheld its consent and is therefore exempt from that aspect of international law that would otherwise hold them to account. This argument is not to be confused with the idea that such individuals are immune from law that is otherwise applicable because they have sovereign immunity or because they are lawful combatants. That is a separate argument which is itself contested (see Chapters 3 and 7). Rather the concern here is the argument that in an international society constituted by state sovereignty, international law cannot apply in any form to the state, or to the citizens of the state, that withholds its consent. As a result a culture of impunity for human rights abuses is allowed to develop and this is out of step with what solidarists see as a growing cosmopolitan consciousness based on humanity.

From the solidarist perspective, therefore, states can be bound by law that reflects a generalized consensus. This finds expression through progressive interpretations of customary international law. This law applies to states even if they have voted against it, withheld their consent from it or if they have generally objected to it. In this regard it can fulfil the function of constitutional law. For Bull, however, this approach threatened a return to natural law, which international society had once rejected because it lacked legitimacy and because it threatened to undermine international order by prompting states to act on principles that were in conflict with state sovereignty and non-intervention. Indeed this concern, which he expressed in *The Anarchical Society*, resonates with many contemporary critics of customary law. The fear that a customary law of humanity will be used by states to intervene in the sovereign affairs of other states and thereby threaten international comity is discussed in Chapter 3 with specific reference to the state practice of universal jurisdiction. This chapter, however, focuses on questions of legitimacy. The concern of contemporary critics is twofold. First, they fear that by widening the process of law creation to include sources other than the explicit agreements between states, solidarists are in fact giving political significance to the

---

[3] Bull, *The Anarchical Society*, 142.

opinions of groups (and indeed individuals) that have no democratic legitimacy. Second, they fear that by binding states that effectively withhold their consent from customary international law, solidarists are ignoring those opinions that do have democratic legitimacy. In short, contemporary positivists argue that customary international law, particularly the more progressive kind pushed by solidarists, is threatening the moral purpose of the state, which is to preserve the social contract between the subjects and the creators of the law. Undermining the principle that law only binds states that consent, they argue, threatens the society of states and the liberty it protects or at least promises.

This chapter proceeds in three main sections. The first examines a normative reason why consent might be considered a constitutional rule of international society and thus worth defending against its solidarist opponents. Clearly, sovereignty and consent can be understood as rules that defend the state because it is a moral value by itself or because separate self-governing states encourage moral diversity. The focus here, however, is on a Vattelian understanding of sovereignty and consent for three reasons: first, because it is widely regarded as a turning point, where international law moved away from the natural law foundations of the past, and embraced the positivist emphasis on state consent. Second, because Vattel's arguments are ultimately grounded in the same natural rights philosophy as the founding documents of the United States and because *The Law of Nations* obviously had an impact on the founding fathers' view of America's relationship to international society.[4] Thirdly, Vattel is important because many of his themes resonate strongly with the reasons given by the United States for opposing the ICC (see Chapter 5). The second section of the chapter examines the efforts of contemporary solidarists who have sought to bypass sovereign consent and to establish an understanding of customary law that is more responsive to an emerging cosmopolitan consciousness. As noted these arguments have prompted forceful counter-arguments from positivists concerned that these attempts to bypass the principle of consent will undermine the moral purpose of the society of states, which in their mind is to defend liberty by preserving the social contract between the individual and the state. The third section demonstrates how this backlash has found particular expression in the American legal and foreign policy discourse as well as the US judiciary.

---

[4] In fact, Vattel has been described as 'by far the most important treatise writer for Americans'. David J. Sylvester, 'International Law as Sword or Shield? Early American Foreign Policy and the Law of Nations', *International Law and Politics*, 32 (1999), 69.

SOVEREIGN CONSENT AS THE FOUNDATION OF
INTERNATIONAL LAW

The idea that international law can only evolve with the consent of sovereign states is closely associated with the idea that an individual's freedom is realized in, and protected by, particular political communities. For Vattel, nature had created a universal society of humankind, yet man's needs were met sufficiently within particular states. 'Nature', he wrote,

obliges every man to work for his own perfection, and in so doing he works for that of civil society, which can not but be prosperous if composed only of good citizens; and as man finds in well-ordered society the greatest help to the fulfilment of the task imposed upon him by nature of becoming better, and therefore happier, he is unquestionably bound to do all in his power to make that society perfect.[5]

Fundamental to a 'well-ordered society' is the Constitution. This establishes the rights and duties of the citizens and those who govern them. Legislative power 'may be confided by a Nation to the Prince, or an assembly, or to both conjointly', however, 'the fundamental laws [of the Constitution] are excepted from their authority'. This does not mean legislators cannot change the Constitution, but Vattel implies that it requires the consent of more than just a majority of citizens, a suggestion that was clearly taken up by America's founding fathers.[6]

Vattel makes it clear that a universally applicable model constitution does not exist. The 'laws and the constitution of different states must vary according *to the character of the people and other circumstances*.'[7] It is for each nation independently to decide its own constitution.

Since the results of a good or bad constitution are of such importance, and since a Nation is strictly obliged to procure, as far as possible, the best and most suitable one, it has a right to all the means necessary to fulfil that obligation. Hence it is clear that a Nation has full right to draw up for itself its constitution, to uphold it, to perfect it, and to regulate at will all that relates to the government, without interference on the part of anyone. . . . To intermeddle in the domestic affairs of another Nation or to undertake to constrain its councils is to do it an injury.[8]

---

[5] E. de Vattel, *The Law of Nations or the Principles of Natural Law Applied to the Conduct and to the Affairs of Nations and of Sovereigns* (Washington, DC: Carnegie Institution of Washington, [1758] 1916) 15.

[6] Vattel, *The Law of Nations*, 18–19. An amendment to the US Constitution can only be proposed by two-thirds of both legislative chambers and then requires the consent of three-fourths of state legislatures to take effect.

[7] Vattel, *The Law of Nations*, 17. Emphasis added.   [8] Vattel, *The Law of Nations*, 18–19.

From Vattel's perspective then, humanity is naturally divided into particular communities. In these communities individuals find liberty and happiness. How those particular communities would relate to each other would be profoundly influenced by the idea that government rested on the consent of the people.

As the individual submits his will to the state in order to advance his own interests Vattel notes that it 'devolves thenceforth upon that body, the state, and upon its rulers to fulfil the duties of humanity towards outsiders in all matters in which individuals are no longer at liberty to act, and it peculiarly rests with the state to fulfil these duties towards other states.'[9] From this perspective, Vattel derives the principle of sovereign equality, which he articulated in the following famous passage.

Since men are by nature equal, and their individual rights and obligations the same, as coming equally from nature, Nations, which are composed of men and may be regarded as so many free persons living together in a state of nature, are by nature equal and hold from nature the same obligations and the same rights. Strength or weakness in this case counts for nothing. A dwarf is as much a man as a giant is; a small republic is no less a sovereign State than the most powerful kingdom. From this equality it necessarily follows that what is lawful or unlawful for one Nation is equally lawful or unlawful for every other Nation.[10]

The form taken by a Nation's government does not affect this principle. 'The honor due to a Nation belongs fundamentally to the body of the people; and it is shown to the sovereign merely as the representative of the Nation.'[11]

A natural obligation to advance human welfare commits a state to respect the sovereignty of other states. Nations must 'put up with certain things although in themselves unjust and worthy of condemnation, because they cannot oppose them by force without transgressing the liberty of individual Nations and thus destroying the foundations of their natural society.'[12] Beyond this, nations are also bound to help others perfect their own society. The 'spirit of mutual assistance' is both right and prudent. It should not be discarded lightly, as one day a sovereign 'may happen to have like need of help'.[13]

The primary obligation of the state, however, is to the liberty of its own citizens and the particular compact they consented to. 'As a consequence of that liberty and independence', Vattel writes,

it follows that it is for each nation to decide what its conscience demands of it, what it can or can not do; what it thinks well or does not think well to do; and therefore it

---

[9] Vattel, *The Law of Nations*, 6.   [10] Vattel, *The Law of Nations*, 7.
[11] Vattel, *The Law of Nations*, 126.   [12] Vattel, *The Law of Nations*, 8.
[13] Vattel, *The Law of Nations*, 114, 225.

is for each nation to consider and determine what duties it can fulfil towards others without failing in its duty towards itself.[14]

For these reasons, obligations between states are always imperfect as they cannot be enforced and 'give but the right of request'.[15] Thus a poor state can request aid from a rich state but it cannot compel it and while it might be immoral to deny such assistance it cannot be considered unlawful.[16]

Imperfect international obligations can be transformed into legally binding, enforceable and therefore perfect obligations if states consent to being so bound. Only under these circumstances can a state be compelled by another to honour an obligation. In this regard a treaty signed by the sovereign acts as an extension of the social contract. It binds the state even if it is found to work injuriously. 'A treaty is valid', writes Vattel, 'if no exception can be taken to the manner in which it has been drawn up; for this, nothing more is required than that the contracting parties be duly authorized to act and that their consent be mutual and properly declared.'[17] Again, Vattel argues, states have an interest in honouring and being seen to honour their obligations to others. Having consented to honour certain commitments, however, the state gives up the right to interpret how that obligation should be met. 'If promises made by treaty impose on the one side a perfect obligation', he concludes, 'they produce on the other a perfect right. Hence, to violate a treaty is to violate the perfect right of the contracting party, and is thus an injury to him.'[18] As international society has an interest in maintaining the faithful observance of treaties, Nations have 'the right to unite together to check a Nation which shows contempt for them'.[19]

Vattel's philosophy is therefore grounded in the natural law tradition, a fact which for some has been overlooked.[20] His emphasis on sovereign consent,

---

[14] Vattel, *The Law of Nations*, 6.   [15] Vattel, *The Law of Nations*, 6.

[16] Vattel, *The Law of Nations*, 116, 119.

[17] Vattel, *The Law of Nations*, 161. He adds, however: 'If a simple injury or some disadvantage does not suffice to render a treaty invalid, the rule does not hold where the results of the treaty are such as to bring about the ruin of the Nation.' This ambiguity informed the early debate between Republicans (represented by Madison as *Helvidius*) and Federalists (represented by Hamilton as *Pacificus*) on US obligations towards revolutionary France. See D. G. Lang, *Foreign Policy in the Early Republic. The Law of Nations and the Balance of Power* (Baton Rouge and London: Louisiana University Press, 1985).

[18] Vattel, *The Law of Nations*, 163.

[19] Vattel, *The Law of Nations*, 188. Again Vattel qualifies this by saying that sovereigns may have good reason for reneging on a treaty. 'It is the sovereign who fails to keep his promise on clearly trivial grounds, or who does not take the trouble to offer reasons, or to disguise his conduct and cover up his bad faith—it is he who deserves to be treated as an enemy of the human race.' Vattel, *The Law of Nations*, 189.

[20] Brown, Nardin, and Rengger suggest that Vattel's modernity has been exaggerated by those seeking the origins of international law. They cite Andrew Hurrell, 'Vattel: Pluralism and Its Limits', in Ian Clark and Iver B. Neumann (eds.), *Classical Theories of International Relations*

however, is widely regarded as marking a turning point in the evolution in international law. From the late eighteenth century onwards, international law is usually understood to be positive, not natural law. It is positive, not in the Austinian sense of being enacted by a superior but in being jointly willed by states, who bind themselves explicitly through treaties or implicitly through customary international law.[21] The opinion of the Permanent Court of International Justice (PCIJ) in the 1927 *Lotus Case* is often cited as the best articulation of this view. This case involved the collision of a French Steamer 'Lotus' with a Turkish merchant ship. The collision killed several Turkish nationals. Turkey claimed that it had jurisdiction over the case and convicted the French officer in charge of the Lotus. France, however, claimed that Turkey had violated international law, which it claimed gave French courts *exclusive* jurisdiction over the case. Rejecting France's claims, the PCIJ found that states were free to extend the application of their laws and the jurisdiction of their courts to persons, property, and acts outside their territory. In fact, it noted that the courts of many countries understood territorial jurisdiction to include acts, the effects of which were felt in that country, even though the perpetrator might have been in another country (or on a ship carrying the flag of another country) at the moment of commission. As an indicator of the positivist nature of international law, the following passage from the Court's opinion is often cited:

International law governs relations between independent States. The rules of law binding upon States therefore emanate from their own free will as expressed in conventions or by usages generally accepted as expressing the principles of law and established in order to regulate the relations between these co-existing independent communities or with a view to the achievement of common aims. Restrictions upon the freedom of States cannot therefore be presumed.[22]

The point here is that this understanding of international law was informed not only by the political reality of nation-states in the modern era. It was also informed by the belief that sovereign nation-states were the best hope of

(London: Macmillan, 1996), 233–55. See Chris Brown, Terry Nardin, and Nicholas Rengger (eds.), *International Relations in Political Thought. Texts from the Ancient Greeks to the First World War* (Cambridge: Cambridge University Press, 2002), 422.

[21] Brown, Nardin, and Rengger (eds.), *International Relations in Political Thought*, 323. See also Terry Nardin, 'Legal Positivism as a Theory of International Society' and Frederick G. Whelan, 'Legal Positivism and International Society', in David R. Mapel and Terry Nardin (eds.), *International Society: Diverse Ethical Perspectives* (Princeton, NJ: Princeton University Press, 1998), 17–35 and 36–53 respectively; and Stephen Hall, 'The Persistent Spectre: Natural Law, International Order and the Limits of Legal Positivism', *European Journal of International Law*, 12 (2001), 269–307.

[22] *The Case of the S.S. 'Lotus'*, Permanent Court of International Justice, 7 September 1927.

realizing the enlightenment ideal of human freedom. Law had to be the product of human reason and reason had determined that, at least according to the Vattelian view, liberty was best secured by nation-states. If international law was to contribute to the enlightenment ideal, therefore, it could only develop with the consent of sovereign states. Of course, this view would be shaken to its core by the inhumanity of sovereign states, which was exposed most clearly by the Second World War. Even before then, however, humanitarians had insisted that standards of civilization existed and sovereign states must respect those standards regardless of whether they had consented to be bound by them.[23] Nonetheless, the view that an international society of sovereign states should be understood not as a 'second best' alternative to a cosmopolitan world society, made necessary by the regrettable reality of a politically significant moral pluralism, but as an end in itself, was and still is a significant one.[24]

CONSENT AND CONSENSUS IN THE CREATION OF INTERNATIONAL LAW

The point that the Vattelian tradition and legal positivism grew out of and, in certain respects, remained dependent on natural law foundations should not be overlooked. Indeed, this fact was at the centre of the post-war solidarist critique, which usually started by noting how contracts could only be considered binding if another source of law had already determined that. So for instance, Brierly argued that

consent of itself cannot create an obligation; it can do so only within a system of law which declares that consent duly given, as in a treaty or a contract, shall be binding on the party consenting. To say that the rule pacta sunt servanda [i.e. promises must be kept and treaties fulfilled] is itself founded on consent is to argue in a circle. A consistently consensual theory again would have to admit that if consent is withdrawn, the obligation created by it comes to an end. Most positivist writers would not admit this, but to deny it is in effect to fall back on an unacknowledged source of obligation,

---

[23] See e.g. the so-called 'Martens Clause' in The Hague Convention II of 1899. This found law in 'the principles of humanity and the dictates of public conscience'. Adam Roberts and Richard Guelff, *Documents on the Laws of War* 3rd edn. (Oxford: Oxford University Press, 2003), 8–9.

[24] Whether international society is best seen as a stepping stone to a better world or as an end in itself is an important question within English School writing. See Chris Brown, 'The "English School": International Theory and International Society', in Mathias Albert, Lothar Brock, and Klaus Dieter Wolf (eds.), *Civilizing World Politics. Society and Community Beyond the State* (Lanham, Boulder, New York, and London: Rowman and Littlefield, 2000), 91–102; see also Chris Brown 'International Theory and International Society: The Viability of the Middle Way?' *Review of International Studies*, 21 (1995), 183–96.

which whatever it may be, is not the consent of the state, for that has ceased to exist.[25]

In fact Vattel also acknowledged this when he wrote that states give up the right unilaterally to decide how to interpret a treaty once it had been accepted as law. Like Vattel some post-war solidarists accepted that the source for *pacta sunt servanda* was to be found in nature. Thus, Lauterpacht argued that the laws which were derived from state consent were only part of what could be understood as international law. 'In a wider sense', he added, 'the binding force even of that part of it that originates in consent is based on the law of nature as expressive of the social nature of man'.[26] More recently, Louis Henkin acknowledges that that 'the normative character of a treaty depends on an antecedent, underlying 'constitutional' principle, rooted perhaps in the natural law, the principle *pacta sunt servanda*, agreements are to be observed'.[27]

For some solidarists, positivism had not only forgotten the natural source of legal obligation, it also had legitimized state actions that violated other aspects of the 'higher law'. So for instance, looking back on the Second World War, Lauterpacht defended as a matter of international law the natural rights and responsibilities of individuals as opposed to states.

Undoubtedly, international law is primarily—though not exclusively—a body of rules governing the relations of states, i.e. of individuals organized as a state. But this circumstance cannot affect decisively the moral content of international law and the dictates of reason and of the general principles which underlie it. It may be true to say that 'after all' states are not individuals; but it is even more true to say that 'after all' states are individuals. For this reason there can be no insuperable difficulty in applying generally recognized principles of law to the conduct of individuals acting as members of state and on behalf of their state.[28]

To those positivists who rejected natural law on grounds of legitimacy and the consequences it might have for order between states, Lauterpacht pointed out the failure of positivism to act as any source of real restraint. 'The law of nature', he wrote, 'has been rightly exposed to the charge of vagueness and arbitrariness. But the uncertainty of the "higher law" is preferable to the arbitrariness and insolence of naked force'.[29]

---

[25] J. L. Brierly, *The Law of Nations. An Introduction to the International Law of Peace*, 6th edn. (Oxford: Clarendon Press, 1963), 53.

[26] Hersch Lauterpacht, 'The Grotian Tradition in International Law', *The British Yearbook of International Law*, 23 (1946), 21.

[27] Louis Henkin, *International Law: Politics and Values* (1995) 28. Quoted by Hall, 'The Persistent Spectre', 285.

[28] Lauterpacht, 'The Grotian Tradition', 28.

[29] Lauterpacht, 'The Grotian Tradition', 24.

Not all solidarists accepted a return to natural law foundations such as this.[30] What united solidarists, however, was their shared frustration with the manner in which international law had in effect reified the state at the expense of other common values. In this way J. L. Brierly noted how positivist assumptions were not only based on mere impressions of what appeared to be 'natural' in the modern era, he also argued that those impressions were out of step with the requirements of an increasingly interdependent world.

By teaching that the 'natural' state of nations is an independence which does not admit the existence of a social bond between them [Vattel] made it impossible to explain or justify their subjection to law; yet their independence is no more 'natural' than their interdependence.... It is true that in Vattel's own day the interdependence of states was less conspicuous in international practice than it is today; and this partly excuses the onesidedness of his system. None the less, by cutting the frail moorings which bound international law to any sound principle of obligation he did it an injury which has not yet been repaired.[31]

The source of legal obligation for Brierly was not consent but custom, which did not depend on the authorization of the state to be legally binding. Of course, positivists do not deny that custom, which is defined as evidence that a general practice is accepted as law, can bind states. Indeed, Vattel recognized that states may 'bind themselves by tacit consent'. This, he added, 'is the foundation of all practices which have been introduced among Nations, and which form the custom of Nations or the Law of Nations founded upon custom'.[32] Yet this formulation has since been interpreted by positivists to mean that states are not bound by custom if they persistently object to such laws. Again Vattel is a source of this. In order to protect the principle of consent, states are 'bound to observe it [custom] towards one another so long as they have not expressly declared their unwillingness to follow it any longer'.[33] The connection between persistent objection and the social contract is easy to see. As Stephen Toope notes, it fits 'neatly within the consent based theory of law creation. The

---

[30] In fact, Lauterpacht himself would later argue that the obligation to respect human rights was found in state practices such as the Nuremberg Trials and treaties like the UN Charter. This interpretation, however, was informed by 'the realisation that there is no rule of international law which definitely precludes individuals and bodies other than states from acquiring directly rights under or being bound by duties imposed by customary or conventional international law, and that the developments of the last quarter of a century have translated that capacity, in many fields and in respect of both rights and duties, into part of positive law'. Hersch Lauterpacht, *International Law and Human Rights* (London: Stevens and Sons, 1950), 4.

[31] J. L. Brierly, *The Law of Nations: An introduction to the International Law of Peace*, 6th edn. (Oxford: Oxford University Press, 1963), 40. See also C. Wilfred Jenks, *Law, Freedom and Welfare* (London: Stevens and Sons, 1963), 71–100; John A. Perkins, 'The Changing Foundations of International Law: From State Consent to State Responsibility', *Boston University International Law Journal*, 15 (1997), 452.

[32] Vattel, *Law of Nations*, 11a.   [33] Vattel, *Law of Nations*, 9.

doctrine was essentially an escape hatch to allow the free operation of the principle of sovereign equality'.[34]

Yet to solidarists like Brierly, customary law cannot be understood as the product of implied consent. Rather 'a customary rule is observed, not because it has been consented to, but because it is believed to be binding, and whatever may be the explanation or the justification for that belief, its binding force does not depend, and is not felt by those who follow it to depend, on the approval of the individual or the state to which it is addressed.'[35] The implication of this, of course, is that customary rules can apply to states that object. In this sense, the constitutive rules of international society are not the product of those treaties that are written and adopted by states, nor are they the product of a jurist's interpretation of natural law. Rather they are customary rules the evidence for which is found in general practices that are recognized as imposing legal obligations. Treaties may help to codify these rules but the constitutive rules of international society are articulated as customary law that is recognized by international society as a whole. To this extent, they define international society as something having an ontological status separate from the will of individual states. The question that then arises, however, is how do we identify customary international law and how do we know that it has achieved a constitutional or peremptory status by articulating the concerns of 'international society as a whole.'

Like Brierly, Richard Falk argued that the actions of individual states took on additional significance in an increasingly interdependent world. A legal framework that allowed such states to avoid legal obligation for the impact their actions had on other states was neither legitimate nor sensible in terms of the common interest. In this context, Falk welcomed what he saw as a discernible trend from consent to consensus as the basis of international legal obligations. If international society was to function effectively under these new conditions, it required, he argued, 'a limited legislative authority, at minimum, to translate an overriding consensus among states into rules of order and norms of obligation despite the opposition of one or more sovereign states.'[36] For Falk this consensus could be found in a supermajority vote at international organizations like the UN General Assembly. While such a vote would require a change in the UN Charter to be formally binding, Falk followed Higgins

[34] Stephen Toope, 'Powerful But Unpersuasive? The Role of the United States in the Evolution of Customary International Law', in Michael Byers and Georg Nolte (eds.), *United States Hegemony and the Foundations of International Law* (Cambridge: Cambridge University Press, 2003), 308.

[35] Brierly, *The Law of Nations*, 52.

[36] Richard Falk, 'On the Quasi-Legislative Competence of the General Assembly', *American Journal of International Law*, 60 (1966), 785.

in arguing that it could act as the kind of customary international law that applied even to those states (i.e. the minority) that objected.[37] To illustrate the new process in action, Falk noted how a consensus in the General Assembly proscribing the practice of apartheid in South Africa contributed to the ICJ's judgment that South Africa's continued presence in what is now Namibia was illegal.[38]

From the solidarist perspective, a shift to consensus would mean a more democratic and thus more responsive means of creating law for international society as a whole. Yet for positivists, Falk's proposal simply exacerbated the problems associated with customary international law. It is generally thought that customary international law is derived not merely from the observance of a pattern of state practice (e.g. the respect for sovereignty) but also an understanding that states follow these practices because they believe there is a legal obligation to do so. This second aspect is commonly referred to as *opinio juris*. It is crucial for developing the notion that common practices provide evidence of law and to distinguish them from those habitual acts that are motivated solely by courtesy or tradition.[39] For instance, a meeting between diplomats might customarily begin with a handshake, but it is not a violation of law if a meeting does not start in this way. More significantly, the jurist requires evidence that a practice occurs because there is an understanding of legal obligation to be able then to claim that customary international law continues to exist even if state practice suggests otherwise. So for instance, states cannot claim a customary right to use torture simply because torture is prevalent in state practice. While states clearly do engage in torture they rarely claim *the right* to do so. Moreover, they usually claim that the act did not actually constitute torture, thereby implicitly recognizing the prohibited nature of torture. In such instances, as Murphy puts it, the problem 'is one of enforcement of a customary norm, not of its lack of existence.'[40]

There is therefore an enormous interpretive burden on the jurist seeking to apply customary international law and for positivists the whole process is far too vague to have any form of legitimacy. This concern is exacerbated by the fact that jurists feel able to call on the opinions of non-state actors to help ease their burden. In fact, Article 38 (4) of the Statute of ICJ explicitly

---

[37] Rosalyn Higgins, *The Development of International Law Through the Political Organs of the United Nations* (Oxford: Oxford University Press, 1963).

[38] Falk, 'On Quasi-Legislative Competence', 790; see also Richard A. Falk, *The Status of Law in International Society* (Princeton, NJ: Princeton University Press, 1970), 70, 87–8.

[39] See Michael Byers, *Custom, Power and the Power of Rules. International Relations and Customary International Law* (Cambridge: Cambridge University Press, 1999) 18; see also Peter Malanczuk, *Akehurst's Modern Introduction to International Law*, 7th edn. (London and New York: Routledge, 2003), 44–5.

[40] John Murphy, *The United States and the Rule of Law in International Affairs* (Cambridge: Cambridge University Press, 2004), 101.

states that the 'judicial decisions and the teachings of the most highly qualified publicists of the various nations' can be regarded as a 'subsidiary means for the determination of rules of law'. This leads positivists to fear that customary international law is not only ignoring the opinion of democratically constituted (and therefore legitimate) states, but that it is empowering a class of international jurists that have little or no legitimacy because they are not accountable to the politicians that represent those people that are subject to customary law. This, of course, goes to the heart of the relationship between the judge and the democratically elected politician, which is discussed in more detail in Chapter 5. The point here is one that is expressed by Hedley Bull in *The Anarchical Society*. For some international lawyers,

the attraction of the consensus [as opposed to consent] doctrine lies in the opportunities it offers to develop international law not in relation to the actual practice of states but in conformity to *their views* as what international order or international justice requires. In this form the doctrine that international law derives from the consensus of states or 'the will of the international community' represents not an attempt to amplify positive international law, but the desire, as it were, to allow natural law to enter by the back door.[41]

While this might not be an entirely accurate portrayal of the solidarist view, Bull's concerns find expression among many contemporary commentators. For instance, Paul Stephan argues that customary international law provides the academic community with a 'hermeneutic monopoly'. This, he adds, is the 'antithesis of democracy'.[42] Mark Weisburd reaches a similar conclusion. He attacks courts for 'relying on sources other than state behaviour to determine the content of customary international law'. This process is dangerous because it

effectively transfers legislative power to groups with little right to claim it—such as judges of international tribunals whose authority is carefully circumscribed in their founding instruments—or no right at all—such as legal academics. . . . The framing of rules of law is necessarily a political act. The ultimate problem with efforts to shift the focus of customary international law determinations from state practice to something else is that the something else, whatever it is, will lack any sort of political legitimacy.[43]

---

[41] Bull, *The Anarchical Society*, 152, emphasis added. See also A. V. Lowe, 'Do General Rules of International Law Exist?' *Review of International Studies*, 9 (1983), 212. Lowe suggests norms based on consensus rather than consent gave natural law 'a new lease of life'; and John Vincent, 'Western Conceptions of a Universal Moral Order', *British Journal of International Studies*, 4 (1978), 34. Vincent argues these developments represent a return to natural law but that this 'might be defended as a source of morality'.

[42] Paul Stephan, 'International Governance and American Democracy', *Chicago Journal of International Law*, 1 (2000), 245–6.

[43] Weisburd, 'American Judges and International Law', 1530. Judge Robert Bork adds that relying on the opinions of professors 'is not only anti-constitutional and undemocratic, it is

This sentiment is echoed by John Bolton. He complains that customary international law effectively takes 'critical political and legal decisions out of the hands of nation-states by operationally overriding their own international decision-making processes.' He charges what he calls 'Globalists' with having 'a very conscious policy…to judicialize key decisions, thus removing them from common political processes, and, in effect to supersede national constitutional standards with international ones.'[44] The point here is not that judges should stop acting as a restraint on a state. After all, liberals expect the courts to protect individuals against the tyranny of the state, even the democratic state. Rather the point is that judges must only interpret laws that have been accepted by the nation or by 'the people'. Customary international law cannot always claim this foundation and judges therefore should not apply it, at least according to this view. As Stephan puts it, it is

one thing for courts, surveying precedent and relying on a variety of substantive and process preferences, to choose a rule that governs our conduct. It is another for courts to take over a prefabricated system of rules and norms, constructed by a loose alliance of like-minded academics and international law specialists through a form of advocacy that involves no democratic checks. These arguments provide a principled basis for rejecting the wholesale incorporation of customary international law into US law.[45]

As these references suggest, these opinions are prominent in US academia and they have found their way into US government. Bolton of course has been a high-profile member of the Bush administration. While these opinions by no means determine the attitudes of either the political or the judicial branches of government, it is clear that the positivist rejection of customary international law is having an influence.

THE UNITED STATES AND CUSTOMARY
INTERNATIONAL LAW

In March 1898, while waging war against Spain, the United States seized the Cuban fishing vessel *Paquete Habana*. The seizure and subsequent sale was later ruled unlawful by the US Supreme Court because under customary international law fishing vessels that posed no risk were exempt from seizure.

class oriented. The professoriat in social matters is way to the left of the American public'. Robert H. Bork, 'Judicial Imperialism', *Wall Street Journal*, 17 June 2003.

[44] John R. Bolton, 'Should We Take Global Governance Seriously?', *Chicago Journal of International Law*, 1 (2000), 212.

[45] Stephan, 'International Governance and American Democracy', 238.

Justice Gray's opinion contained this often quoted passage defending the application of customary international law.

International law is pa⸳   ⸳w. and must be ascertained and administered by the courts of jus⸳⸳⸳⸳ ⸳⸳ ⸳⸳⸳⸳⸳⸳⸳⸳⸳⸳ ⸳⸳⸳⸳⸳⸳⸳⸳⸳⸳⸳ as often as questions of right depending ⸳⸳⸳ ⸳⸳ are d⸳⸳⸳ presen⸳⸳d for the⸳⸳ de⸳ermination. For this purpose, where there is no trea⸳⸳ ⸳⸳d ⸳⸳ ⸳⸳⸳⸳⸳olling e⸳⸳⸳⸳utive or le⸳⸳⸳⸳⸳ve ac⸳ or judicial decision, resort must be had ⸳⸳ ⸳⸳⸳ ⸳⸳⸳⸳⸳⸳⸳ ⸳⸳⸳ ⸳⸳⸳⸳⸳ ⸳⸳ ⸳⸳⸳⸳⸳⸳⸳ ⸳⸳ations, and, as evidence of these, to the works of ⸳⸳⸳⸳⸳⸳ ⸳⸳⸳ co⸳⸳⸳⸳⸳⸳⸳⸳⸳⸳s who by years of labor, research, and experience have made themsel⸳⸳⸳ ⸳⸳⸳uliarly well acquainted with the subjects of which they treat. Such ⸳⸳ ⸳⸳⸳⸳orted to by judicial tribunals, not for the speculations of their authors concerning what the law ought to be, but for trustworthy evidence of what the law really is.[46]

In 1997, however, this approach was challenged by Curtis Bradley and Jack Goldsmith in their seminal article 'Customary International Law [CIL] as Federal Common Law: a Critique of the Modern Position'.[47] There were two aspects to their critique. First, they joined those who considered customary international law to be so vague that it in effect turned judges with no democratic mandate into legislators. While some argued that judges merely interpreted what was good for international society as a whole based on the evidence of general practice, Bradley and Goldsmith argued that this 'interpretation' merely reflected the judge's subjective opinion of what the law should be. In other words, those who argued custom was a valid source of law assumed that a clear distinction existed

between law-interpretation and lawmaking that cannot survive even the mildest of legal realist critiques. More importantly, it ignores the character of CIL lawmaking: CIL is often unwritten, the necessary scope and appropriate sources of 'state practice' are unsettled, and the requirement that states follow customary norms from a 'sense of legal obligation' is difficult to verify. Given [...this...] it makes no sense to say judges 'discover' an objectively identifiable CIL. In fact, the process of identifying and applying CIL is at least as subjective as the domestic common law process. This is particularly true of the new CIL, which is less tied than traditional CIL to 'objective' evidence of state practice.[48]

---

[46] The Paquete Habana, 175 U.S. 700 (1900).

[47] Curtis A. Bradley and Jack L. Goldsmith, 'Customary International Law as Federal Common Law: A Critique of the Modern Position', *Harvard Law Review*, 110 (1997), 815–76.

[48] Bradley and Goldsmith, 'Customary International Law', 855. For an elaboration that stresses the distinction between old and new customary international law, where the latter deals with the relationship between the state and its citizen, see Bradley and Goldsmith, 'Commentary: Federal Courts and the Incorporation of International Law', *Harvard Law Review*, 111 (1998), 2250–75.

Second, even if judges could discern 'objective' practice, customary international law was by no means applicable in US courts because its source is 'the international community as a whole' and not the American people. Only those treaties that had been ratified by a two-thirds majority of the US Senate could become what the US Constitution called 'the supreme Law of the Land'. Without being codified by such a treaty or statute the application of customary international law would be

in tension with basic notions of American representative democracy. When a federal court applies CIL as federal common law, it is not applying law generated by US law-making processes. Rather, it is applying law derived from the views and practices of the international community. The foreign governments and other non-U.S. participants in this process 'are neither representative of the American political community nor responsive to it.'[49]

However, the centrepiece of Bradley and Goldsmith's argument was their reading of the 1938 US Supreme Court decision in *Erie Railroad Co.* v. *Tompkins*. While this specific case did not involve customary international law, it did involve the application of federal common law to a dispute involving parties from two different states in the union. In Bradley and Goldsmith's article, federal common law is analogous to customary international law to the extent that it is a body of unwritten rules developed by courts in the absence of clear and direct constitutional or statutory provision. Federal law had grown as a response to the increased interdependence of the states in the union. For instance, federal common law was often used to resolve interstate disputes concerning boundaries, water rights, and transportation. In the 1938 *Erie* decision, however, the Supreme Court ruled that federal common law did not apply and reaffirmed the positivist assumption that 'law in the sense of which courts speak of it today does not exist without some definite authority behind it.'[50] In other words, the law that applied should be statutory not common law, because only the former could guarantee the kind of legitimacy expected of a democracy. Indeed, this ruling was in part a response to the concern that federal common law 'is often little less than what the judge advancing the doctrine thinks at the time should the general law on a particular subject'.[51] The Supreme Court in other words had adopted a strictly positivist approach to the source of law and from this Bradley and Goldsmith drew the conclusion

---

[49] Bradley and Goldsmith, 'Customary International Law', 857. Citing Phillip R. Trimble, 'A Revisionist View of Customary International Law', *UCLA Law Review*, 33 (1986), 721.

[50] Justice Brandeis for the majority in *Erie Railroad Co.* v. *Tompkins* US (1938), quoted by Bradley and Goldsmith, 'Customary International Law', 853.

[51] Justice Brandeis for the majority in *Erie Railroad Co.* v. *Tompkins* US (1938), quoted by Lawrence Lessig, '*Erie*-Effects of Volume 110: An Essay on Context in Interpretive Theory', *Harvard Law Review*, 110 (1997), 1793–4.

that contrary to the Paquete Habana decision customary international law could no longer be applied in US courts without prior statutory authority. 'This strand of Erie', they concluded,

requires federal courts to identify the sovereign source for every rule of decision. Because the appropriate 'sovereigns' under the U.S. Constitution are the federal government and the states, all law applied by federal courts must either be federal or state law. After Erie, then, a federal court can no longer apply CIL in the absence of some domestic authorization to do so . . . After Erie, CIL no more applies in federal courts in the absence of domestic authorization than does the law of France or Mars.[52]

Bradley and Goldsmith's argument provoked 'a firestorm of protest from the academy'.[53] At the heart of the response was the claim that *Erie* did not rule out federal common law but limited it to the determination of federal issues. It was, the critics added, clearly the intent of the founding fathers to ensure respect for 'law of nations' by assigning responsibility for its enforcement to the three branches of federal government including the courts.[54] This might have been a consequence of US weakness and a concern to avoid giving the great powers a pretext for war;[55] or it might have been be seen as 'a badge of honour' for the new republic (i.e. enforcing the law of nations helped the United States constitute itself as an independent sovereign state).[56] Either way the founders clearly intended that customary international law, or what was then called the 'law of nations', could be used in federal courts without statutory authorization.

Bradley and Goldsmith's critics further noted that US courts had in fact continued to apply customary international law long after *Erie*. Perhaps the best-known example is the 1980 *Filártiga* v. *Peña-Irala* decision. In this case, Dr. Joel Filártiga, a political opponent of the Paraguayan dictator General Stroessner, along with his daughter Dolly Filártiga, sued Norberto Peña-Irala, a former Inspector General of Police in Asunción, for the torture and murder in 1976 of their son and brother Joelito Filártiga. Both plaintiffs were citizens of Paraguay, but Dolly had applied for permanent political asylum while visiting the United States in 1978. Peña-Irala, who had been living in the

---

[52] Bradley and Goldsmith, 'Customary International Law', 853–4.

[53] Murphy, *The United States*, 97.

[54] Gerald L. Neuman, 'Sense and Nonsense about Customary International Law: a Response to Professors Bradley and Goldsmith', *Fordham Law Review*, 66 (1997), 371–92; Harold Hongju Koh, 'Commentary: Is International Law Really State Law', *Harvard Law Review*, 111 (1998), 1824–59.

[55] Beth Stephens, 'The Law of Our Land: Customary International Law as Federal Law after Erie', *Fordham Law Review*, 66 (1997), 419–25.

[56] Anne-Marie Burley, 'The Alien Tort Statute and the Judiciary Act of 1789: A Badge of Honor', *American Journal of International Law*, 83 (1989), 461–93.

United States, was arrested in April 1979 in the United States as an illegal alien. Although the court for the Eastern District of New York where the suit was originally filed dismissed the case on grounds that such issues were beyond the scope of the law of nations, the Second Circuit Court of Appeals overturned this. Citing the §1350 of the 1789 Judiciary Act [otherwise known as the Alien Tort Claims Act (ATCA)] it noted that the First US Congress established district court jurisdiction over 'all causes where an alien sues for a tort only (committed) in violation of the law of nations'. The Court of Appeals continued:

Construing this rarely-invoked provision, we hold that deliberate torture perpetrated under color of official authority violates *universally accepted norms of the international law of human rights*, regardless of the nationality of the parties. Thus, whenever an alleged torturer is found and served with process by an alien within our borders §1350 provides federal jurisdiction.[57]

This followed the submission of the affidavits of a number of distinguished international legal scholars (Richard Falk, Thomas Franck, Richard Lillich, and Myres MacDougal) who stated unanimously that the law of nations prohibits absolutely the use of torture.[58] The State Department, under the political direction of the Carter administration, also submitted a statement arguing that 'international law now embraces the obligation of a state to respect the fundamental human rights of its citizens'.[59] The Filártigas were ultimately awarded $10 million. Unfortunately for the Filártigas, they were never able

---

[57] *Filártiga* v. *Peña-Irala*, 630 F.2d. 30 June 1980. Emphasis added.

[58] A more recent case shows that federal courts might be willing to apply customary international law, but they are less willing to accept academic opinion such as this. On 5 September 1996, a federal jury found Ramzi Yousef guilty of the bombing of a Philippine Airline in August 1994, which had been flying from Manila to Japan. The attack did not harm any American citizen, but it killed one Japanese national and injured a number of others. In finding jurisdiction on this charge, the district court relied, in part, on the universality principle, which gives states the right to apply their laws abroad if the act in question rises to the level of a universal crime. Bombing an aircraft, they ruled, was equivalent to hijacking, which, according to the Third Restatement of Foreign Relations (a document written by the American Law Institute to help clarify the law), is a universal crime under customary international law. At appeal, however, the 2nd Circuit Court attacked the district court's reliance on a form of scholarly treatise, i.e. the Restatement. 'This notion—that professors of international law enjoy a special competence to prescribe the nature of customary international law wholly unmoored from legitimating territorial or national responsibilities, the interests and practices of states, or (in countries such as ours) the process of democratic consent—may not be unique, but it is certainly without merit'. *U.S.* v. *Yousef*, 327 F.3d 56 (2nd Cir. 2003). See Anthony Clark Arend, 'International Law, Terrorism and U.S. Courts', paper presented at the International Studies Annual Convention, Montreal, 20 March 2004. See also Weisburd, 'American Judges and International Law', 1507–8, 1517.

[59] Quoted by Neuman, 'Sense and Nonsense', 380. A similar position was taken by the Clinton administration in *Kadic* v. *Karadzic*, where a federal court awarded $745 million to the victims of the Bosnian Serb leader. See Koh, 'Commentary: Is International Law Really State Law', 1824.

to collect damages and US immigration officials deported the Paraguayan officer.[60]

In this case, a statute (i.e. the 1789 Judiciary Act) reaffirms the constitutional duty of the courts to punish those who offend the law of nations, but the argument that human rights are protected under the law of nations is contested on several levels. At one level the conservative Judge Robert Bork argues that the Judiciary Act applies to the law of nations as it existed in 1789. At that time, the rights in question were those of foreign ambassadors and certainly not the conception of human rights applied in *Filártiga*.[61] This new expression of customary international law he argued

is a serious incursion by courts into the domain of Congress, involving, as it does, the enactment of world-wide law by an unholy alliance of imperialistic judges and a leftish cadre of international law professors. In 1789 the law of nations was just that, a law governing the relationship of nations, not of individuals.[62]

This distinction between 'old' custom that articulated the rights of states and 'new' custom that articulates the rights of individuals is also evident in Bradley and Goldsmith's argument. 'The judicial incorporation of new CIL', they write, goes to 'the heart of what the Constitution permits states to regulate unless and until the federal political branches, in which the states and their citizens have a voice, pre-empt state law through democratic processes.'[63] In this sense, Bradley and Goldsmith's argument is more concerned with a particular kind of customary international law, one that was no longer, in their eyes, 'benign'.[64] Given this, they might be guilty of using positivism in the way they accuse certain judges of using custom. That is, to paraphrase Lessig, positivism is not an objective or apolitical standard of law-making. Rather it is a means of organizing opposition to a practice that is no longer considered benign by those threatened by it.

---

[60] For an overview of the case and its consequences, see Richard Alan White, *Breaking Silence: The Case That Changed the Face of Human Rights* (Washington, DC: Georgetown University Press, 2004).

[61] *Tel-Oren* v. *Libyan Arab Republic* 726 F.2d 774 (DC Cir. 1984). The plaintiffs in this case were survivors and representatives of persons murdered in an armed attack on a civilian bus in Israel in March 1978. They filed suit for compensatory and punitive damages in a district court, naming as defendants the Libyan Arab Republic and the Palestine Liberation Organization among others. The district court dismissed the case citing lack of jurisdiction.

[62] Robert H. Bork, 'Judicial Imperialism', *Wall Street Journal*, 17 June 2003.

[63] Bradley and Goldsmith, 'Commentary: Federal Courts and the Incorporation of International Law', 2268.

[64] Lawrence Lessig argues that *Erie* should be understood not as a decision that overturned incorrect past arguments, but as an expression of a new interpretive context. The legal positivism that underpinned the judgment became a way 'of organizing opposition to a practice that was no longer...benign'. Lawrence Lessig, 'Erie-Effects of Volume 110: An Essay on Context in Interpretive Theory', *Harvard Law Review*, 110 (1997), 1794.

Since *Filártiga*, the Supreme Court has rejected the view that only customary international adopted and made enforceable by the political branches can
be applied in US courts. On 29 June 2004, Justice Souter delivered the Court's
opinion in *Sosa* v. *Alvarez-Machain*, a case that involved claims under the Alien
Tort Statute.[65] The facts of this case are as follows: in 1985 a Drug Enforcement
Agent in Mexico was captured and tortured to death. In response, US and
Mexican agents arrested Alvarez-Machain and took him to the United States
for trial. Alvarez-Machain was acquitted and he subsequently sued Mexican
nationals in US courts for unlawful arrest under the ATCA. On the question
of whether ATCA applied, the majority found that

no development in the two centuries from the enactment of [the ATCA] to the birth
of the modern line of cases beginning with *Filártiga* v. *Peña-Irala* ... has categorically
precluded federal courts from recognizing a claim under the law of nations as an
element of common law; Congress has not in any relevant way amended [the ATCA]
or limited civil common law power by another statute.[66]

The Supreme Court also directly addressed the question posed by Bradley and
Goldsmith on *Erie*. For the Supreme Court *Erie*

did not in terms bar any judicial recognition of new substantive rules, no matter
what the circumstances, and post-*Erie* understanding has identified limited enclaves
in which federal courts may derive some substantive law in a common law way. For
centuries we have affirmed that the domestic law of the United States recognizes the
law of nations.... It would take some explaining to say now that the federal courts
must avert their gaze entirely from any international norm intended to protect individuals.... The position we take today has been assumed by federal courts for 24 years
ever since the Second Circuit decided *Filártiga* v. *Peña-Irala*.... Congress, however,
has not only expressed no disagreement with our view of the proper exercise of the
judicial power, but has responded to its most notable instance by enacting legislation
supplementing the judicial determination in some detail.[67]

The legislation referred to was the 1992 Torture Victim Protection Act, which
enabled all persons (i.e. foreign nationals and US citizens) subject to extraju-
dicial killings or torture by foreign government officials to seek compensation
in US courts.

The Supreme Court did, however, take on board some of the criticism of
customary international law. For instance, the majority opinion added that

---

[65] Tort Claims Act. *Sosa* v. *Alvarez-Machain* No. 03-339, Supreme Court of the United States,
2004.

[66] *Sosa* v. *Alvarez-Machain* No. 03-339, Supreme Court of the United States, 2004, 30.

[67] *Sosa* v. *Alvarez-Machain* No. 03-339, Supreme Court of the United States, 2004, 35–7.

there are good reasons for a restrained conception of the discretion that a federal court should exercise in considering a new cause of action of this kind. Accordingly, we think courts should require any claim based on the present-day law of nations to rest on a norm of international character accepted by the civilized world and defined with a specificity comparable to the features of the 18th century paradigms we have recognized.[68]

Thus, customary international law could be applied in US courts and the Alien Tort Statute was not limited to the consideration of eighteenth-century torts, that is violation of safe conducts, infringement of the rights of Ambassadors, and piracy. Yet in this particular case, the Supreme Court found that the prohibition of arbitrary arrest did not meet the specificity requirements they required to apply that prohibition as a matter of customary international law. Alvarez's failure to prove this, the Supreme Court concluded, was underscored by the Restatement (Third) of Foreign Relations Law, which noted that only 'prolonged' arbitrary detention was prohibited by such law. Justice Souter concluded by noting that '[w]hatever may be said for the broad principle Alvarez advances, in the present, imperfect world, it expresses an aspiration that exceeds any binding customary rule having the specificity we require.'[69]

CONCLUSION

If the rules that constitute international society are customary rules then the debate about how customary international law is created is a matter of constitutional politics.[70] At the centre of this debate is the claim that sovereign consent must be preserved as the foundation of international law because it helps to protect liberty based on the social contract between the sovereign and citizen. This is countered by the solidarist argument that a sovereign's actions often have an impact on the lives of individuals who are not citizens. As this impact increases in an interdependent world, then the need to renegotiate the social contract becomes more obvious. For solidarists like Falk, this need could be addressed by shifting the focus of international law away from consent and towards a consensus that could speak for international society as a whole. The fact that positivists in the United States oppose this view reveals two things. It demonstrates that they are not necessarily committed to democratic

---

[68] *Sosa* v. *Alvarez-Machain* No. 03-339, Supreme Court of the United States, 2004, 30.

[69] *Sosa* v. *Alvarez-Machain* No. 03-339, Supreme Court of the United States, 2004, 44.

[70] Bruce Ackerman, 'Constitutional Politics/Constitutional Law', *The Yale Law Journal*, 99 (1989), 453–547.

accountability per se but that they are committed to a concept of democratic accountability that is based on particular nation-states. The question is therefore, not necessarily one of democracy but one of boundaries. Those less attached to the idea that nations are naturally and irrevocably divided are more willing to see customary international law as a democratizing influence. See for instance Beth Stephens' spirited defence of customary internation*l law. 'Given the tremendous clout of the United States in the international arena' she writes, 'complaints that international law is imposed on this country ring false.... Such whining from the dominant force in world affairs lacks credibility and fails to reflect the process by which customary international law norms develop.' She continues:

It is true that the United States occasionally loses on such issues, despite its clout. But U.S. citizens can be confident that their views have been fairly aired and that their government is deeply involved in developments of importance to this country. That the result might on rare occasions be disappointing does not make the process less democratic, because minority views usually lose in a democratic process.... Enforcement of norms that the United States, a full participant in the international law community, has willingly become bound by, poses no threat to democracy.[71]

Stephens may very well be correct. However, a reluctance to accept the binding nature of customary international law can be seen in several examples. For instance the State Department takes a view of state practice that emphasizes the acts of governments but not UN General Assembly resolutions.[72] Indeed the United States only adopted the persistent objector rule when decolonization altered the political balance in the General Assembly and the ICJ found the United States in breach of customary international law when it mined Nicaraguan harbours in the 1980s.[73] More recently, Attorney General

---

[71] Stephens, 'The Law of Our Land', 457–8; see also Koh, 'Commentary: Is International Law Really State Law?', 1853, 1859.

[72] Murphy, *The United States and the Rule of Law*, 15.

[73] Murphy, *The United States and the Rule of Law*, 14–5; J. P. Kelly, 'The Twilight of Customary International Law', *Virginia Journal of International Law*, 40 (2000), 514. In the *Nicaragua* case the ICJ ruled 'that the United States of America, by training, arming, equipping, financing and supplying the *contra* forces or otherwise encouraging, supporting and aiding military and paramilitary activities in and against Nicaragua,... by certain acts on Nicaraguan territory in 1983–84, namely [the mining of Nicaraguan harbours]...has acted, against the Republic of Nicaragua, in breach of its obligations under customary international law not to intervene in the affairs of another State'. Case concerning the Military and Paramilitary Activities in and against Nicaragua (*Nicaragua* v. *United States of America*), Judgment of June 1986. For discussions of the erosion of the state practice requirement in the *Nicaragua* case, see Theodor Meron, *Human Rights and Humanitarian Norms as Customary Law* (Oxford: Clarendon Press, 1989), 107; Anthony D'Amato, 'Trashing Customary International Law', *American Journal of International Law*, 81 (1987), 102–3.

John Ashcroft argued that the 'law of nations' covered by the ATCA did not include international human rights treaties and that abuses committed outside of the United States could not be covered under the law.[74] Finally, the Department of Justice (DOJ) documents released after the Abu-Ghraib prisoner abuse scandal reveal the profound influence positivist arguments have had in creating the legal space for powerful states like the United States to wield their power. Indeed Assistant Attorney General James Bybee dismissed any thought that the United States might be restrained in its war on terror by customary international law by citing Bradley and Goldsmith's argument. 'The spurious nature of this type of law' he concludes, 'led the Supreme Court in the famous case of *Erie R.R. Co.* v. *Tompkins* ... to eliminate general federal common law.'[75]

As noted above, this reading of *Erie* has been rejected by the Supreme Court in Sosa, but it is worth focusing on the positivist argument for two reasons. Underlying Bybee's adoption of Bradley and Goldsmith's argument was not merely a concern that incorporating customary international law into US federal law is unconstitutional. There clearly was an attempt to use this normative argument to release the President from unwanted legal restraints in the war on terrorism. As a summary of the Vattelian position, Bybee's argument is worth quoting at length. It should be read, however, in the context of an argument that was designed to release the President from any form of legal restraint, because the argument here is that while positivism may defend liberty based on the nation-state, it can also help the nation-state to justify very illiberal foreign policies. Bybee argued that

---

[74] This argument is found in a May 2003 amicus brief for the defence in a civil case alleging that the oil company Unocal was complicit in forced labour and other abuses committed by the Burmese military during the construction of the Yadana gas pipeline. The Justice Department brief went well beyond the scope of the Unocal case, however, and argued for a radical reinterpretation of ATCA. Human Rights Watch, 'Ashcroft Attacks Human Rights Law', 15 May 2003. It echoes Judge Bork's arguments on ATCA (see above) and the October 1987 amicus brief filed by the Reagan administration in *Trajano* v. *Marcos*. This case involved a citizen of the Philippines who was suing the former Philippine President Ferdinand Marcos for torture. The Reagan administration, however, argued for 'a much narrower interpretation of the Alien Tort Statute, one that would exclude cases between aliens for human rights violations committed outside the United States'. Burley, 'The Alien Tort Statute', 463. See also Brief for the United States as Respondent Supporting the Petitioner *Sosa* v. *Alvarez-Machain* (2004).

[75] Memo 6, Re: Application of Treaties and Laws to al-Qaeda and Taliban Detainees, Memorandum to Alberto Gonzales, Counsel to the President and William J. Haynes, General Counsel, Department of Defense, from Jay S. Bybee, Assistant Attorney General, Department of Justice, 114, in Karen J. Greenberg and Joshua L. Dratel (eds.), *The Torture Papers. The Road to Abu-Ghraib* (Cambridge: Cambridge University Press, 2005). In fact, Goldsmith himself served as Special Counsel to the Department of Defense in 2002–3, before moving to the Department of Justice as Assistant Attorney General.

allowing customary international law to rise to the level of federal law would create severe distortions in the structure of the Constitution: Incorporation of customary international law directly into federal law would bypass the delicate procedures established by the Constitution for amending the Constitution or for enacting legislation. Customary international law is not approved by two-thirds of Congress and by three-quarters of the State legislatures, it has not been passed by both houses of Congress and signed by the President, nor is it made by the President with the advice and consent of two-thirds of the Senate. In other words, customary international law has not undergone the difficult hurdles that stand before enactment of constitutional amendments, statutes, or treaties. As such, it can have no legal effect on the government or on American citizens because it is not law. Even the inclusion of treaties in the Supremacy Clause does not render treaties automatically self-executing in federal court, not to mention self-executing against the executive branch. If even treaties that have undergone presidential signature and senatorial advice and consent can have no binding legal effect in the United States, then it certainly must be the case that a source of rules that never undergoes any process established by our Constitution cannot be law.[76]

An unwillingness to accept the binding qualities of 'new' customary international law does not mean that positivists in the United States object to the idea of an international society existing independently of state action. Their general acceptance of the idea that states can be bound by treaties—aside from Bybee—is evidence that they accept 'old' custom (i.e. *pacta sunt servanda*) as a source of legal obligation. An unwillingness to see consent removed as a constitutional principle of international law does demonstrate, however, a concern for the *type* of international society that can develop. Positivists would accept this and argue that they are concerned to protect the possibility that liberty can develop in independent nation-states. They tend not to acknowledge, however, that this also guarantees a kind of international society that might be described in other contexts as 'individualist' rather than 'communitarian'. In other words, this kind of society guarantees the freedom of its individual members (in this case states) by restricting the development of a conception of the common good that would otherwise demand further sacrifice of its citizens. In 'individualist' societies of course, those with power have more freedom than those without power and it is often the case that the weaker members can only find liberty in a 'communitarian' society, which curtails the freedom of the powerful. Defending a society constituted by the rule of sovereign consent in other words is a means of defending the freedom that the powerful can more easily exercise in individualist societies. This argument is of course implicit in the title of Hedley Bull's classic, *The Anarchical Society*. The rules of sovereignty and sovereign consent help constitute a society of states,

[76] Memo 6, Memorandum for Alberto Gonzales, 113.

but they limit it to an 'anarchical' society where there is no law higher than that willed by states. In such a society, the powerful usually flourish because they are able to negotiate contracts that suit their particular interests and are thus able to construct a normative order that is convenient to themselves. Defending the society of states constituted by the rules of sovereignty and sovereign consent, therefore, is not only about defending the principle of liberty based on the nation-state, it is also about defending the privileges that powerful nation-states have in that particular society.

3

International Society—The Duty Either to
Extradite or Prosecute

Chapter 2 discussed alternative sources of international law. This chapter
builds on that discussion by asking who has the right to prosecute individuals for violations of international law. The two questions (and thus the two
chapters) are of course closely linked. Whether a state can claim the right
to prosecute those violating international law depends on the scope of the
law and the legitimacy of the processes that made that law. The solidarist
who recognizes the legitimacy of a universal consensus on 'war crimes', for
instance, will likely support a state's claim to assert jurisdiction over those
who commit such acts, even though that state might not have a direct connection to the crime. On the other hand, a positivist unwilling to accept the
invocation of a universal consensus would be interested to know whether
specific treaties exist indicating an agreement between states over the exercise
of criminal jurisdiction or whether the prosecuting state has some kind of
connection to the particular crime.[1] The positivist position on the source
of international law, in other words, is the starting point for the pluralist
position on universal jurisdiction. To assert jurisdiction when a treaty is not
present would put at risk the two principles of pluralist international society.
First, it would be undemocratic as a state would be holding an individual to
account before a law he, by not being a citizen of that state, had not consented
to. Indeed, the actions that the prosecuting state might deem unlawful may
very well have been sanctioned by the perpetrator's state and may even have
been conducted on behalf of that state. This would not necessarily make
those actions democratic (the state may after all be a dictatorship), but to

---

[1] Other than the universality principle, it is generally considered that a state can claim jurisdiction based on three other principles: the territorial principle, where a state claims jurisdiction
over crimes committed on its territory; the national principle, where a state claims jurisdiction
over crimes committed by their nationals (active nationality principle) or against their national
(passive personality principle); and finally the protective principle, which allows a state to
prosecute acts that threaten its security even when they are committed by foreigners abroad.
Malanczuck, *Akehurst's*, 109–12.

the extent that 'democracy' can only be attained by a contract between an independent nation and its sovereign, the exercise of power by the sovereign of another nation in this manner is inevitably undemocratic. Second, the assertion of jurisdiction by one state over the citizens of another, particularly when those individuals are acting with the consent of the state, is a fundamental challenge to good relations between states and to international order more generally.

This chapter illustrates how this debate has manifested itself in contemporary international society. The first section establishes how the duty either to extradite or prosecute those charged with committing crimes that 'in some way affect human society'[2] is recognized by international society. Where Grotius and indeed Vattel grounded this responsibility in natural law, it is obvious from treaties with near universal ratification (e.g. the Geneva and Torture Conventions) that contemporary international society still considers it the right and duty of states to exercise universal jurisdiction. Despite this grounding in treaty law states have been reluctant to punish individuals whose crimes do not in some way impact on their particular interests. Where states have responded, moreover, they have provoked a pluralist backlash and often found the political costs to be prohibitive. The second and third sections of this chapter illustrate this concern with reference to the Pinochet case before the British House of Lords and the Yerodia case before the ICJ. The issue here was not so much the right of states to exercise universal jurisdiction, although the decision of the House of Lords to rely on treaty law rather than customary law to justify extradition did have significant implications in this regard. Rather the issue was the exercise of jurisdiction over individuals who could claim sovereign or diplomatic immunity under other aspects of customary and treaty law. The debate surrounding these cases illustrates at its starkest the dispute over the character of contemporary international society. Should it prioritize relations between states, in which case former Heads of State and diplomats should be entitled to immunity from prosecution, or should it prioritize human rights and criminal accountability for individuals who abuse those rights, in which case it should abandon such immunities?

The opinions of the Law Lords and the Judges of the ICJ in the Pinochet and Yerodia cases are significant for interpreting where the balance lies in contemporary international society. Where the Pinochet decision was interpreted as a breakthrough for supporters of human rights and international

---

[2] Hugo Grotius [translated by Francis W. Kelsey et al.], *De Jure Belli ac Pacis Libri Tres* (Oxford: Clarendon Press, [1646] 1925), 526.

criminal justice the Yerodia decision and its warning of international 'chaos' was seen as something of a setback. The opinions of judges, however, by no means determine the priority that a state gives to international criminal justice. The final section therefore examines the attitude of governments to the subject and concludes that the conservatism of the ICJ is matched by the conservatism of the powerful states, notably the United States. Governments that have been willing to exercise universal jurisdiction in the area of international human rights and humanitarian law have come under intense pressure from the United States to revert to a more pluralist approach. This is particularly apparent in the US response to Belgian laws that provided for universal jurisdiction over crimes against humanity. While the US policy drew on Vattelian arguments, which warn against the implications for democracy and international order, it is apparent that such concerns are usually acted upon only when America's particular interests are at stake.

AUT DEDERE, AUT JUDICARE: THE DUTY EITHER TO EXTRADITE OR PROSECUTE IN INTERNATIONAL SOCIETY

The idea that states have a right and even a duty to prosecute individuals who 'in some way affect human society' can be found in Grotius's *De Jure Belli ac Pacis*. For Grotius punishment 'should be left to the states themselves and their rulers'. But

so comprehensive a right has not been granted to states and their rulers *in the case of crimes which in some way affect human society, and which it is the right of other states and their rulers to follow up* . . . Much less do states and their rulers possess this full authority in the case of crimes by which another state or its ruler is in a special sense injured, and on account of which that ruler or state, for the sake of dignity or security, has the right to exact punishment, in accordance with our previous conclusions. Therefore the state in which the guilty person dwells, or its ruler, ought not to interfere with this right.

In order to avoid a war 'for the purpose of exacting punishment', it followed that the custodial state 'should either punish the guilty person as he deserves, or it should entrust him to the discretion of the party making the appeal'.[3]

A similar formulation can be found in Vattel. The same remnant of natural law that allowed Vattel to condemn slavery and piracy allowed him to make an exception to the rule that a nation 'has no right to punish [an individual] for an offense committed in a foreign country'. While

---

[3] Grotius, *De Jure Belli ac Pacis*, 526–7. Emphasis added.

nature only confers upon men and Nations the right to punish...only those who have done us an injury... *an exception must be made against those criminals who, by their character and frequency of their crimes, are a menace to public security everywhere and proclaim themselves enemies of the whole human race.* Men who by profession are poisoners, assassins, or incendiaries may be exterminated wherever they are caught; for they direct their disastrous attacks against all Nations, by destroying the foundations of their common safety. Thus pirates are hanged by the first persons into whose hands they fall. If the sovereign of the country in which crimes of this nature have been committed requests the surrender of the perpetrators for the purpose of punishing them, they should be turned over to him as being the one who has first interest in inflicting exemplary punishment upon them.[4]

Despite arguments that seek to distinguish the advice of Grotius and Vattel on this issue, it is clear that the principle of *aut dedere aut punier* [either extradite or punish] can be seen as a maxim common to what Martin Wight called the rationalist tradition of international theory.[5] As Bassiouni and Wise point out, the principle stemmed not merely from prudential concerns of avoiding war between states, but from a duty to a broader conception of community. This duty of *aut dedere, aut judicare* [either extradite or prosecute], they write,

was linked to the concept of *civitas maxima*. Grotius assumed the existence of a common social or moral order which the criminal law of every state aims to secure. He treated the duty to extradite or punish not as a bilateral obligation, but rather as derived from the common interest which all states have in suppressing all forms of crime, and therefore as an obligation owing to all other states, to the whole 'international community', the *civitas maxima*.[6]

Rarely is the 'common social and moral order' of contemporary international society derived from natural law. Vattel may have been able to identify a duty to extradite or punish 'enemies of the human race' by continuing to appeal to natural law, but the positivist implications of his contract theory became more significant in the centuries that followed publication of the *Law of Nations*. Yet, as the Geneva Conventions show, the duty either to extradite or prosecute individuals charged with breaches of the common social and moral order continues to be expressed in treaty law and continues to gain the consent of sovereign states. Thus, Articles 49, 50, 129, and 146 of the respective four Conventions state that

---

[4] Vattel, *The Law of Nations*, 93. Emphasis added. Remec claims that unlike Grotius, Vattel 'did not recognize any general right to punish crimes for the sake of human society in general'. Extradition of a criminal was merely a means of avoiding state responsibility for the acts of private individuals. *The Position of the Individual in International Law According to Grotius and Vattel* (The Hague: Martinus Nijhoff, 1960), 231–2.

[5] Wight, *International Theory*.   [6] Bassiouni and Wise, *Aut Dedere Aut Judicare*, 22.

Each High Contracting Party shall be under the obligation to search for persons alleged to have committed, or to have ordered to be committed, such grave breaches, and shall bring such persons, regardless of their nationality, before its own courts. It may also, if it prefers, and in accordance with the provisions of its own legislation, hand such persons over for trial to another High Contacting Party concerned, provided such High Contracting party has made out a prima facie case.

'Grave breaches' are defined in each of the conventions by a list of acts. The precise content varies in each of the four conventions, but a common core contains prohibitions on 'wilful killing, torture, or inhuman treatment,... wilfully causing great sufferance and serious injuries... extensive destruction or appropriation of property not justified by military necessity and carried out unlawfully and wantonly'. 'Serious violations' of the Geneva Conventions have traditionally not been considered as criminal offences that are subject to universal jurisdiction.

A further example of the duty to extradite or prosecute is the 1984 Convention against Torture under which state parties acquire similar though less exacting obligations. They are obliged to make the crime of torture, as defined in the Convention, an offence under national law (Article 4). They are also required to establish jurisdiction over the crime when it is committed on its territory, by one of its nationals, against one of its nationals (if the state feels it appropriate), or over any case in which the accused is present on its territory (Article 5). The state party is obliged, if it does not extradite the person, to submit the case to its authorities for prosecution (Articles 6, 7, and 12). The Convention against Torture, therefore, does not go as far as the Geneva Conventions, which contain a duty *to search for* persons even when they are outside the territories of states' parties. Both treaties, however, establish a duty to extradite or prosecute individuals accused of the relevant offence regardless of where it is alleged to have taken place.

The regimes created by the Geneva and Torture Conventions relate only to the 'contracting parties' and are only applicable, therefore, to a closed set of state parties. As these Conventions can boast near universal ratification this is somewhat beside the point. It is appropriate to note, however, that the phrase 'universal jurisdiction' is more accurately applied when it is considered a peremptory norm of customary international law. Only then, as Chapter 2 noted, can it be considered binding on all states regardless of the actions of their sovereigns.[7] Understanding this, some commentators have claimed that conventions like those relating to war crimes and torture are themselves declaratory of customary law from which no state can derogate, regardless of

---

[7] Rosalyn Higgins, *Problems and Process—International Law and How to Use It* (Oxford: Clarendon Press, 1994), 62–5.

its status relative to the treaty.[8] Under customary international law, all states are entitled, although not obliged, to exercise universal jurisdiction in respect of grave breaches of the Geneva Convention and torture. Indeed, the ICRC study on customary international law establishes as Rule 157 the right of states to vest universal jurisdiction in their courts over war crimes. This is supported by 'treaty practice' (i.e. near universal adherence to the Geneva Conventions), by extensive national legislation and, although less extensively, by military manuals.[9]

The ICRC study also points to state practice such as the trial of war criminals in national courts. Such instances are admittedly rare. Cases that might first appear to be pursued under universal jurisdiction do in fact fall under the active or passive personality principle. This allows states to exercise jurisdiction where the accused or victim of a crime is a national. Many of the non-Nuremberg post-Second World War tribunals, for instance, tried war crimes committed by or against their nationals.[10] For example, in 1990 a Canadian court tried and acquitted the former Hungarian *Gendamerie* officer Imre Finta, because he was by then a Canadian citizen; and in 1987 a French court convicted former Gestapo chief of Lyon, Klaus Barbie.[11] However, some individuals suspected of committing war crimes in the Second World War have been prosecuted under the universality principle. In Israel, for instance, the universality principle allowed a state that did not exist at the time of the conflict to prosecute former Nazi officers Adolf Eichmann and John Demjanjuk.[12] More recently, trials have been held in Danish, German, Dutch, Belgian, and Swiss courts that involve war crimes in the former Yugoslavia and Rwanda.[13] As the ICRC study notes, it is significant for the development of a customary right in this area, 'that the states of nationality of the accused did not object to the exercise of universal jurisdiction in these cases'.[14]

With regards to universal jurisdiction for the crime of torture, perhaps the best-known case is the request made by Spain, Belgium, France, and

---

[8] Theodor Meron, 'The Geneva Conventions as Customary Law', *American Journal of International Law*, 81 (1987), 352.

[9] Jean-Marie Henckaerts and Louise Doswald-Beck, *Customary International Humanitarian Law, Volume I, Rules* (Cambridge: Cambridge University Press, 2005), 604–7.

[10] Axel Marschik, 'The Politics of Prosecution: European National Approaches to War Crimes', in T. L. H. McCormack and G. J. Simpson (eds.), *The Law of War Crimes. National and International Approaches* (The Hague, the Netherlands: Kluwer, 1997), 74–93.

[11] Sharon Williams, 'Laudable Principles Lacking Application: The Prosecution of War Criminals in Canada', in McCormack and Simpson (eds.), *The Law of War Crimes*, 151–70; Marschik, 'The Politics of Prosecution', 82–7.

[12] Jonathan M. Wenig, 'Enforcing the Lessons of History: Israel Judges the Holocaust', in McCormack and Simpson (eds.), *The Law of War Crimes*, 103–22.

[13] See Menno T. Kamminga, 'Lessons Learned form the Exercise of Universal Jurisdiction in Respect of Gross Human Rights Offenses', *Human Rights Quarterly*, 23 (2001), 940–74.

[14] Henckaerts and Doswald-Beck, *Customary International Humanitarian Law*, 605.

Switzerland that the UK extradite the Chilean Senator, Augusto Pinochet.[15] Much of the controversy surrounding this case revolved around the principle of sovereign immunity, which is addressed below. It is worth pointing out here, however, that the UK arrested Pinochet only after the basis for extradition was changed from the murder of Spanish citizens in Chile, to general acts of torture. Spain's request that the UK extradite Senator Pinochet was initially based on the passive personality principle and evidence that between 1973 and 1983 he had murdered Spanish citizens in Chile. As this was not considered sufficient grounds for the UK to extradite Pinochet a second request was made based on evidence of torture. On this basis the UK could, under the universality principle recognized by the 1988 UK Criminal Justice Act, arrest Pinochet and extradite him to Spain.[16]

It is also worth noting that the Law Lords' ultimate decision, which was delivered on 24 March 1999 and ruled 6 to 1 in favour of extradition, relied on treaty rather than customary law.[17] The decisive fact was that all three states involved—Chile, the UK, and Spain—had consented to be bound by the terms of the 1984 Convention against Torture. As Lord Browne-Wilkinson explained, prior to the Convention the prohibition against torture may have been accepted as a *jus cogens* norm, but 'there was no international tribunal to punish torture and no general jurisdiction to permit or require its punishment in domestic courts'. Consent to the Convention, therefore, was necessary for national courts to claim jurisdiction.

Not until there was some form of universal jurisdiction for the punishment of the crime of torture could it really be talked about as a fully constituted international crime. But in my judgment the Torture Convention did provide what was missing: a worldwide universal jurisdiction.[18]

---

[15] More recently, a UK court tried Afghan warlord Faryadi Sarwar Zardad on charges of torture, and Dutch courts prosecuted Sebastian Nzapali, a former military officer from the Congo, for violations of the Convention against Torture. Sandra Laville, 'UK Court Convicts Afghan Warlord', *The Guardian*, 19 July 2005.

[16] Diana Woodhouse (ed.), *The Pinochet Case. A Legal and Constitutional Analysis* (Oxford: Hart, 2000), 3. As Lord Lloyd put it: 'unlike murder, torture is an offence under English law wherever the act of torture is committed. So unlike the first provisional warrant, the second provisional warrant is not bad on its face.' *Regina v. Bartle and the Commissioner of Police for the Metropolis and Others Ex Parte Pinochet (On Appeal from a Divisional Court of the Queen's Bench Division)*, 28 November 1998.

[17] Of the 6 only Lord Millet relied extensively on customary international law. *Regina v. Bartle and the Commissioner of Police for the Metropolis and Others Ex Parte Pinochet (on appeal from a Divisional Court of the Queen's Bench Division)*, 24 March 1999. The 28 November decision, which had ruled 3 to 2 in favour of proceeding with extradition, was made void after it was revealed that Lord Hoffmann had direct links with Amnesty International. See *In re Pinochet*, 15 January 1999.

[18] *Ex Parte Pinochet*, 24 March 1999.

Relying on treaty law and the principle of sovereign consent, however, had serious implications for the charges that Pinochet had to answer. Spain and Chile had ratified the Convention with effect from 21 October 1987 and 30 October 1988, respectively. It was, however, determined that Pinochet could not be extradited to Spain for acts of torture that occurred before the UK's ratification came into effect, which was 8 December 1988. As the crimes Pinochet allegedly committed took place between 1973 and 1990 this radically reduced the number of extraditable offences. Such evidence demonstrates how sovereign consent can protect individuals from accountability before a law that may have otherwise been applicable as custom.

In this case a majority of Law Lords ruled that Pinochet could still be extradited, yet Lord Goff argued that the reduced number of extraditable cases made the allegations of insufficient gravity to override Pinochet's immunity as a former head of state. Lord Hutton addressed this issue head on:

a single act of torture carried out or instigated by a public official or other person acting in an official capacity constitutes a crime against international law, and that torture does not become an international crime only when it is committed or instigated on a large scale. Accordingly I am of the opinion that Senator Pinochet cannot claim that a single act of torture or a small number of acts of torture carried out by him did not constitute international crimes and did not constitute acts committed outside the ambit of his functions as head of state.[19]

The separate issue of sovereign immunity is addressed below. The key point here is that the Law Lords may have recognized the right of the UK and Spanish courts to exercise jurisdiction over this case but they did so only because the other state involved (Chile) had consented to be bound by such a regime. Of course, the judgment was a breakthrough for human rights activists but its implications were not as far-reaching as some might have assumed.

To complete this review of the duty to extradite or prosecute in contemporary international society it is necessary to consider the 1948 Genocide Convention. A state's obligation here is slightly different to that under the Geneva or Torture Conventions. The Convention states that '[p]ersons who commit genocide...shall be punished' (Article 4) and it affirms that states parties 'undertake to prevent and punish' those who commit genocide (Article 1). However, the Convention only refers to trials before tribunals of the state where the act of genocide occurred or before an international criminal court (Article 6). It is silent as to any right or obligation to extradite or prosecute. Indeed in 1948 states were not prepared to recognize the

---

[19] *Ex Parte Pinochet*, 24 March 1999.

notion of universal jurisdiction over genocide, in part because the United States insisted that prosecution could only take place with the consent of the state upon whose territory the crime was committed.[20] It is now widely agreed, however, that the offence of genocide is subject to universal jurisdiction as a principle of customary international law.[21] Recent state practice regarding the exercise of universal jurisdiction in respect of genocide supports this view. In September 1997, for instance, a court in Düsseldorf, Germany found Nikola Jorgic, a former leader of a Serb paramilitary group, guilty of eleven counts of genocide and sentenced him to life imprisonment. Two years later Djuradi Kuslij was convicted of genocide by a court in Munich, Germany and he too was sentenced to life imprisonment. The same court had earlier acquitted Novislav Djajic of having been an accessory to genocide.[22]

PLURALISM AND SOLIDARISM IN INTERNATIONAL CRIMINAL JUSTICE: THE PINOCHET CASE

As noted, the first aspect of the pluralist response to these developments is the argument that universal jurisdiction is undemocratic and even neocolonial. For instance, Henry Kissinger has argued that the most appropriate solution to the question of how to deal with Senator Pinochet was for the Chilean Supreme Court to withdraw his immunity making it possible for courts

of the country most competent to judge this history and to relate its decisions to the stability and vitality of its democratic institutions.... The instinct to punish must be related, as in every constitutional democratic political structure, to a system of checks and balances that includes other elements critical to the survival and expansion of democracy.[23]

The fact that there are those who argue that Kissinger should face international prosecution for his part in the crimes that took place in Chile will inevitably

---

[20] William A. Schabas, 'United States hostility to the International Criminal Court: It's All about the Security Council', *European Journal of International Law*, 15 (2004), 706–7.

[21] Henckaerts and Doswald-Beck, *Customary International Humanitarian Law*, 605. The Preamble of the 1998 Rome Statute, which set up the ICC, recalls 'that it is the *duty* of every state to exercise its criminal jurisdiction over those responsible for international crimes' [emphasis added]. However, as Louise Arbour points out, 'there is no other express provision in the Statute that *requires* state to exercise universal jurisdiction over such crimes.' Louise Arbour, 'Will the ICC Have an Impact on Universal Jurisdiction?', *Journal of International Criminal Justice*, 1 (2003), 586.

[22] Kamminga, 'Lessons Learned', 970.

[23] Henry Kissinger, 'The Pitfalls of Universal Jurisdiction', *Foreign Affairs*, 80 (2001), 90–1.

influence how this particular argument is perceived.[24] It is important to note, however, that Kissinger did not argue that Pinochet should be immune from prosecution—just that it should be for the *Chilean* courts to decide. Whether he would agree to a Chilean court seeking the extradition of those foreign leaders who assisted Pinochet is left unsaid, but it is logical to assume that Kissinger would claim that the actions he conducted on behalf of President Nixon and the American people during his time in power should be judged only by American courts. This position may have a democratic appeal to it, but it recalls the Kantian/solidarist criticism introduced in the previous chapters. Politicians that have a domestic democratic mandate do not always behave democratically internationally and as long as domestic courts defer to executives in matters of foreign affairs a culture of impunity will grow in the kind of pluralist society of sovereign states that Kissinger advocates. This possibility is discussed further in Chapter 7.

The communitarian conception of accountability, therefore, may conveniently suit powerful politicians who seek to avoid liability for their actions in the anarchical world of international relations. It does have normative value, however, and it is supported by observers with no particular interest a stake. For instance, Lord Lloyd offered the following explanation of his decision to support Pinochet's request for immunity:

quite apart from any embarrassment in our foreign relations, or potential breach of comity, and quite apart from any fear that, by assuming jurisdiction, we would only serve to 'imperil the amicable relations between governments and vex the peace of nations' ... we would be entering a field in which we are simply not competent to adjudicate. We apply customary international law as part of the common law, and we give effect to our international obligations so far as they are incorporated in our statute law; but we are not an international court. For an English court to investigate and pronounce on the validity of the amnesty in Chile would be to assert jurisdiction over the internal affairs of that state at the very time when the Supreme Court in Chile is itself performing the same task. In my view this is a case in which, even if there were no valid claim to sovereign immunity, as I think there is, we should exercise judicial restraint by declining jurisdiction.[25]

Such an opinion is clearly sympathetic not only to the pluralist concern for international order, but also to the communitarian or contractarian position outlined in Chapter 2. Justice at the level of the state is, according to this view, simply much more effective in rebuilding strong communities. As one observer of the debate put it, 'justice at a distance often fails because it is at a

---

[24] For reasons why 'Mr. Kissinger would seemingly have good reason to be concerned', see Phillipe Sands, *Lawless World. America and the Making and Breaking of Global Rules* (London: Allen Lane, 2005), 44.

[25] *Ex Parte Pinochet*, 28 November 1998.

distance'.[26] Or, as the President of the ICJ, Judge Guillame put it in his Separate Opinion on the Yerodia judgment,

[t]he primary aim of the criminal law is to enable punishment in each country of offences committed in the national territory. That territory is where the evidence of the offence can most be gathered. That is where the offence generally produces its effects. Finally, that is where the punishment imposed can most naturally serve as an example.[27]

Foreign judges may be well meaning, but from this perspective, justice done internationally weakens the restorative value it is meant to have.[28] Indeed, this very same point was made by those political leaders in Chile who advocated further democratic reforms. They had opposed Pinochet in the past, but now they supported the Chilean government's position, which was to see Pinochet return home. Pro-democracy forces campaigned for the lifting of Senatorial immunity, but they feared that the movement for wider constitutional reforms would suffer if 'the Pinochet issue' were dealt with overseas. As Lagos and Muñoz put it at the time, 'if Pinochet does not return to Chile to be tried, the democratic forces will not feel the urgency to create the conditions for justice, thus losing an opportunity to right some of the wrongs of the transition'.[29]

Some have argued in less instrumental terms. From their perspective, the exercise of universal jurisdiction does not only reduce the possibility of reforms that might promote or restore democracy, it actually negates the very idea of popular sovereignty. For instance, Casey and Rivkin point out that the exercise of judicial power by one sovereign over the actions of another inevitably raises the spectre of neocolonialism. In their criticism of the Mexican decision to allow the extradition to Spain of Miguel Cavallo, the

[26] Chandra Lekha Sriram, 'Review Article. New Mechanisms, Old Problems? Recent Books on Universal Jurisdiction and Mixed Tribunals', *International Affairs*, 80 (2004), 975.

[27] Case Concerning the Arrest Warrant of 11 April 2000 (*Congo* v. *Belgium*), 14 February 2002, Separate Opinion of President Guillame, para. 4.

[28] See David Miller, 'Bounded citizenship', in K. Hutchings and R. Dannreuther (eds.), *Cosmopolitan Citizenship* (Basingstoke, UK: Macmillan, 1999), 74–5; George P. Fletcher, 'Against Universal Jurisdiction', *Journal of International Criminal Justice*, 1 (2003), 583. Fletcher also notes how the exercise of universal jurisdiction potentially violates the prohibition of double jeopardy (i.e. no person can be tried for the same crime twice). An example of this, he suggests, was Belgium's attempt to prosecute Ariel Sharon for crimes committed in Sabra and Shatila refugee camps despite the Kahan Commission determining that he was not criminally liable. For a response, see Georges Abi-Saab, 'The Proper Role of Universal Jurisdiction', *Journal of International Criminal Justice*, 1 (2003), 596–602.

[29] Richard Lagos and Heraldo Muñoz, 'The Pinochet Dilemma', *Foreign Policy*, 114 (1999), 36. Lagos was the Chilean Minister of Education from 1990 to 1992 and Minister of Public Works from 1994 to 1998. Muñoz served as the Ambassador of Chile to the Organization of American States from 1990 to 1994 and to Brazil from 1994 to 1998.

former Argentine officer who was accused of torture during the time of the military junta, Casey and Rivkin write:

It is neither the right nor the place of the Spanish judiciary to deny the validity of Argentina's laws [which gave Cavallo an amnesty], any more than it is, say, Britain's ᵗᵗᵍht to correct perceived deficiencies in the American judicial system. Argentina is ᵢᵢ₋ longer a colony. It made a choice. Perhaps it chose badly. Perhaps it paid too high a price for democracy.... That, however, is for Argentina, not Garzon [the Spanish Prosecutor] or anybody else, to decide.[30]

Criminal prosecutions are not the only way a society may choose to deal with its troubled past. Alternative processes might be inspired by a willingness to forgive, or by prudential reasons that see an amnesty on criminal prosecutions as a price worth paying for peace. Which way is best is not necessarily the issue for pluralists. Their objection to the exercise of universal jurisdiction is that it should be for the particular community to decide what is suited to its own particular circumstances. Only then can the liberty provided by the social contract between the individual and society be observed. From this perspective, the trial of Senator Pinochet in Spain would have made a mockery of Chile's social contract, part of which was his amnesty from prosecution.[31]

To a certain extent, the House of Lords bypassed this criticism by relying on treaty law and the fact that Chile had consented to be bound by the 1984 Convention against Torture. Indeed, Chile had become a party to the treaty while Pinochet was head of state. The issue that the Law Lords had to decide, therefore, was not whether the Torture Convention applied to Chile but whether as a former head of state Pinochet could nonetheless claim immunity from prosecution. Immunities, which differ from amnesties in that they are granted before the commission of an act, have played a central role in the development of a pluralist society of states. A state's right to engage in lawful combat, for instance, is based on the assumption that its soldiers are immune from prosecution. International humanitarian law places conditions on that right by imposing restrictions on the conduct of hostilities, but it also protects prisoners of war from criminal prosecution. Without such immunities, the

[30] David B. Rivkin Jr. and Lee A. Casey, 'Crimes Outside the World's Jurisdiction', *New York Times*, 22 July 2003. Although the Spanish extradition request relied on the principle of universal jurisdiction, Cavallo's imprisonment in June 2003 was based on the fact that his victims included Spaniards. This was a response to the Spanish High Court's ruling in the *Guatemalan Generals* case in February 2004, see below. Antonio Cassese, 'Is the Bell Tolling for Universality? A Plea for a Sensible Notion of Universal Jurisdiction', *Journal of International Criminal Justice*, 1 (2003), 590.

[31] The amnesty, however, was controversial within Chile. See Pablo De Greiff, 'Comment: Universal Jurisdiction and Transitions to Democracy', in Stephen Macedo (ed.), *Universal Jurisdiction: National Courts and the Prosecution of Serious Crimes Under International Law* (Philadelphia, PA: University of Pennsylvannia Press, 2006), 127–30.

very concept of 'war' would make no sense.[32] The Pinochet case, however, contested the legal priority that international society gave to sovereign and diplomatic immunity.

Sovereign immunity allows a state to claim freedom from the jurisdiction of another state. It derives from the Vattelian principle that states are independent and legally equal. Historically the ruler was associated with the state and thus possessed complete immunity from prosecution.[33] Diplomatic immunity allows a state's representative to claim freedom from the criminal jurisdiction of the receiving state. Acceptance of this as a norm of international society is reflected in the almost universal accession to the 1961 Vienna Convention on Diplomatic Relations, which notes in the Preamble that 'privileges and immunities would contribute to the development of friendly relations among nations, irrespective of their differing constitutional and social systems'. This is codified in Article 31, which states that 'a diplomatic agent shall enjoy immunity from the criminal jurisdiction of the receiving state'. Under Article 39 of that Convention, immunity lasts until the agent leaves the country and continues thereafter with respect to acts performed in the exercise of that person's official functions. The norm has been described by the ICJ in the *Tehran Hostages Case*, as 'essential for the maintenance of relations between states'. It is moreover 'accepted throughout the world by nations of all creeds, cultures, and political complexions'.[34]

The Law Lords in the Pinochet case did not disagree with this and they used Article 39 of the Convention as a starting point for their judgment on the immunities that a former head of state was entitled to. However, the majority ruled that in contemporary international society the obligation to prosecute those charged with the crime of torture prevailed over the obligation to respect such immunities. There were two aspects to their reasoning, one based on custom, the other based on an interpretation of the 1984 Convention against Torture. Those that were willing to rely on custom pointed to judgments at Nuremberg and more recently at the international criminal tribunals for the former Yugoslavia (ICTY) and Rwanda (ICTR) as evidence that public officials were no longer entitled to immunity from prosecution for international crimes. This interpretation was opposed by Lord Slynn in the first hearing and Lord Goff in the second. The sources cited in order to elevate the prohibition against torture to a peremptory norm were deemed inappropriate for the case. According to Lords Slynn and Goff these sources established that immunities

---

[32] For further discussion of the distinction between lawful and unlawful combat see Chapter 7.

[33] Malanczuk, *Akehurst's*, 118–9.

[34] *Tehran Hostages Case (USA v. Iran), ICJ Rep. 1980*. Quoted by Malanczuk in *Akehurst's*, 123.

were not valid before *international* courts but they said very little to challenge the status of sovereign immunity in *national* courts. Lord Goff also found that treaty law, specifically the Convention against Torture, did not challenge the peremptory status of sovereign immunity. The failure of the Convention to state explicitly that Heads of State were not immune from prosecution implied that acts committed by Heads of State in furtherance of their public duties were exempt from the Convention. 'It is surely most unlikely', he reasoned

that during the years in which the draft was under consideration no thought was given to . . . waiving state immunity. Furthermore, if agreement had been reached that there should be such a waiver, express provision would inevitably have been made in the Convention to that effect. Plainly, however, no such agreement was reached. . . . Furthermore, if immunity [for the act of torture] was excluded, former heads of state and senior public officials would have to think twice about travelling abroad, for fear of being the subject of unfounded allegations emanating from states of a different political persuasion. In this connection, it is a mistake to assume that state parties to the Convention would only wish to preserve state immunity in cases of torture in order to shield public officials guilty of torture from prosecution elsewhere in the world. Such an assumption is based on a misunderstanding of the nature and function of state immunity, which is a rule of international law restraining one sovereign state from sitting in judgment on the sovereign behaviour of another.[35]

Of course, Lord Goff was merely interpreting the meaning of the Convention against Torture and not stating what he thought international law should be. Yet the above reasoning suggests that a normative concern for relations between states did influence his opinion. The idea that Heads of State would be forced to 'think twice' *before engaging in torture* and that this was always the intention of the Convention against Torture obviously had less of an influence on his opinion. Unfortunately for Pinochet, the travel plans of alleged torturers did not move the majority to grant immunity.

Those in favour of maintaining Pinochet's immunity also argued that the reference to 'public officials' in the Torture Convention did not apply to Heads of State. Article 1 of the Convention against Torture defines torture as the intentional infliction of severe pain or suffering 'by or at the instigation of or with the consent or acquiescence of *a public official* or other person *acting in an official capacity'*. For Lord Hope, the words 'public official' might be thought to refer to someone of lower rank than the head of state. 'But', he added, 'a head of state who resorted to conduct of the kind described in the exercise of his function would be clearly "acting in an official capacity"'. From this perspective, therefore, the Torture Convention did apply to Heads

[35] *Ex Parte Pinochet*, 24 March 1999.

of State. However, the question remained as to whether the duty to extradite or prosecute in the Torture Convention overrode the immunity that former Heads of State could claim under Article 39 of the Vienna Convention with regard to acts performed in exercise of their official functions. Six of the seven Law Lords disagreed with Lord Goff and answered that it did. Lord Hutton put it most clearly:

Therefore having regard to the provisions of the Torture Convention, I do not consider that Senator Pinochet or Chile can claim that the commission of acts of torture after 29 September 1988 were functions of the head of state. The alleged acts of torture by Senator Pinochet were carried out under colour of his position as head of state, but they cannot be regarded as functions of a head of state under international law when international law expressly prohibits torture as a measure which a state can employ in any circumstances whatsoever and has made it an international crime.[36]

Thus, the Torture Convention applied to Pinochet because as a head of state he had been a 'public official' at the time it was in effect. Yet he could not claim the immunities entitled to a former head of state under the Vienna Convention on Diplomatic Relations because torture was not considered an act consistent with the functions of a head of state.

PLURALISM AND SOLIDARISM IN INTERNATIONAL CRIMINAL JUSTICE: THE YERODIA CASE

Academic criticism of the *ex parte Pinochet* decision echoed the normative position of Lord Goff. Jonathan Black-Branch for instance, argued that the 'smooth working of international relations' or the 'comity of nations' could be considered 'a more pressing international concern'. His own justification for this clearly echoes the kind of prudent judgement that informed the pluralism of English School writers like Hedley Bull.

The principles of comity, as it pertains to heads of state, are even more fundamental to international law and politics than many others and thus must be respected. That is not to say that human rights issues are not important. It is only to say that fostering good relations between, and among, states may be more productive in the long run. It is not a principle extended to everyone, only heads and former heads of state. Non-heads or former heads who commit acts of torture can, and indeed should, be tried. Additionally, this will not give world leaders a carte blanche to commit torture and other atrocities. It highlights that these are issues which are not adequately provided for under international law and those desiring a world-wide jurisdiction for crimes of

[36] *Ex Parte Pinochet*, 24 March 1999.

this nature, including for heads of state, should press for clarity on this point under law.[37]

'The comity of nations' argument appears in a more significant guise in the ICJs judgment in the so-called *Arrest Warrant* or *Yerodia* case.

On 11 April 2000, a Belgian magistrate signed an arrest warrant against the incumbent foreign minister of the Democratic Republic of the Congo, Abdulaye Yerodia Ndombasi, for grave breaches of the Geneva Conventions and for crimes against humanity. These crimes were punishable in Belgium under the Law of 16 June 1993 'concerning the Punishment of Grave Breaches of the International Geneva Conventions', which was amended by the Law of 19 February 1999 'concerning the Punishment of Serious Violations of International Humanitarian Law'. Article 7 of that law stated that Belgian courts 'shall be competent to deal with breaches provided for in the present Act, irrespective of where such breaches have been committed'. A finding of jurisdiction did not necessarily mean that immunities were redundant. As noted above, a strict reading of Article 39 of the Vienna Convention would have guaranteed Yerodia absolute immunity from prosecution while he remained in office. Under Article 5 of the Belgian law, however, Yerodia was stripped of this immunity and could thus be prosecuted while he was serving in his official capacity. Article 5 stated that immunity attaching to the official capacity of a person would not prevent the application of the law.[38]

The acts Yerodia was alleged to have committed, which included speeches inciting attacks on the Tutsi population in Kinshasa, were in fact perpetrated *before* he took office. If the Belgian Prosecutors had waited for Yerodia to leave office their claim that he was not immune from prosecution for these acts would have been consistent with Article 39. As noted above, this states that an official only has absolute immunity while he is in office. On leaving government a former official can be prosecuted for acts occurring before or after his time in office or for 'private acts' while in office. By seeking to prosecute an incumbent foreign minister, however, the DRC argued that Belgium was acting contrary to international law and they took the dispute to the ICJ. The DRC filed two specific complaints: first, that the actions by the Belgian magistrate represented interference in its internal affairs and

---

[37] Jonathan Black-Branch, 'Sovereign Immunity Under International Law: The Case of Pinochet', in Woodhouse (ed.), *The Pinochet Case*, 102. For similar arguments, including the deterrent effect universal jurisdiction may have on peacekeeping, see the objection of Lord Browne-Wilkinson to the 'Princeton Principles', in Macedo (ed.), *Universal Jurisdiction*, 272. See also Madeline H. Morris, 'Universal Jurisdiction in a Divided World', *New England Law Review*, 35 (2001), 337–61.

[38] Luc Reydams, 'Universal Criminal Jurisdiction: The Belgian State of Affairs', *Criminal Law Forum*, 11 (2000), 190–7.

second, that this was incompatible with the diplomatic immunity of its foreign minister. In its final submission to the ICJ, however, the DRC referred only to a violation of customary international law concerning the absolute inviolability and immunity from criminal process of incumbent foreign ministers. For some, the ICJ could not make a judgment on the question of immunities without first dealing with the issue of jurisdiction.[39] Yet both parties and the Court as a whole agreed that the issues could be dealt with separately. On 14 February 2002, the ICJ held by a vote of 13 to 3 that a sitting foreign minister was immune from prosecution in another country's court system regardless of the seriousness of the crimes with which he was charged.[40] It was considered a setback for advocates of universal jurisdiction and a reassertion of a fundamental principle of pluralist international society.[41]

In its final judgment, the ICJ concluded that it was

unable to deduce from [state] practice that there exist under customary international law any form of exception to the rule according immunity from criminal jurisdiction and inviolability to incumbent Ministers for Foreign Affairs, where they are suspected of having committed war crimes or crimes against humanity.... The Court has also examined the rules concerning the immunity or criminal responsibility of persons having an official capacity contained in the legal instruments creating international criminal tribunals.... It finds that these rules likewise do not enable it to conclude that any such exception exists in customary international law *in regard to national courts.*[42]

Judge Koroma's Separate Opinion gives insight into the reasoning behind this judgment. The 'paramount legal justification' for such immunities, he claimed, is 'not only functional necessity but increasingly these days the foreign minister represents the state, even though his or her position is not assimilable to that of Head of State'.[43] This was either rejected in whole, as in the Dissenting Opinion of Judge Van den Wyngaert,[44] or in part as in

---

[39] *Arrest Warrant Case, Joint Separate Opinion of Judges Higgins, Kooijmans, and Buergenthal.*

[40] *Arrest Warrant Case*, para. 78.

[41] See also the March 2001 ruling by the French *Cour de Cassation*, which accepted that heads of state are entitled to absolute immunity from international prosecution and thus declined jurisdiction on the case brought against Libyan leader, Ghaddafi, for his alleged role in a September 1989 airline bombing. For a critique of the decision, which argues that an exception could have been made if terrorism was classed as an international crime and that exception could be enforced if Ghaddafi ever travelled to France in a *private* capacity see Salvatore Zappalà, 'Do Heads of State in Office Enjoy Immunity from Jurisdiction for International Crimes? The *Ghaddafi* Case before the French *Cour de Cassation*', *European Journal of Law*, 12 (2001), 595–612.

[42] *Arrest Warrant Case*, para. 58–9.

[43] *Arrest Warrant Case. Separate Opinion of Judge Koroma*, para. 6.

[44] *Arrest Warrant Case. Dissenting Opinion of Judge Van den Wyngaert*, which states that 'it is not sufficient to compare the *rationale* for the protection from suit in the case of diplomats, Heads of State and Foreign Ministers to draw the conclusion that there is a rule of customary

the Joint Separate Opinion of Judges Higgins, Kooijmans, and Buergenthal, which nonetheless recognized 'that the purpose of the immunities attaching to ministers for foreign affairs under customary international law is to ensure the free performance of their functions on behalf of their respective states'.[45]

Yerodia was thus immune from prosecution while he was in office. The Court noted, however, that 'the *immunity* from jurisdiction enjoyed by an incumbent Minister of Foreign Affairs does not mean that they enjoy *impunity* in respect of any crimes they might have committed, irrespective of their gravity'.[46] He or she may be prosecuted in their own countries and in foreign jurisdiction if the state which they represented waived their immunity. Furthermore, incumbent ministers may be subject to criminal proceedings before international courts.[47] Finally, and perhaps most controversially, the ICJ ruled that

After a person ceases to hold the office of Minister of Foreign Affairs, he or she will no longer enjoy all the immunities accorded by international law in other states. Provided that it has jurisdiction under international law, a court of one State may try a former Minister of Foreign Affairs of another State in respect of acts committed prior or subsequent to his or her period of office, as well as in respect of acts committed during that period in office *in a private capacity.*[48]

This seemingly overturned the implications of the Pinochet decision. The House of Lords had, as noted, ruled that the immunity former state representatives were entitled to with regard to acts committed in the pursuit of their official capacities did not apply to the prohibition against torture. Now the ICJ ruled that once a foreign minister leaves office he or she would continue to enjoy *absolute* immunity for acts performed in their official capacity, even if those acts were allegedly war crimes or crimes against humanity. The Separate Joint Opinion by Judges Higgins, Kooijmans, and Buergenthal recognized

international law protecting Foreign Ministers ... Foreign Ministers do not 'impersonate' the State in the same way as Heads of State, who are the State's alter ego. State practice concerning immunities of (incumbent and former) Heads of State does not, *per se*, apply to Foreign Ministers. There is no State practice evidencing an *opinio juris* on this point' (para. 11–16).

[45] *Arrest Warrant Case. Joint Separate Opinion of Higgins, Kooijmans, and Buergenthal,* para. 81.

[46] *Arrest Warrant Case,* para. 60.

[47] The distinction between immunities before international (or at least internationalized) and national courts was made even more apparent when in May 2004 the Appeals Chamber of the Special Court for Sierra Leone rejected the applicability of the *Arrest Warrant* ruling and found the Court competent to exercise jurisdiction over a serving foreign President, as was Charles Taylor at the time of his indictment. Zsuzsanna Deen-Racsmány, '*Prosecutor* v. *Taylor*: The Status of the Special Court for Sierra Leone and Its Implications for Immunity', *Leiden Journal International Law,* 18 (2005), 299–322.

[48] *Arrest Warrant Case,* para. 61. Emphasis added.

that it was 'increasingly claimed in the literature... that serious international crimes cannot be regarded as official acts' and noted the judgment in *ex parte Pinochet* to this effect.[49] By accepting the final judgment of the Court, however, they presumably did not see this as evidence of settled practice.

As noted above, the ICJ judgment only addressed the issue of immunities. Yet it is clear from the Separate Opinion of the Court's President, Gilbert Guillaume, that the ICJ also had major reservations concerning Belgium's claim to exercise universal jurisdiction. His opinion imitates the pluralist warnings about what the exercise of universal jurisdiction might mean for democracy based on the nation-state and for international order. Guillame explicitly links the reaction against universal jurisdiction to the contractarian philosophy of Montesquieu and Rousseau. 'Their views', he notes, 'found expression in terms of criminal law in the works of Beccaria, who stated in 1764 that 'judges are not the avengers of humankind in general... A crime is punishable only in the country where it is committed'.[50] Moreover, he refers to Grotius but to establish what might be termed custodial jurisdiction, where the alleged criminal is already on the territory of the prosecuting state, rather than to establish universal jurisdiction. Grotius, according to Guillame, did nothing more than point out 'that *the presence on the territory of a state* of a foreign criminal peacefully enjoying the fruits of his crimes was intolerable'.[51] The idea that a state could exercise jurisdiction without the crime affecting its territory, property, or citizenry was not recognized by international law.

President Guillame did recognize that a 'system corresponding to the doctrines espoused long ago by Grotius' had since been 'set up *by treaty*'. Yet even here, he argued that states are only ever obliged to exercise jurisdiction over the offences covered by the various conventions 'whenever the perpetrator... is found on the territory of the state. ....' In this way international society could, in instances where treaties were universally adhered to, provide universal punishment and perpetrators would be denied refuge. Yet, Guillame concluded, 'none of these texts has contemplated establishing jurisdiction over offences committed abroad by foreigners against foreigners when the perpetrator is not present in the territory of the state in question. Universal jurisdiction *in absentia* is unknown to international conventional law'.[52] Nor could it be

---

[49] *Arrest Warrant Case. Joint Separate Opinion of Higgins, Kooijmans, and Buergenthal,* para. 85.

[50] *Arrest Warrant Case. Separate Opinion of President Guillame,* para. 4.

[51] Ibid. While the ICJ did not pass judgment on universal jurisdiction in *Yerodia*, it has since been presented with an opportunity to do so in the case of *Certain Criminal Proceedings in France (Republic of Congo v. France).* At the time of writing, the case was pending.

[52] *Arrest Warrant Case. Separate Opinion of President Guillame,* para. 9.

found in international customary law. Legislation in France, Germany, and the Netherlands was cited to demonstrate that there needed to be a 'link' to the state exercising its jurisdiction before criminal prosecutions could proceed.[53]

Finally, Guillame dealt with the contention that even in the absence of treaty and customary rules that allowed Belgium to exercise jurisdiction in this case, a state still enjoyed total freedom of action. The source for this claim was the *Lotus* judgment referred to in Chapter 2. It will be recalled that in this case the PCIJ ruled that Turkey could exercise jurisdiction over a French citizen for crimes committed at sea. The PCIJ judgment noted:

Far from laying down a general prohibition to the effect that States may not extend the application of their laws and the jurisdiction of their courts to persons, property, and acts outside their territory, [international law] leaves them in this respect a wide measure of discretion which is only limited in certain cases by prohibitive rules.[54]

For President Guillame, however, this did not justify Belgian actions. The *Lotus* case did not mimic the *Arrest Warrant* case, as the PCIJ found that the 'effects' of the offence had impacted directly on Turkey (Turkish sailors had died). More significantly, Guillame argued that contemporary international society had explicit rules which would prohibit the kind of freedom Belgium now claimed.

The adoption of the United Nations Charter proclaiming the sovereign equality of States, and the appearance on the international scene of new States, born of decolonization, have strengthened the territorial principle. International criminal law has itself undergone considerable development and constitutes today an impressive legal *corpus*. It recognizes in many situations the possibility, or indeed the obligation, for a State other than that on whose territory the offence was committed to confer jurisdiction on its courts to prosecute the authors of certain crimes where they are present on its territory. International criminal courts have been created. But at no time has it been envisaged that jurisdiction should be conferred upon the courts of every State in the world to prosecute such crimes, whoever their authors and victims and irrespective of the place where the offender is to be found. *To do this would, moreover, risk creating total judicial chaos. It would also be to encourage the arbitrary for the benefit of the powerful, purportedly acting as an agent for an ill-defined 'international community'. Contrary to what is advocated by certain publicists, such a development would represent not an advance in the law but a step backward.*[55]

---

[53] See also *Arrest Warrant Case, Separate Opinion of Judges Higgins, Kooijmans, and Buergenthal,* para. 19–21.

[54] *The Case of the S.S. 'Lotus'*, Permanent Court of International Justice, 7 September 1927, 15.

[55] *Arrest Warrant Case. Separate Opinion of President Guillame,* para. 15. Emphasis added.

There were two aspects to Guillame's Separate Opinion which prompted other judges to respond: his comments on universal jurisdiction and the separate issue of immunities. First, on the issue of jurisdiction, the Separate Joint Opinion of Judges Higgins, Kooijmans, and Buergenthal and the Dissenting Opinion of Judge Van den Wyngaert both reject Guillame's assertion that the rules of international society prohibit a state's right to exercise universal jurisdiction. Judge Van den Wyngaert contradicts President Guillame by noting instances of state practice where jurisdiction was exercised without a national 'link' to the crime. Moreover, the practice of requiring a link is more a practical one (such as the capacity of national courts and the difficulty of obtaining evidence) than a juridical one. She also states that the 1949 Geneva Conventions do not require the presence of the suspect for states to act on their duty to search for and extradite or prosecute a war criminal. 'Reading into Article 146 of the Fourth Geneva Convention (see above) a limitation on a state's right to exercise universal jurisdiction would fly in the face of a *teleological interpretation* of the Geneva Conventions. The purpose of these Conventions, obviously, is not to restrict the jurisdiction for crimes under international law'.[56] As with the Pinochet Case, then, there was a different interpretation of the meaning and indeed intention of the relevant treaties.

In the Separate Joint Opinion of Judges Higgins, Kooijmans, and Buergenthal it was argued, contrary to the position implied by President Guillame, that prosecutions in foreign courts are often the more likely and thus the more credible alternative to prosecutions in domestic or international courts.[57] Yet on the second issue of immunities they agree with Guillame. Their Joint Opinion added that if 'a state may choose to exercise a universal criminal jurisdiction *in absentia*, it must also ensure that certain safeguards are in place'. One of these safeguards is respect for the immunities entitled under international law. 'They are', they conclude, 'absolutely essential to prevent abuse and to ensure that the rejection of impunity does not jeopardize stable relations between states'.[58] This pluralist position is tempered by their view that cosmopolitan sentiments can grow in strength. Like Hedley Bull, these

---

[56] *Arrest Warrant Case. Dissenting Opinion of Judge Van den Wyngaert*, para. 54–5, 65.

[57] *Arrest Warrant Case. Separate Joint Opinion of Judges Higgins, Kooijmans, and Buergenthal*, para. 78.

[58] In order to balance the claims of criminal justice with the need for international order, they further recommend that the Prosecutor bringing charges should be independent of government and that the state contemplating exercising universal jurisdiction should first 'offer to the national state of the prospective accused person the opportunity itself to act upon the charges concerned'. As the following chapter demonstrates, these principles (an Independent Prosecutor and a jurisdiction that complements that of national courts) have been adopted by the ICC in Articles 15 and 17 of the Rome Statute respectively. *Arrest Warrant Case, Separate Opinion of Judges Higgins, Kooijmans, and Buergenthal*, para. 59.

judges are keen not to rule out this possibility but stress that in the meantime international law has an important function in balancing normative priorities. As a statement of the pluralist–solidarist problem at the heart of the English School inquiry, it is worth quoting at length.

These trends reflect a balancing of interests. On the one scale, we find the interest of the community of mankind to prevent and stop impunity for perpetrators of grave crimes against its members; on the other, there is the interest of the community of States to allow them to act freely on the inter-State level without unwarranted interference. A balance therefore must be struck between two sets of functions which are both valued by the international community. Reflecting these concerns, what is regarded as a permissible jurisdiction and what is regarded as the law of immunity are in constant evolution. The weights on the two scales are not set for all perpetuity. Moreover, a trend is discernible that in a world which increasingly rejects impunity for the most repugnant offences, the attribution of responsibility and accountability is becoming firmer, the possibility for the assertion of jurisdiction wider and the availability of immunity as a shield more limited. The law of privileges and immunities, however, retains its importance since immunities are granted to high State officials to guarantee the proper functioning of the network of mutual inter-State relations, which is of paramount importance for a well-ordered and harmonious international system.[59]

The ICJ approach to the tension between international stability and criminal justice in the Yerodia case caused Judge Van den Wyngaert to write a dissenting opinion. 'By issuing and circulating the warrant', she argued, 'Belgium may have acted contrary to international comity. It has not, however, acted in violation of an international legal obligation.'[60] Siding with the majority of Law Lords in the Pinochet case, she argues that full immunity cannot possibly apply to the 'official acts' of state representatives. Customary international law has criminalized certain acts, such as war crimes, crimes against humanity, and genocide, which can 'for practical purposes, only be committed with the means and mechanisms of a state and as part of state policy'. These acts, in other words, are almost inevitably 'official acts'. It makes no legal sense therefore to grant immunity to state officials for crimes that can only be committed by state officials. The implication of this would be that international criminal law is redundant and, as Lord Steyn pointed out, orders such as Hitler's 'final solution' could not be punished because they were the 'official acts' of a head of state.[61]

---

[59] *Arrest Warrant Case. Separate Opinion of Judges Higgins, Kooijmans, and Buergenthal*, para. 75.

[60] *Arrest Warrant Case. Dissenting Opinion of Judge Van den Wyngaert*, para. 1.

[61] *Arrest Warrant Case. Dissenting Opinion of Judge Van den Wyngaert*, para. 36.

The solidarist perspective in Van den Wyngaert's position is evident in the manner by which she reached the conclusion that the acts Yerodia was charged with were criminal acts under customary international law. For instance, she cited 'a plethora of recent scholarly writings' and 'the opinion of *civil society*, an opinion that cannot be completely discounted in the formation of customary international law today'.[62] Furthermore, the solidarist argument that states have a responsibility to prosecute nationals charged with committing these acts is evident in her criticism of the DRC. 'The Congo was ill placed when accusing Belgium of exercising universal jurisdiction in the case of Mr. Yerodia', she noted.

If the Congo had acted appropriately, by investigating charges of war crimes and crimes against humanity allegedly committed by Mr. Yerodia in the Congo, there would have been no need for Belgium to proceed with the case.... [A]s Hersch Lauterpacht observed in 1951, 'the dignity of a foreign state may suffer more from an appeal to immunity than from a denial of it'. The International Court of Justice should at least have made it explicit that the Congo should have taken up the matter itself.[63]

This concern for the normative implications of the ICJ judgment is also evident in Judge Van den Wyngaert's final observations, which directly addressed President Guillame's warning of 'judicial chaos'.

In the abstract, the chaos argument may be pertinent. This risk may exist, and the Court could have legitimately warned against it in its Judgment without necessarily reaching the conclusion that a rule of customary international law exists to the effect of granting immunity to Foreign Ministers. However, granting immunities to incumbent Foreign Ministers may open the door to other sorts of abuse. It dramatically increases the number of persons that enjoy international immunity from jurisdiction.... Perhaps the International Court of Justice, in its effort to close one box of Pandora for fear of chaos and abuse, may have opened another one: that of granting immunity and thus *de facto* impunity to an increasing number of government officials.

The danger that Judge Van den Wyngaert warned against recalls the solidarist criticism of pluralist IR theory. As John Vincent put it, the concern for international order between states causes us 'to act as if other states are legitimate, not because they are legitimate but because to do otherwise would lead to chaos'. It betrays a 'morality of states' that rationalizes a

---

[62] *Arrest Warrant Case. Dissenting Opinion of Judge Van den Wyngaert*, para. 27.

[63] *Arrest Warrant Case. Dissenting Opinion of Judge Van den Wyngaert*, para. 35, quoting Hersch Lauterpacht, 'The Problem of Jurisdictional Immunities of Foreign States', 28 *British Yearbook of International Law*, 28 (1951), 232.

blindness to the central moral issues in the treatment of individuals (for example, slavery), or of groups (for example, the principle of national self-determination), or in a certain sense of the world as a whole (for example, the obligations attending travel on 'spaceship earth'). A morality giving no sight of such central issues would be a third-rate morality whatever the argument of prudence that supported it.[64]

The Bull–Vincent, pluralist–solidarist split in English School theory, in other words, is clearly apparent in the Opinions of the judges deciding the Yerodia case.

THE POLITICS OF INTERNATIONAL CRIMINAL JUSTICE

In her Dissenting Opinion on the Yerodia judgment, Judge Van den Wyngaert recognized that Belgium may have been 'naive in trying to be a forerunner in the suppression of international crimes and substantiating the view that, where the territorial state fails to take action, it is the responsibility of their states to offer a forum to victims'.[65] This, however, was a political matter that the Court need not have concerned itself with. 'Belgium's conduct', she notes, 'may show a lack of *international courtesy*'. But,

[e]ven if this were true, it does not follow that Belgium actually violated (customary or conventional) international law. *Political wisdom* may command a change in Belgian legislation, as has been proposed in various circles. *Judicial wisdom* may lead to a more restrictive application of the present statute, and may result from proceedings that are pending before Belgian courts. This does not mean that Belgium has acted in violation of international law by applying it in the case of Mr Yerodia.[66]

In other words, the right to exercise universal jurisdiction exists, at least according to Judge Van den Wyngaert, but deciding to exercise that right inevitably involves other normative criteria. The idea that statespeople 'operate with multiple responsibilities when they engage in the activity of foreign policy' is again a familiar one to those working within English School IR theory.[67] For instance, Robert Jackson links Martin Wight's three traditions of international theory, as discussed in Chapter 1, to notions of national responsibility (realism), international responsibility (rationalism), and humanitarian responsibility (revolutionism or cosmopolitanism). This kind of linkage has

---

[64] Vincent, *Human Rights and International Relations*, 124.

[65] *Arrest Warrant Case. Dissenting Opinion of Judge Van den Wyngaert*, para. 86.

[66] *Arrest Warrant Case. Dissenting Opinion of Judge Van den Wyngaert*, para. 3.

[67] Robert Jackson, *The Global Covenant. Human Conduct in a World of States* (Oxford: Oxford University Press, 2000), 169.

been partly responsible for the confusion on how English School theory distinguishes solidarist international society from world society. This is addressed in Chapter 4. If they are true to their position in Wight's revolutionist category cosmopolitans advocate bypassing the state rather than giving it additional responsibilities. When talking about state responsibilities, as opposed to individual or non-state responsibilities, it is therefore essential to recognize that one is necessarily talking from within the rationalist tradition of IR theory. But it is also necessary to recognize that within the rationalist tradition one can identify pluralist and solidarist approaches to international society. Where the former prioritizes the principles of sovereign consent, sovereign immunity, and international comity (e.g. Guillame), the latter gives greater weight to an international consensus among a wider range of political actors and empowers states to punish human rights abusers rather than let them escape accountability behind a veil of international order (e.g. Van den Wyngaert).

Given this qualification, Jackson's emphasis on 'normative pluralism' is helpful in sensitizing us to the difficulties that states like Belgium and the UK face when they claim to act as agents of humanity. Any claim to be a good citizen of international society should seek to balance each of the responsibilities that Jackson identifies.[68] As well as balancing the interests of their own citizens against the interests of international society they should, in the words of Judges Higgins, Kooijmans, and Buergenthal, balance 'two functions which are both valued by the international community', that is international comity and international criminal justice. Whether a judge should let these political issues influence his or her interpretation of the law is a matter of dispute but as the two cases examined above demonstrate, it is somewhat unavoidable. What is not in dispute, at least from those writing from the perspective of good international citizenship, is that governments should give due consideration to their national, international, *and* humanitarian responsibilities when deciding how to respond to the law and when deciding whether new law is needed.

If such criteria help to illuminate the issue, they do not necessarily provide the politician with definitive answers. An assessment of whether a specific decision to sacrifice one value in order to protect another is justified is inevitably going to be subjective. The pluralist criticism of international criminal justice, examples of which one can find in the above opinions of

---

[68] The idea of 'good international citizenship' has been developed by academics working broadly within the English School tradition. See Andrew Linklater, 'The Good International Citizen and the Crisis in Kosovo', in Albrecht Schnabel and Ramesh Thakur (eds.), *Kosovo and the Challenge of Humanitarian Intervention* (Tokyo, New York, and Paris: United Nations University Press, 2000), 482–95; Tim Dunne and Nicholas J. Wheeler, 'Good International Citizenship: A Third Way for British Foreign Policy', *International Affairs*, 74 (1998), 847–70.

Lord Goff and President Guillame, is often premised on the belief that such actions will lead to a breakdown of international society and the proliferation of 'chaos'. If this were so, then abandoning this practice would probably be justified. Rarely are these issues as clear-cut as this however. The perception of the threat to international order posed by universal jurisdiction is probably overstated. Moreover, as Judge Van den Wyngaert notes, the cost of sticking to a pluralist society of independent sovereign states in terms of impunity for egregious human rights abuses is often underestimated. The fact that these judges disagree on what international law entitles states to do exacerbates the politician's dilemma.

The politics of the Pinochet and Yerodia cases further illustrates this aspect of good international citizenship. The judgment of the British Law Lords in the Pinochet case was seen as an important victory for advocates of international criminal justice, but its immediate impact was limited. The House of Lords judgment did not mean that Pinochet *would* be extradited, merely that the British Home Secretary, at that time Jack Straw, *could* under the 1989 Extradition Act make the decision to send him to Spain for trial. For Michael Byers, the Home Office's reluctance to support the case for extradition was evident in its refusal to take a position on the question of sovereign and diplomatic immunity. This, Byers further notes, was in marked contrast to the position the UK government had taken at the negotiations to set up the ICC.[69] There was no shortage of voices reminding the Home Secretary of the costs to Britain should the extradition of Senator Pinochet go ahead. Conservative leaders, such as Lady Thatcher and Lord Lamont, were outspoken in support for Pinochet, reminding the British people of what they saw as a debt of gratitude owed to the former Chilean leader for his support during the Falklands war. Church leaders reminded Straw of the spiritual costs. The Archbishop of Canterbury Dr. George Carey, for instance, called upon Jack Straw to listen to Lady Thatcher and 'to be compassionate in this situation'.[70] More significantly, the Foreign Office and the Ministry of Defence warned Straw that trade and diplomatic problems would inevitably result from a decision to proceed with extradition.[71] This was made clear when the Chilean military ditched a

---

[69] Michael Byers, 'The Law and Politics of the Pinochet Case', *Duke Journal of Comparative and International Law*, 10 (2000), 425. The British government also rejected a call by Amnesty International to charge Pinochet itself rather than merely respond to the initiative of a Spanish court.

[70] Ewen Macaskill, David Pallister, and Ian Black, 'Straw Hints has Deal with Chile over Pinochet', *The Guardian*, 23 October 1998; see also Christopher Morgan, 'Carey Pleads for Pinochet to Be Released', *Sunday Times*, 31 October 1999; on the Vatican's intervention on behalf of Pinochet, see Joan Smith, 'The Elitists Stand Exposed', *The Independent*, 21 February 1999.

[71] Kim Sengupta, 'The Flight of Pinochet', *The Independent*, 3 March 2000.

£100 million deal with the British tank-maker Vickers. Thousands of jobs were reportedly put at risk.[72]

In March 2000, Straw allowed Pinochet to return to Chile on grounds that he was unfit to stand trial, a medical judgement that had been confirmed by British doctors but was not immediately released to the public because of medical confidentiality. For some, the medical evidence was, despite being seen to be genuine following its eventual leak to the press, a convenient excuse 'for Straw to do what he had wanted to do all along'.[73] Support for this interpretation can be found in news reports that political leaders in the UK, Spain, and Chile had secretly discussed ways in which they could reach a mutually beneficial end to the affair. According to one report, Prime Minister Tony Blair 'undertook to do what he could within the law provided that exchanges between the two leaders [himself and President Eduardo Frei of Chile] were kept secret'.[74] The full picture of what happened has yet to emerge but it is implied in these reports that out of these discussions a plan emerged to return Pinochet to Chile. The Chilean government would raise the matter of the Senator's health, which would then allow the British Home Secretary to use his discretion under the 1989 Extradition Act. The hope that this would be seen to be legally above board while delivering a politically suitable outcome was, however, thwarted by another international treaty, the 1957 European Convention on Extradition. It did not include medical unfitness as a reason for a refusal to extradite. Ultimately, Jack Straw chose to ignore it despite his claim to attach 'great importance to the international obligations of the United Kingdom'.[75]

The conclusion that the British government had put the national interest ahead of its responsibilities to the solidarist conception of international society as articulated by the Law Lords in their interpretation of the Torture Convention is hard to avoid. Any defence of the New Labour government's decision to put British jobs in the defence industry (the prospects of which improved following Jack Straw's decision)[76] have to be weighed next to the continuing sense

[72] David Robertson, 'Jobs Crisis at Vickers as Chile kills £100 Million Tank Deal', *Scotland on Sunday*, 13 December 1998.

[73] Byers, 'The Law and Politics of the Pinochet Case', 438. The refusal to release the medical report was legally challenged by the Belgian government, who had their claim upheld by the Courts of Appeal on 15 February 2000. They were leaked to the press shortly after this decision.

[74] Hugh O' Shaughnessy, 'Secret Deal Freed Pinochet', *The Observer*, 7 January 2001. The report was based on the publication of *Augusto Pinochet: 503 Dias Atrapado en Londres* by Monica Perez, Editorial Los Andes, 2000. See also Sengupta, 'The Flight of Pinochet'.

[75] Sands, *Lawless World*, 40–2.

[76] Chile reportedly resumed negotiations to purchase three out-of-service Royal Navy frigates in a deal worth £500 million. Mark Watts and Conal Walsh, 'Chile Restarts UK Arms Talks', *Sunday Business*, 23 January 2000. However, continuing anger over the detention reportedly influenced the decision by the Chilean air force to buy 16 F-16 fighter jets from Lockheed Martin

of injustice that the victims of the Pinochet regime feel. Yet any criticism of the government's decision also has to be assessed not merely alongside the social and economic interests of certain British citizens, but also alongside the communitarian argument that returning Pinochet to Chile was the right thing to do. Either way it is hard to accept the argument of those who complained that the financial cost of simply debating the issue in the British courts made the detention of Pinochet unjustifiable. Lord Lamont, for example, argued that the legal costs alone made the judicial process an 'expensive political farce that should have been killed off long ago'.[77] The legal fees that lawyers involved charged may have been extortionate, but the Pinochet case was far from being a political farce because it helped to expose the normative assumptions of contemporary international society and its constituent members.

Regardless of the judgement to be made on the UK government's decision not to extradite Senator Pinochet, the case clearly illustrates the additional burdens a state takes on when seeking to respond to the solidarist agenda of international criminal justice. What is apparent in the Pinochet case, and clear in cases involving Belgium, is that United States foreign policy has tended to exacerbate those burdens. In the Pinochet case for instance, it was reported that the United States joined the Chilean government in putting pressure on Straw to release Pinochet. Although these reports were publicly denied by officials, it is clear that the Clinton administration was split on how best to approach the issue. On one side, there were those who wanted to see Pinochet extradited, but on the other side, there were those who supported the public positions of Henry Kissinger and President Bush Sr, which was to oppose extradition.[78] The administration's public stance, which was described as one of 'determined neutrality', was designed not to jeopardize Washington's strong relations with Chile's government. By referring to the two pluralist concerns of international order and a state's progress towards democracy, moreover,

---

of the United States instead of the Gripen combat aircraft manufactured by a joint venture involving BAE Systems. Jimmy Burns and Mark Mulligan, 'Pinochet Cloud over Straw's Chilean Defence Contracts Push', *Financial Times*, 28 March 2002.

[77] Quoted in 'Taxpayers to Foot Pinochet's Legal Bill', *The Guardian*, 8 July 1999.

[78] Pail Waugh, 'Pinochet Backed by Old Ally Bush', *The Independent*, 12 April 1999; see also Ewen Macaskill, Elizabeth Love, and Nick Hopkins, 'US Urges Pinochet Return. Quiet Pressure by Washington Adds to Dilemma for Straw', *The Guardian*, 30 November 1998. The link between Kissinger and Pinochet noted above also applied to Bush. He was director of the CIA in the 1970s, and it was thus easy to interpret his stance as part of an effort to avoid being embarrassed by American links to Pinochet. The CIA reportedly resisted President Clinton's order to release intelligence documents detailing what the agency knew about Pinochet's dictatorship. Attention focused on the murder in September 1973 of American journalist Charles Horman. A State Department document released by the Clinton administration implied that US intelligence might have played 'an unfortunate part' in his death. George Gedda, 'Documents at Odds over Death of American in Chile', *Associated Press*, 9 October 1999. The document is available at: foia.state.gov/documents/Chile2/000002A9.pdf

Clinton administration officials gave the impression that they would be happy to see Pinochet return to Chile. For instance, Secretary of State Madeleine Albright drew the distinction between international criminal justice in failed states such as Rwanda and Yugoslavia and the same process in Chile, where 'the citizens of a democratic state are wrestling with the very difficult problem of how best to balance the need for justice and the requirements of reconciliation'. 'Significant respect', she concluded, 'should be given to their conclusions'. On the other hand, officials drew attention to the so-called 'Arafat question'. How, they asked, 'could the US reconcile its desire to bring terrorists and brutal leaders to justice with the fact that some of those people are now legitimized in their own country?'[79]

The Bush administration's response to the Belgian legislation that was at the centre of the Yerodia case was certainly less discreet, but then the threat to American citizens and to US allies was much more direct. Following the conviction in June 2001 of four Rwandans for their part in the 1994 genocide, the Belgian courts became the focus of human rights activists seeking justice for past abuses. Just one week after the verdict, a group of Palestinians living in the Lebanon filed a complaint against Ariel Sharon for his alleged role, when he was Israeli defence minister, in the 1982 massacre in the Sabra and Shatila refugee camps outside Beirut. The diplomatic tension between Israel and Belgium developed into a full-blown crisis following the *Cour de Cassation*'s rule that the universal jurisdiction law did not require Sharon's presence in Belgium for it to be effective. Israel withdrew its ambassador from Belgium and the potential economic costs for Belgium were made apparent when the American Jewish Congress wrote to Belgian Prime Minister Guy Verhofstadt, warning that the 'legal climate' in Belgium made foreign investment 'highly unlikely'.[80]

From March 2003, the political costs of Belgium's Law Concerning the Punishment of Serious Violations of International Humanitarian Law became intolerable. In that month a group of Iraqis, sponsored by an organization reported to have links to Saddam Hussein's government, brought a complaint against former President Bush, Vice-President Cheney, Secretary of State Colin Powell, and retired General Norman Schwarzkopf for their alleged roles in the 12 February 1991 missile attack on the Amiriya bunker in Baghdad. At least 200 Iraqi civilians were reportedly killed in the attack. In an effort to pre-empt the diplomatic fallout, Belgian legislators rushed through an amendment to the law, which stipulated along the lines of President Guillame's Separate Opinion in the Yerodia case that an investigation could only take place if the

[79] Thomas W. Lippman, 'US Keeps Low Profile on Pinochet. Officials Don't Want Precedent Set', *Washington Post*, 6 December 1998.
[80] Uri Dan, 'Pointing the Finger at Brussels', *The Jerusalem Post*, 6 March 2003.

complaint had a direct link to Belgium. Otherwise the Justice Minister could intervene to return the case to the country of origin. However, the diplomatic pressure increased when in May 2003 another group of Iraqis filed a complaint against US General Tommy Franks who was then commanding US forces in Iraq.[81]

In many respects, the Bush administration was pushing on an open door when they complained to the Belgian government. Belgian human rights activists, such as Senator Alain Destexhe, sought reform and Foreign Minister Louis Michel argued that Belgium 'must not impose itself as the moral conscience of the world'. Yet, if any doubt existed, the Bush administration made clear that any failure to repeal the law would be extremely costly. Secretary of Defense Donald Rumsfeld, for instance, publicly threatened to withhold funding for construction of a new NATO headquarters should the law remain in place. It was he stated, 'perfectly possible' for NATO 'to meet elsewhere'.[82] In August 2003 the law was replaced in a manner that granted automatic immunity from prosecution for any official from a NATO or EU nation and limited jurisdiction to complaints where either the victim or defendant was a Belgian national or resident. The following month Belgium's highest Court upheld the new legislation by formally dismissing the complaints filed against Sharon, Bush, and others.[83] While these revisions satisfied the United States such that the State Department could look back on what it described as 'a major bilateral irritant',[84] human rights groups lamented the fact that prosecution of former dictators, such as Hissène Habré, was once more postponed.[85]

---

[81] Glen Frankel, 'Belgian War Crime Law Undone by its Global Reach', *Washington Post*, 30 September 2003.

[82] C. S. Smith, 'Rumsfeld Says Belgian Law Could Prompt Alliance to Leave', *International Herald Tribune*, 13 June 2003' and 'Belgians Are Incensed by American Pressure on War Crimes Law', *International Herald Tribune*, 14 June 2003.

[83] 'War Crimes Cases Dropped', *New York Times*, 25 September 2003.

[84] US State Department, Background Note: Belgium.

[85] Habré, the former President of Chad, had initially been arrested in Senegal but released when the constitutional court there found that they did not have jurisdiction over extraterritorial crimes in the absence of implementing legislation applicable to acts at the relevant time. Chadian victims then filed charges against Habré in Belgium. See R. Brody and H. Duffy, 'Prosecuting Torture Universally: Hissène Habré, Africa's Pinochet?' in H. Fischer and C. Kress, and S. R. Lüder (eds), *International and National Prosecutions of Crimes under International Law. Current Developments* (Berlin: Berlin Verlag Arno Spitz, 2001). The case was put on hold because of the uncertain status of the Belgian legislation, but in September 2005 a Belgian judge issued an arrest warrant charging Habré with crimes against humanity, war crimes, and torture. At the time of writing, Senegal had rearrested Habré but refused to hand him over to Belgium. It had instead requested the African Union to recommend a 'competent jurisdiction' for the trial. Human Rights Watch, 'The Case Against Hissène Habré, an "African Pinochet" ', www.hrw.org/justice/habre

CONCLUSION

Like Belgium, Spain has reconsidered the role it wishes its legal system to play as an agent of solidarist international society. This followed a February 2003 ruling by the Spanish Supreme Court in the so-called *Guatemalan Generals* case, which provided there must be a link between the foreign offence and Spain before a Spanish court can exercise jurisdiction.[86] These reforms are in line with the opinion of President Guillame in the Yerodia case, which ruled that customary international law could only accommodate extraterritorial and not universal jurisdiction. This was also an important, if often overlooked implication of the manner in which the Law Lords reached their decision in the Pinochet case. In the absence of a direct link to the UK and Spain those states could continue to assert their jurisdiction over acts that took place in Chile, *but only because Chile had consented to be bound by the terms of the 1984 Convention against Torture*. If these cases are representative, then it is clear that any trend towards a solidarist conception of international society has been checked. As Cassese notes, these trends may sound the death knell for '*absolute* jurisdiction (which one could also term "universality unbound" or "wild exercise of extraterritorial judicial authority")'. Yet the future does not look so bad for 'conditional universality' where 'jurisdiction may only be triggered when the territorial or national state fails to act, and provided the prosecuting state shows an acceptable link with the offence'.[87]

The positivist/pluralist check on recent trends demonstrates that the principle of sovereign consent is still considered significant in the creation of international criminal law, and indeed the principles of sovereign and diplomatic immunity are still considered important exceptions to that law. It should be noted, however, that these exceptions relate to law between states. As Chapter 4 notes there is no place for immunity in the law applied by international courts. Perhaps the more telling fact, however, is the unwillingness on the part of international society as a whole to show any kind of enthusiasm even for the more limited conditional universality now exercised by states like Spain and Belgium. As Van Elst noted, most states have been unwilling to act on the judicial obligations they acquire under treaties such as the Geneva Conventions. Writing in 2000, for instance, he calculated that 'if the numbers of countries that have penalized all or some of the grave breaches (73) are combined with the numbers of countries that have established universal jurisdiction (54), it turns out that only 30 countries have established universal jurisdiction over

---

[86] Cassese, 'Is the Bell Tolling for Universality,' 590.
[87] Cassese, 'Is the Bell Tolling for Universality,' 595.

all grave breaches'.[88] Given 192 states are party to the Conventions, this figure suggests that a commitment to abide by IHL is not matched by a willingness to enforce it through national courts. Some of the reasons behind a state's unwillingness to act on the obligations to extradite or prosecute have been covered in this chapter. First, there is the communitarian or contractarian view of accountability, which not only sees justice as better served at the national level but sees in international criminal justice a threat to democracy. Second, there is the view that the use of national courts to implement international criminal justice is a threat to good relations between states and international order more generally.

The critical observer must constantly be aware not only of the normative value of these arguments, but also of the manner in which they can be used either by those seeking to avoid accountability for their own actions or by those unwilling to accept the burdens of confronting those seeking to avoid accountability. What is clear from the two cases studied above is that United States administrations have been reluctant to support those states that claim universal jurisdiction over crimes that offend humanity. Far from being seen in terms of states acting as agents of humankind, the exercise of universal jurisdiction is seen in geopolitical terms whereby America's enemies can co-opt America's allies to pursue politically motivated prosecutions against the United States. It should be noted that this opposition to the principle of universal jurisdiction is not absolute. At least in civil cases the US judiciary continues to hold foreigners accountable for human rights abuses through the ATCA. Yet even here, the Bush administration has, as noted in Chapter 2, sought to rein in the scope of the act and the type of cases it is applicable to. It should also be noted that the US political branch has been less than conservative in its application of extraterritorial jurisdiction when it is in its particular interests. For example, Michael Scharf notes how the United States indicted, apprehended, and prosecuted Fawaz Yunis, a Lebanese national, for hijacking from Beirut airport a Jordanian airliner whose passengers included two US citizens. The US-asserted jurisdiction based on the Hostage Taking Convention, a treaty that provides jurisdiction over hostage takers, despite the fact that Lebanon was not party to the treaty and did not consent to the prosecution of Yunis in the United States.[89] This is an example of what will become, in the following chapters, a familiar story of the selective and self-serving view of international criminal justice held by the US government.

[88] Richard Van Elst, 'Implementing Universal Jurisdiction over Grave Breaches of the Geneva Convention', *Leiden Journal of International Law*, 13 (2000), 831.

[89] Michael Scharf, 'The ICC's Jurisdiction over the Nationals of Non-Party States', in Sarah B. Sewall and Carl Kaysen (eds.), *The United States and the International Criminal Court* (London: Rowman and Littlefield, 2000), 220–2.

4

The Rome Statute and the Constitution
of World Society

The purpose of Chapter 3 was twofold. First, it sought to illustrate how debates in the area of international criminal justice help illustrate the pluralist–solidarist divide in English School conceptions of international society. Second, it sought to illustrate the reluctance of states to fulfil what solidarists see as a state duty to extradite or prosecute individuals charged with international crimes. The present attitude of the US government towards universal jurisdiction helps to reinforce that reluctance. Its reaction to the legislation that allowed Belgian courts to exercise universal jurisdiction is likely to act as a powerful deterrent to any other state thinking along such lines. More accurately, US policy is likely to deter those states who seek the *impartial* application of international law, for it is clear that the US government is only concerned when the law has an impact on its particular interests or on those of its allies. There has been, for instance, no discernible objection to the use of Belgian courts for the 2005 prosecution of two Rwandan businessmen implicated in the 1994 genocide.[1] This insight into the way power and law interact might lead some to conclude that international criminal justice is simply a neocolonial tool of the powerful. The politically significant response, however, has been a reaffirmation of the normative value of international criminal justice and an attempt to separate it from the vagaries of power politics. In other words, the reluctance of states to exercise universal jurisdiction, the danger that such practices pose to interstate relations and the perception that justice will always be selective because of the corrupting influence of power politics, has not led international society to abandon international criminal justice. Rather these arguments strengthened the political significance of those calling for the creation of international criminal courts that are independent of states.

The purpose of this chapter is to locate these most recent developments in the English School framework and by doing so to demonstrate how the issue

---

[1] '2 Go on Trial in Brussels in 1994 Rwanda Massacre', *International Herald Tribune*, 10 May 2005.

of international criminal justice can help English School theory distinguish solidarist conceptions of international society from world society. Central to the argument is the point introduced in Chapter 3. In liberal conceptions of solidarist international society individuals might be the bearers of rights, but it is still deemed the responsibility *of states* to provide an environment in which those rights can be enjoyed. Where solidarists differ from pluralists is that they recognize the universality of certain humanitarian values and argue that it is the duty of states, as good international citizens, to intervene in the affairs of another state when it is either unwilling or unable to protect those values. A state might respond to this responsibility unilaterally, that is by using its courts to exercise universal jurisdiction, or it might do so multilaterally through the institutions of the UN. As this chapter shows, however, the criticism of universal jurisdiction (i.e. that it threatens interstate relations, is corrupted by power politics, and is therefore inevitably selective) has also been applied to the so-called ad hoc courts created by the UN. Once again, this criticism has not weakened the support for international criminal justice. Rather, it has contributed to the creation of a permanent international criminal court that is independent of the UN and the society of states. It is argued here that the Rome Statute's definition of core crimes and its provision of a Prosecutor that can act without the authorization of the UN Security Council help to constitute world society. Central to that claim, however, is the difference between a revolutionary conception of world society and the Kantian conception of world society, which was outlined in Chapter 1. The following section elaborates on that distinction and relates the two conceptions of world society to other English School works on the subject.

FROM INTERNATIONAL TO WORLD SOCIETY

The reason the English School has had difficulty distinguishing solidarist international society from world society is the lack of specificity at the level of constitutive rules. The idea that both types of society share a common cosmopolitan consciousness based on humanity, as well as a common interest in seeing individuals punished for crimes that offend humanity, has been generally accepted. The difference between the two societies, however, lies at the level of rules and institutions. As Chapter 1 argued, solidarist international society is dependent on the willingness and ability of states to act as agents of humanity. It lacks the kind of institutions that can reinforce the cosmopolitan consciousness 'at the moment it meets with opposition' if states are unwilling or unable to do so. A revolutionary conception of world society, on the other hand, has supranational institutions that fulfil this function but it does not accommodate states. Revolutionists are willing to cast the state into the rubbish bin of history. A Kantian conception of world society has supranational institutions but these complement states and the society of states when these institutions act to reinforce the cosmopolitan consciousness. From this perspective, and based on the conclusions of Chapter 3, one might conclude that world society did not exist prior to the creation of a permanent criminal court that was independent of states and the UN Security Council. As Chapter 3 noted, the institution of criminal justice was dependent on states using their national courts, or on the UN Security Council setting up international courts, in order to sustain a global consciousness that valued humanity. To be clear, this is *not* what is being suggested here. Obviously world society existed prior to the formation of the ICC. The argument that is being advanced, however, is that such a society was weaker because it lacked the institution of criminal justice to help maintain societal cohesion when its core value (i.e. humanity) was so obviously violated.

To elaborate on this point, it is again helpful to draw on Barry Buzan's revision of the traditional English School framework. Buzan argues that English School scholarship should not merely be interested in answering 'what' questions, which are addressed by identifying the constitutional *structures* that distinguish types of society, it should also be interested in 'why' and 'how' questions, which are concerned with the *processes* that hold these structures in place.[2] Drawing on the social theory of Alexander Wendt, Buzan adds a new dimension to the traditional English School spectrum.[3] Thus, the values around which international societies might unite (e.g. diversity, humanity, and religion) can be held in place as a result of belief, calculation, or coercion. Clearly, a cosmopolitan consciousness based on humanity existed as a matter of belief before the creation of the ICC and this found expression in the declarations of international humanitarian and human rights law, as well as the movement to create a permanent court. But if individuals could violate these values with impunity, then the common consciousness and the sense of society would clearly be damaged and possibly destroyed. As Durkheim noted (see Chapter 1), the sociological function of criminal justice is not to deter possible offenders, rather it is to provide 'the emotional reaction' that says the criminal act will not become the normal state of affairs. It is 'to maintain inviolate the cohesion of society'.

---

[2] Buzan, *From International to World Society?*, 106.
[3] Alexander Wendt, *Social Theory of International Politics* (Cambridge: Cambridge University Press, 1999).

To the extent that the criminal process can deny them their liberty, then clearly there is an element of coercion designed to make would-be offenders recalculate their actions; and in this respect, criminal justice adds to the institutional depth of a society. The most significant function of international criminal justice, however, is that it officially documents and condemns the criminal act so that it does not undermine the bonds that hold a society together. Prior to the establishment of the ICC, non-governmental organizations (NGOs) acted as unofficial institutions with a similar sociological purpose. That is they helped to reconstitute humanity by publicly exposing the perpetrators of inhumane acts. Of course, they often did this when states and the society of states were willing to turn a blind eye to such acts; and in this respect, the 'publicity' created by the likes of Amnesty International and Human Rights Watch was an institution that helped to develop and then sustain the common values that world society rests on. Yet, from this perspective, world society was exceedingly 'thin' and underdeveloped. It existed, to use Bull's language, in embryonic form. It is argued below that the creation of the ICC is an indication that world society has developed beyond that stage. This is not only because its practices—that is criminal justice—address Buzan's 'how/why' question (i.e. it helps to restore 'faith in humanity'), but also because it answers the 'what' question in a very different way to previous international criminal courts.

Before elaborating on that point, it is necessary to address other aspects of Buzan's conception of world society, most notably his claim that individuals, transnational actors (TNAs), and states are all members of such a society. To get to this point Buzan initially argues that interhuman, transnational, and interstate societies each have a distinct ontological status. Yet this turns out to be a temporary move and ultimately Buzan argues that a world society exists when

> no one of the three domains or types of unit is dominant over the other two, but all are in play together.... A world society... would be based on principles of functional differentiation among the various types of entities in play, and agreements about the rights and responsibilities of different types of unit in relations both to each other and to different types.... Each type of unit would be acknowledged by the other as holding legal and political status independently, not as a gift from either of the others. Individuals and firms would thus become subjects of international law in their own right. Humankind has not yet seen a world society in this sense, though the EU may be heading in that direction.[4]

In certain respects, this reflects what is called in this book a Kantian conception of world society. It recognizes individuals, states, and other collective

---

[4] Buzan, *From International to World Society?*, 203.

actors (e.g. transnational corporations) as members. It also captures John Williams's argument that there are good normative reasons why we should value collective actors other than states and reconstitute world society in order to protect those values.[5] However, such arguments need to be treated with caution on both normative and empirical grounds.

First, Buzan's argument that world society need not be universal is conceptually confusing. For instance, there is no need to call the EU a 'world' society when 'European' society will do. But more importantly this move has normative implications that are easy to overlook. The reason that a Kantian conception of world society is based on humanity with the individual human being at its core is not because it is the normative order preferred by powerful Western liberal democratic states. Rather, it is because that principle is possibly the only one that can be universalized. This does not mean that Western governments or corporations are exempt from the rules that constitute a world society on these grounds. Liberal democracies do have safeguards against the abuse of human rights, but the need for cosmopolitan law stems in part from the fact that liberal democracies do not always respect the human rights of foreigners.[6] Neither does it mean that non-Western governments or non-state communities organized along non-liberal lines will be excluded from world society. Williams's concern to protect diversity in world society and Buzan's argument to include the rights claims of TNAs need not be dismissed. It does, however, mean that the rights world (i.e. a universal) society extends to states and non-state groups must be relative to the universal value of humanity. In order to do this, it is *necessary* that the rules that constitute world society reflect a legal hierarchy. If humanity is the only value that is held in common across world (not regional) society, then it must, to use Onuf's language, be recognized in law that is *jus cogens* or constitutional. In other words, the rights of transnational corporations to do business must be considered unconstitutional by world society if the consequence of that trade is the perpetuation of gross human rights abuses, just as the right of states to wage war is also limited by *jus cogens* norms in IHL.[7] Recognizing a hierarchy of rules such as this is

---

[5] John Williams, 'Pluralism, Solidarism and the Emergence of World Society in English School Theory', *International Relations*, 19 (2005), 19–38.

[6] Daniele Archibugi, 'Immanuel Kant, Cosmopolitan Law and Peace', *European Journal of International Relations*, 1 (1995), 448.

[7] For example, the right to trade freely does not prevent sanctions 'targeting *jus cogens* violations such as genocide'. Sarah H. Cleveland, 'Human Rights Sanctions and International Trade: A Theory of Compatibility', *Journal of International Trade Law*, 5 (2002) 133. For a discussion on how international criminal law extends past state agents to include individual private business people, see Andrew Clapham, 'Issues of Complexity, Complicity and Complementarity: From the Nuremberg Trials to the Dawn of the International Criminal Court', in Phillipe Sands (ed.), *From Nuremberg to The Hague. The Future of International Criminal Justice* (Cambridge: Cambridge University Press, 2003) 30–67. Note also the early statements by Luis Moreno Ocampo,

necessary in order to avoid the reification of collective actors at the expense of what is held in common across a truly global society (i.e. humanity). It is also necessary because a world society on these terms actually exists and for Buzan to argue that '[h]umankind has not yet seen a world society' is therefore empirically wrong. Demonstrating the existence of a world society on these terms is the subject of the rest of this chapter.

EXTENDING THE 'SOLIDARIST MOMENT'

The idea that the superpowers could cooperate to maintain a balance of power and could respect the spheres of great power influence, if not the sovereignty of all states, demonstrates that pluralist conceptions of international society were not entirely absent from IR during the cold war.[8] With the rise of 'new political thinking' in the Eastern bloc, moreover, a deeper consensus on common values began to emerge and states began to respond to a different set of priorities. In this immediate post-cold war period, international society experienced what Nicholas Wheeler has called a 'solidarist moment'. This is derived from his analysis of the laws that legitimize the use of force and the possibility that a new norm of humanitarian intervention might have evolved in this period. He demonstrates how in the early 1990s the UN Security Council was willing to interpret the humanitarian emergencies in Iraq and Somalia as threats to international peace and security and then give member states the authority (either tacitly or explicitly) to use force to support relief operations.[9]

There were many concerns with such interventions, but two stand out. At the legal level, a number of states had made it clear that these interventions in the affairs of sovereign states were only legitimized by unique and exceptional circumstances. It was clear that states like China and India were nervous at the prospect that sovereignty would no longer be a restraint on the use of force, a fear that would be voiced much more audibly when NATO used force against Yugoslavia at the end of the decade.[10] A second concern was political and this involved the willingness of member states to risk their national interest on

the ICC Prosecutor, which noted that the directors of transnational corporations could be investigated if their companies were implicated in trade that sustains situations where crimes against humanity are being committed. John Malpas, 'If You're Going to San Francisco', *Legal Week*, 18 September 2003; Marlise Simons, 'Prosecutor Turns Focus to New War Crimes Court', *New York Times*, 29 September 2003.

[8] Bull, *The Anarchical Society*, 194–222.
[9] Nicholas J. Wheeler, *Saving Strangers. Humanitarian Intervention in International Society* (Oxford: Oxford University Press, 2000).
[10] Wheeler, *Saving Strangers*, 186, 275.

behalf of humanitarianism. The reaction to the death of American service-members in Somalia demonstrated that the suffering of strangers was quickly forgotten when the images turned to the suffering of nationals.[11] As the experience in Somalia reminded Americans of the limitations of using force, crimes against humanity and genocide took place in Bosnia and Rwanda. Again the concern for the welfare of nationals imposed strict limits on the commitment of states to humanitarian goals. In Bosnia, British and French concerns for their troops reinforced the perceived importance of impartiality to the peacekeeping mission. To rely on the consent of the combatants in these conflicts—where the egregious abuse of human rights was not a side effect of the war but a war aim—was of course a tragic misconception.[12] It was, however, one that was reinforced by a moral calculation that prioritized the lives of nationals over those of strangers.

International society's commitment to solidarism was, from this perspective, short-lived. In other contexts, however, the solidarist moment was extended. The ICTY and ICTR, which were created by UN Security Council resolutions, demonstrated that states and the society of states considered it necessary to prosecute those charged with core crimes even if they were not able or willing to prevent them from committing those crimes.[13] The experience of these so-called 'ad hoc tribunals', however, further revealed the limitations of a solidarist international society that is dependent on the political will of the permanent powers of the UN Security Council. Former president of the ICTY, Antonio Cassese, makes several important observations in this regard. First, creating such courts *after* the criminal acts had been committed diminished the deterrent effects of international humanitarian and human rights law. This, of course, assumes the law does have such an effect, which is not necessarily the case. It is nevertheless logical to argue that if the law is to deter crimes there must be evidence that it will be enforced. Such arguments pushed towards the creation of a permanent court. This was reinforced by Cassese's second point. Following the creation of the ICTY and ICTR the Security Council began to suffer from 'tribunal fatigue'. Cassese writes that 'the logistics of setting up the ad hoc tribunals for the former Yugoslavia and Rwanda had strained the capabilities and resources of the United Nations and consumed the Security Council's time. The Security Council, as the organ that created both tribunals, found itself frequently seized with issues and problems

[11] Wheeler, *Saving Strangers*, 188–200.

[12] United Nations, *Report of the Secretary-General Pursuant to General Assembly Resolution 53/35. The Fall of Srebrenica*, 1999; *Report of the Independent Inquiry into the Actions of the United Nations During the 1994 Genocide in Rwanda*, 1999.

[13] Security Council Resolution 808 (1993); Security Council Resolution 827 (1993); Security Council Resolution 955 (1994).

concerning these tribunals and their administration, and as a result became less inclined to establish other similar organs.'[14]

These two points exacerbated the more general problem, which involved the charge of 'selective justice'. The criminal tribunals for Rwanda and the former Yugoslavia suited the political purpose of the great powers because those states could be seen to be making amends for their past failures while not exposing their own nationals to international prosecutions. Of course, the ICTY did have jurisdiction over acts committed by NATO officials during its 1999 campaign against the Milosevic regime and one might accept the Prosecutor's conclusion that the allegations of NATO war crimes lacked substance.[15] This conclusion, however, did not satisfy opponents of the ICTY and it did nothing to mitigate the impression that it was a tool used by the great powers to promote their particular interests.[16] Nor did it address the wider criticism, which was that international criminal justice would inevitably be tainted so long as it was dependent on the will of the Security Council. For instance, there may have been a case for international courts to investigate the situations in Colombia, Chechnya, Tibet, and Northern Ireland, but these courts would never be created so long as the interested (and possibly accused) parties could veto the enabling resolution at the Security Council. The fact that the Security Council was 'fatigued' by the creation of such tribunals thus exacerbated what was already a significant problem with international criminal justice as it was implemented by the society of states.

These problems led logically to calls for a court that was permanent *and* independent of states.[17] To this end, Cassese notes the positive lessons drawn from the UN experience with ad hoc tribunals. The ICTY and the ICTR had an important practical impact. Both tribunals had accumulated jurisprudence regarding the interpretation of offences that 'could be drawn upon by those seeking a permanent, effective, and politically uncompromised system of international criminal justice'. Of more significance, however, was the moral legacy created by these tribunals. The events in the former Yugoslavia and

---

[14] Antonio Cassese, 'From Nuremberg to Rome: International Military Tribunals to the International Criminal Court', in Cassese, Gaeta, and Jones (eds.), *The Rome Statute*, 15. For evidence that the United States accepted that a permanent Court would be cost-effective and would 'ensure uniformity in the evolution of case law', see David J. Scheffer, 'The United States and the International Criminal Court', *The American Journal of International Law*, 93 (1999), 12–13.

[15] For discussion and criticism of the decision, see Paolo Benvenuti, 'The ICTY Prosecutor and the Review of the NATO Bombing Campaign Against the Federal Republic of Yugoslavia', *European Journal of International Law*, 12 (2001), 503–30.

[16] See e.g. Christopher Black, 'The International Criminal Tribunal for the Former Yugoslavia: Impartial?', *Mediterranean Quarterly*, 11 (2000), 29–40.

[17] See e.g. M. C. Bassiouni, 'From Versailles to Rwanda in Seventy-Five Years: The Need to Establish a Permanent International Criminal Court', *Harvard Human Rights Journal*, 10 (1997).

Rwanda and the process of publicizing them through tribunals helped 'shock the world out of its complacency'. He concludes,

the idea of prosecuting those who committed international crimes now acquired a broad-based support in world opinion and many governments. The international community in turn became more vocal about a permanent institution with universal recognition that would not suffer from the problems of *ad hoc* institutions.[18]

In this respect, one might argue that the ad hoc tribunals helped to constitute world society. By punishing individuals whose actions offended humanity they helped to maintain a common consciousness at the moment it met with opposition in Bosnia and Rwanda. Yet, in these specific circumstances, one cannot call criminal justice an institution of world society because the ad hoc courts were dependent on the will of the Security Council for their mandate, which was restricted both geographically and temporally. Moreover, these courts existed only because impunity for egregious human rights abuses was deemed, by the Security Council, to be a threat to *international* peace and security.[19] Ending impunity was not a common interest, rather it was an interest to the extent it restored order to international society. Interhuman relationships, in other words, continued to be mediated by states and the society of states. The ad hoc tribunals were, therefore, an expression of solidarist international society.

What is interesting, however, is that the response to these courts, in particular the criticism that they were tainted by the selectivity of the Security Council, demonstrated that a cosmopolitan consciousness had evolved to a point where the moral inconsistencies of a solidarist international society were not merely apparent, they were no longer tolerated. In other words, the experience of the ad hoc tribunals provided reason for changing the constitutive rules of global politics. In this respect, the period between the creation of the ad hoc courts and the creation of the permanent ICC can help answer the question posed by Buzan: at what point does solidarism change the rules so that the label 'society of states' is no longer appropriate?[20] The answer suggested here is as follows: states in a solidarist international society create institutions—such as international criminal justice—that seek to sustain and strengthen a cosmopolitan consciousness based on common values such as humanity. In this type of society, however, states continue to maintain control of that process by, for instance, limiting the jurisdiction of judges

[18] Cassese, 'From Nuremburg to Rome', 16.

[19] So, for instance, resolution 808 (1993) had to determine that ethnic cleansing was 'a threat to international peace and security' before it could under resolution 827 (1993) set up an international tribunal under Chapter VII of the Charter.

[20] Buzan, *From International to World Society?* 181.

that are notionally independent. There is, however, a 'tipping point' when the cosmopolitan consciousness becomes so well-developed that the state and indeed the UN Security Council are perceived to be obstacles in the way of institutions designed to protect common values. This is the constitutional moment where the fundamental rules of society are changed. The ICTY and the ICTR, like the Nuremberg Tribunals before them, made a positive contribution to that process by helping to sustain a cosmopolitan consciousness based on humanity. Yet they also contributed to this process by being examples of what is wrong with a society where human relations are mediated by a few powerful states. That is they contributed to the call for new institutions that are independent of the society of states because the old ones were tainted by the charges of selective and victor's justice.

A CONSTITUTIONAL MOMENT: THE ROME CONFERENCE

A key focal point for the campaign to establish a permanent ICC was the 1994 proposal for a permanent court by the United Nations International Law Commission (ILC). This, however, was far from revolutionary. James Crawford, for instance, notes how the Draft Statute proposed by the ILC set its sights extremely low, particularly by limiting the Court's jurisdiction to treaty crimes.[21] This was based on a political judgement that states would only support the court if they had explicitly consented to be bound by the law it asserted jurisdiction over. To assert jurisdiction on the basis of customary international law or to begin the effort of developing substantive law in those areas that were not yet covered by a specific treaty was considered too difficult. This conservatism was also evident in the fact that the ILC Draft provided no independent powers of investigation for the Prosecutor. Investigations would depend on the acceptance of states or on the authorization of the Security Council under Chapter VII. In this sense, the initial proposal was more akin to what might have been described as a permanent ad hoc court. It was permanent but it was not independent of the society of states.

It is testament to the power of the emerging cosmopolitan consciousness that human rights groups and a coalition of 'like-minded states' were able radically to change this initial draft.[22] The final Statute not only defined the crimes over which the Court could exercise jurisdiction, some of which were regarded as new, but it also gave the Prosecutor the power to decide

[21] James Crawford, 'The Work of the International Law Commission', in Cassese, Gaeta, and Jones (eds.), *The Rome Statute*, 23–34.

[22] For a list of states, see Schabas, *An Introduction*, p. 16.

independently of states and the Security Council whether it was appropriate to launch an investigation. The significant legislative activity in this regard took place at the Rome Conference during the summer of 1998. The fact that this conference was creating new law is emphasized by Sadat. She notes, for instance, that it is possible to view the delegates in Rome as scribes merely writing down existing customary international law. This is partly true, 'as all revolutions build upon pre-existing ideas'. But, she adds,

it would be disingenuous to suggest that the Rome process was in no way legislative, given that most of the crimes were very poorly defined in customary international law. Moreover, even where there was general agreement on the existence of a particular crime, drafting the Statute required clarifying and elucidating the precise content of the offense in a way that often moved the 'law' of the Statute far beyond existing customary international law understandings.[23]

Sadat actually concludes that the delegates at Rome 'were generally quite conservative in crafting definitions of crimes'. This does not, however, detract from the fact that the conference was 'a quasi-legislative process'.

By the criteria outlined in Chapter 2, solidarists would argue that this kind of legislative activity was legitimized firstly by the level of participation in the Rome Conference and secondly by the overwhelming majority of states that voted in favour of adopting the Statute. For instance, in the final vote on whether to adopt the Statute for ratification 120 states voted in favour, 21 abstained, and 7 voted against. Although the vote was officially not recorded, it is widely held that China, Libya, Iraq, Yemen, Qatar, Israel, and the United States voted against the Statute.[24] Additional legitimacy, solidarists might argue, can be derived from the input of states that decided not to vote against the Statute or register an abstention. The conference was in fact attended by no less than 160 states. Perhaps more significantly, 250 NGOs nominally represented those voices that might otherwise have been excluded had the conference only invited states.[25] In fact, the NGO movement was able to

---

[23] Sadat, *The International Criminal Court*, 11–12.

[24] There were several significant votes in the final hours of the conference. The first involved a final US attempt to restrict the Independent Prosecutor's jurisdiction. Norway countered this proposal with a no-action motion. This was supported by Sweden and Denmark, with Qatar and China speaking against. This motion was adopted by a vote of 113 against, 17 for, and 25 abstentions. This followed a similar vote (114 in favour, 16 against, and 20 abstentions) to stop India proposing that the conference prohibit nuclear weapons. Philippe Kirsch, QC and Darryl Robinson, 'Reaching Agreement at the Rome Conference', in Cassese, Gaeta, and Jones (eds.), *The Rome Statute*, 67. Kirsch and Robinson do not speculate on how individual states voted. The source for the list of states voting against the Statute is Lawrence Weschler, 'Exceptional Cases in Rome: The United States and the Struggle for an ICC', in Sewall and Kaysen (eds.), *The United States and the International Criminal Court*, 107–8.

[25] 137 NGOs had official credentials for the Rome Conference; however, Sadat claims 250 were present. Sadat, *The International Criminal Court*, 1.

amass its strength through the formation of a coalition, the Coalition for an International Criminal Court (CICC), which originated under the auspices of the World Federalist Movement and ultimately represented 800 NGOs from all over the world.[26]

It is possible to argue, therefore, that the overwhelming nature of the vote in favour of the Statute and NGO participation gives the Statute the legitimacy it requires to bind those citizens of states that have otherwise objected to it. This would be strongly contested by positivists, not least among them the US government, who emphasize the central importance of sovereign consent. For their part, the NGOs insist that their participation in the drafting of the Statute helped to democratize and thus legitimize the legislative process. For instance William Pace, who headed the CICC, explains that the main role of the NGO coalition was to 'level the playing field between large and small delegations'. Along with Jennifer Schense, he adds that the NGOs sought to encourage 'universal participation in the ICC process and undertook serious efforts to ensure that smaller countries would be not only present but active in the Prep-Com and Rome Conference'.[27] In so doing, the CICC helped increase political support for the Statute by increasing in the eyes of many the legitimacy of the negotiating process.

One might expect this kind of analysis from Pace, as he continues to head the CICC. Yet his analysis of the role played by NGOs need not be discarded, since it is echoed by other observers with much less of a stake in history. Sadat, for instance, argues the success of the conference 'can be credited, at least in part, to the enormous lobbying and informational efforts of NGOs, which conducted a tireless campaign in support of the Court and came together in a new example of global civil society'.[28] For Marc Weller, NGOs helped make the representation at Rome 'virtually universal'. Given that, he argues, the conference legitimately 'exercised the function of an international constitutional convention'.[29] Bruce Broomhall also credits the NGO coalition with a

---

[26] Sadat, *The International Criminal Court*, 6.

[27] William R. Pace and Jennifer Schense, 'The Role of Non-Governmental Organization', in Antonio Cassese, Gaeta, and Jones (eds.), *The Rome Statute*, 116–17. On the relative success of gender-based NGOs, see Pam Spees, 'Women's Advocacy in the Creation of the International Criminal Court: Changing Landscapes of Justice and Power', *Signs: Journal of Women in Culture and Society*, 28 (2003), 1233–54. It is also worth noting here that UN Secretary-General trust funds assisted 35 delegates from 33 least-developed countries and 19 delegates from 19 developing countries to attend. Philip Nel, 'Between Counter-hegemony and Post-hegemony: The Rome Statute and Normative Innovation in World Politics', in Andrew F. Cooper, John English, and Ramesh Thakur (eds.), *Enhancing Global Governance: Towards a New Diplomacy?* (Tokyo: United Nations University Press, 2002), 157–8.

[28] Sadat, *The International Criminal Court*, 5–6.

[29] Marc Weller, 'Undoing the Global Constitution: UN Security Council Action on the International Criminal Court', *International Affairs*, 78 (2002), 700.

significant role in the evolution of international law. They helped to create, he argues, 'a new legitimation environment in which states are under increased pressure to justify their decisions and account for their conduct towards their own citizens'. Only through the further growth of this kind of activity, he concludes, can states be held accountable to laws they may not otherwise adopt.[30]

CONSTITUTING WORLD SOCIETY: THE ROME STATUTE

There are two ways in which a legal document like the Rome Statute helps to constitute society. The first is that it identifies the form a society takes by codifying fundamental principles. The second is the manner in which it structures social processes that help to construct and then to reaffirm the common values articulated in the document. In this latter respect, the Rome Statute is not unique and is perhaps best understood as the latest development in the historical process discussed above. From this perspective, the ICC is not qualitatively different to the ad hoc courts created by the UN. By exposing the activities of those that abuse human rights on a massive scale, by identifying those activities as crimes that offend humanity, and by punishing the perpe-trators of those crimes, these courts have helped to reaffirm humanity as a value worth defending and have thus contributed to the social construction of a cosmopolitan consciousness. Yet, in both of these historical cases, the judicial process has been contingent on the behaviour of states, either as victors in an interstate conflict or as members of the Security Council which was able to define crimes against humanity as threats to international peace and security. In other words, these ad hoc courts may be part of a social process that has historically helped constitute a cosmopolitan consciousness, but it is one that is very much controlled by powerful states. In this respect, the Rome Statute is different. It builds on the legacy of Nuremberg and the UN courts by crim-inalizing actions that offend humanity, but it also creates a judicial process that is (at least theoretically) independent of the corrupting influences of the state and the national consciousness that the state must take into account. As this section shows, this claim is subject to important qualifications, but to the extent that it codifies common interests, values, and institutions that are notionally independent of states, the Rome Statute helps to establish the character of world society.

[30] Broomhall, *International Criminal Justice*, 5.

The Rome Statute articulates a common interest in seeing individuals prosecuted for what are called core universal crimes—genocide, war crimes, and crimes against humanity. These crimes are defined in Articles 6–8 and the Court assumed jurisdiction over them on 1 July 2002 (or the first day of the month after the sixtieth day following the deposit of the sixtieth ratification of the Treaty of Rome at the UN).[31] It is significant that the Statute also contains the crime of aggression, which deals with *jus ad bellum* and not *jus in bello* actions, but it does not empower the Court immediately to exercise jurisdiction over such a crime as the Rome Conference could not produce a definition that commanded a consensus. The Statute thus reaffirms the illegality of aggression in principle but it specifies in Article 5 that the Court may not exercise jurisdiction until the Assembly of State Parties is able to define it and not within seven years of the Statute entering into force. For some, this was a mistake and the 'failure to reach a consensus definition should have required its removal from the final text'.[32] The compromise, however, has allowed others to claim that the Court exercises 'dormant jurisdiction' over the crime of aggression.[33] It also demonstrates an unwillingness to claim jurisdiction over crimes that do not command a consensus across the international community as a whole.

While this compromise may have been sensitive to the view that law rests on a broad-based consensus among states, it has not prevented critics of the ICC from arguing that international criminal law is biased in favour of the powerful states. Aggression would not be criminalized, they argue, because the powerful states wish to preserve the right to be aggressive. As Thomas Smith put it, the 'second-class treatment' of aggression probably stemmed 'from the fact that hi-tech states can adhere to the letter of *in bello* laws, but find *jus ad bellum* hazier and compliance harder to establish'.[34] The propensity of the great powers to challenge and violate what might be considered a customary prohibition on the use of force is certainly significant to the context of the debate, particularly after NATO's war against Yugoslavia in 1999 and the

---

[31] Rome Statute, Article 126.

[32] Scheffer, *The United States and the International Criminal Court*, 21.

[33] Kirsch and Robinson, 'Reaching Agreement at the Rome Conference', 78. This uncertainty has been used by supporters of the Court to argue that the United States must remain engaged as either a state party or a signatory state and therefore observer at the Assembly of State Parties and by opponents of the Court to indicate the flawed nature of the Statute. For the former, see Bartram Brown, 'US Objections to the Statute of the International Criminal Court: A Brief response', *NYU Journal of International Law and Policy*, 31 (1999), 868; for the latter, see Senator Helms, S. Hrg 105–724 'Is a U.N. International Criminal Court in U.S. National Interests', Hearing Before the Subcommittee on International Operations of the Committee of Foreign Relations, United States Senate, 105th Cong. 2nd Sess. 23 July 1998.

[34] Thomas W. Smith, 'Moral Hazard and Humanitarian Law: The International Criminal Court and the Limits of Legalism', *International Politics*, 39 (2002), 175–92.

US-led war against Iraq in 2003. There are, however, genuine differences on how to define aggression and one of the main sticking points is the role of the Security Council in deciding when a particular act constitutes aggression.[35] In addition, as these two examples demonstrate, the hi-tech states do not always adhere to *in bello* laws and these states do not therefore escape the jurisdiction of the court. Smith's critique of humanitarian law is perhaps on stronger ground when he notes that the failure of the Statute to criminalize the use of nuclear weapons leads to a conclusion that the Statute favours the 'haves' over the 'have nots'.[36] Given the fact that such weapons by their nature violate fundamental principles of IHL (i.e. their use is likely to be indiscriminate and disproportionate), it is easy to conclude that the decision not to criminalize their use was purely a political one. Such arguments, however, do not prevent the obvious conclusion that a crime against humanity remains a universal crime whether it is committed systematically by machete or instantly by the use of a nuclear weapon.

The revolutionary impact of the Statute, however, is not to be found in its definition of common values and its reaffirmation of a common interest in international criminal justice. As noted above and in Chapter 3, states in a solidarist international society hold similar values and interests in common. Rather, the revolutionary impact of the Rome Statute can be found in the means by which a situation is referred to the Court. There are three ways that this can happen. Under Article 13, the UN Security Council acting under Chapter VII of the Charter can request that the Prosecutor investigate a particular situation. For some, most notably the United States, this should have remained one of two referral mechanisms, the other being that of a state party. For others, however, this would have done nothing to address the complaint that as an institution of international society international criminal justice was selective and therefore illegitimate. Thus, Article 15 allows the Court's Prosecutor to initiate investigations *proprio motu* (i.e. on his own accord) if he has sufficient evidence to convince a panel of pre-trial judges that crimes within the jurisdiction of the Court had been committed.[37] In other words, if the Prosecutor believes that there are reasonable grounds to proceed, he can investigate a situation without receiving a mandate from the Security

---

[35] See William A. Schabas, 'The Unfinished Work of Defining Aggression: How Many Times Must the Cannonballs Fly, Before They Are Forever Banned?', in Dominic McGoldrick, Peter Rowe, and Eric Donnelly (eds.), *The Permanent Court International Criminal Court. Legal and Policy Issues* (Oxford and Portland Oregon, Hart, 2004), 123–41.

[36] Thomas W. Smith, 'The New Law of War: Legitimizing Hi-tech and Infrastructural Violence', *International Studies Quarterly*, 46 (2002), 359.

[37] Olivier Fourmy, 'Powers of the Pre-Trial Chambers', in Cassese, Gaeta, and Jones (eds.), *The Rome Statute*, 1207–30.

Council or a state party.[38] What is more, his investigation can be launched and his case can rest on evidence supplied to him by NGOs. In other words, an investigation and (because the judges are also independent) a trial can be done without states being involved. The process of criminal justice is in this respect a 'world' and not an 'international' institution.

To be sure there are obvious qualifications to this rather bold claim. First, the physical location of the Court (The Hague) requires the cooperation of the Netherlands and the physical arrest and incarceration of criminals will be done by state authorities.[39] More significantly, the Court is financed by state parties who also elect key officials like the judges and the Prosecutor.[40] A successful investigation, moreover, is likely to require the cooperation of states to make sure all relevant evidence is available to both the prosecution and the defence. The Court is not, therefore, entirely independent of international society. There is, however, an intriguing possibility that a revolutionary vision of world society is contained within the Statute. It will be recalled from Chapter 1 that in a revolutionary conception of world society human relations are no longer mediated by states. In effect, supranational institutions replace states as the agents of common values. It is contended here that this vision is evident in Article 116 of the Rome Statute. This states that the Court can

receive and utilize, as additional funds, voluntary contributions from governments, international organizations, individuals, corporations and other entities, in accordance with relevant criteria adopted by the Assembly of State Parties.

The final parenthesis reminds us of the check maintained by states. However, the idea that the institution of international criminal justice can not only be legally separated from states but also materially supported by 'individuals, corporations, and other entities' does add depth to the revolutionary vision of a world society where interhuman relations are no longer mediated by states. It is, moreover, a vision that is not wholly utopian, particularly when one takes note of the global public goods that have been supported by donations from individuals such as Ted Turner.[41] If one also adds, without necessarily recommending, the possibility that private military companies could provide

---

[38] Luis Moreno Ocampo, an Argentinian lawyer who helped bring the leaders of his country's former military dictatorship to justice, was elected as Prosecutor in March 2003.

[39] See Rome Statute, Parts 9 and 10, International Cooperation and Judicial Assistance, and Enforcement. See also Alistair D. Edgar, 'Peace, Justice and Politics: The International Criminal Court, "New Diplomacy", and the UN System', in Cooper, English, and Thakur (eds.), *Enhancing Global Governance*, 133–51.

[40] Rome Statute, Article 112 (Assembly of State Parties), Article 36 (Qualification, nomination, and election of judges), Article 42 (Office of the Prosecutor).

[41] In 1997, Turner donated $1 billion over 10 years to the United Nations. For further discussion, see Richard Falk, *Law in an Emerging Global Village. A Post-Westphalian Perspective* (New York: Transnational 1998) 218–9.

the arrest and detention capabilities when states are unwilling or unable to do so, then this vision comes into even better focus. After all, this is not too far removed from the offer by such companies to provide the capabilities necessary for humanitarian relief missions.[42] To be sure, there is no evidence to suggest that the drafters of the Statute aspired to this kind of society.[43] The aim was certainly to create a Court that was independent of the society of states, but the drafters were keen to make sure that the Court would work with states and with the UN. In this respect, the Statute is best described as offering a Kantian vision of world society. The evidence for this alternative view is best demonstrated by focusing on Articles 17 and 16 of the Rome Statute, which deal specifically with the relations between the Court, individual states, and the society of states in general.

A long-standing concern of English School theory is the potential for world society to undermine the order that the society of states brings to international politics. For instance, Buzan writes how English School theory reveals

the possibility of an ontological tension between the development of world society (particularly human rights) and the maintenance of international society. The argument is that the development of individual rights threatens external, or juridical, sovereignty by facilitating grounds for outside intervention in the domestic life of the state. It threatens internal, or empirical, sovereignty by restricting the rights of the state against its citizens. In other words, regardless of whether a measure of common culture is required as a foundation for international society, any serious attempt to develop world society (by advancing a universalist human rights law for example) will tend to undermine the states that are the foundation of international society.[44]

At first glance, this might describe the relationship between the Court and international society. Clearly, the Rome Statute alters the constitutional status of state sovereignty. States are expected to punish individuals whose actions offend humanity and to accept that the ICC can intervene in the legal affairs of states as they relate to core universal crimes. Yet the Court's relationship with the state is conditioned by the principle of complementarity, which finds clearest expression in Article 17 of the Rome Statute. This provides that the Court must always defer to states that are able and willing to investigate and

---

[42] Letter from Sandline to *The Atlantic* in response to Samantha Power's article 'Bystanders to Genocide', 23 August 2001 at <www.sandline.com>.

[43] On Nordic enthusiasm for non-state contributions and Chinese concerns that 'he who pays the piper calls the tune', see Mahnoush H. Arsanjani, 'Financing', in Cassese, Gaeta, and Jones (eds.), *The Rome Statute*, 325–6.

[44] Buzan, 'The English School', 478. Andrew Hurrell made a similar point when he highlighted the need for an empirical focus not only on 'the tensions that exist both between pluralism and solidarism, but also between solidarism and transnational law'. Andrew Hurrell, 'Keeping History, Law and Political Philosophy Firmly within the English School', *Review of International Studies*, 27 (2001), 492.

to prosecute in those cases they have jurisdiction over. In this sense, national courts have *primary* jurisdiction over a situation involving allegations of core crimes, which differs from the regime operating in the ICTY where the tribunal took precedent over national law.[45] Under the Rome Statute, however, national courts do not have *exclusive* jurisdiction. If there is an unjustified delay in national proceedings or if those proceedings were not conducted independently or impartially, or deemed to have been 'for the purpose of shielding the person concerned from criminal responsibility', the ICC can resume jurisdiction over a situation.[46]

It is this last point that is controversial, not least in the US policymaking community. Yet, for some commentators, the principle of complementarity eases any tension by encouraging states to meet their own obligations to humanity. In other words, it is hoped that in order to pre-empt any interference in their internal affairs, states will pass legislation that will enable them to prosecute their own nationals for crimes that offend humanity. If that kind of legislation leads to the prosecution of individuals who would have otherwise escaped justice, then it can be considered a success for the ICC even though it may not play a direct role in the particular case.[47] Indeed, this view is held by Luis Moreno Ocampo, the Court's first Independent Prosecutor.[48] In this sense, 'the ontological tension' that Buzan talks about 'between the development of world society . . . and the maintenance of international society' is not as acute as might first appear.[49] A solidarist international society of states that responds to the universal interest in seeing individuals punished for core crimes by pre-empting the ICC will not be in tension with world society. David Turns evokes this kind of harmonization when he writes of a simultaneous 'internationalization of national criminal law' and 'nationalization of international criminal and humanitarian law'.[50] Indeed, the Statute's preference for

---

[45] Statute of the International Tribunal for the Former Yugoslavia, Article 9. On the role played by the United States in broadening the complementarity regime 'to include a deferral to national jurisdiction at the outset of a referral of an overall situation to the ICC rather than only at a preliminary stage of the work on any particular case', see Scheffer, 'The United States and the International Criminal Court', 13.

[46] Rome Statute, Article 17. See John T. Holmes, 'The Principle of Complementarity', in Lee (ed.), *The International Criminal Court*, 41–78.

[47] A. Hays Butler, 'The Growing Support for Universal Jurisdiction in National Legislation', in Stephen Macedo (ed.), *Universal Jurisdiction. National Courts and the Prosecution of Serious Crimes Under International Law* (Philadelphia, PA: University of Pennsylvania Press, 2004), 67–76.

[48] See his inaugural address to the Assembly of State Parties, 22 April 2003 available at: www.iccnow.org

[49] Buzan, 'The English School', 505.

[50] 'Aspects of National Implementation of the Rome Statute: The United Kingdom and Selected Other States', in McGoldrick et al. (eds.), *The Permanent International Criminal Court*, 340, 387.

state enforcement of universal laws acknowledges the benefits of a solidarist international society.

This poses the obvious question of how the Statute's vision of Kantian world society with the constitutive rule of complementarity differs from the solidarist conception of international society. It is helpful here to recall the distinction made in Chapter 1, which drew on Buzan's distinction between Convergence and Confederative international societies. It was argued there that it would be more helpful to equate what Buzan called Confederative inter-state societies with the Kantian conception of world society and to see what Buzan called Convergence societies at the outer end of the solidarist spectrum. It was also argued that in Confederative or Kantian world societies states no longer expect (nor indeed welcome) intervention by other states because they have given up their sovereignty to supranational institutions. The corollary of this is that in a Kantian world society it is no longer acceptable for states to intervene in the affairs of other states in order to protect common values because it is expected that supranational institutions will do that. In the area of international criminal justice this means that in a solidarist international society that lacks supranational courts states are still expected to exercise universal jurisdiction despite the questions concerning the legitimacy of such action and the possible threat it poses to comity between states. However, in a Kantian world society national governments need not take these risks (even if they were willing to) because the ICC can exercise impartial jurisdiction without the attendant dangers to international society. Of course, the idea that states should refrain from interfering in the affairs of other states while still observing cosmopolitan law was exactly what Kant had in mind when he warned against what we might now call humanitarian intervention.

The idea that states are handicapped in their pursuit of justice because they are responsible for maintaining good relations with other states is evident in the *Yerodia* decision that was discussed in detail in Chapter 3. There the ICJ considered it necessary to uphold the principle of diplomatic immunity for serving foreign ministers when the case related to the exercise of universal jurisdiction by *national* criminal courts. This was partly for reasons of comity between nations. However, these reasons were seemingly not as important to the ICJ when it came to the jurisdiction of *international* criminal courts. According to the ICJ, international courts could exercise jurisdiction over incumbent state officials because the threat to international order was less.[51] This is reflected in the Rome Statute. Article 27 (1), for instance, states that the

---

[51] *Arrest Warrant Case*, para. 60. See also Zsuzsanna Deen-Racsmány, '*Prosecutor* v. *Taylor*: The Status of the Special Court for Sierra Leone and Its Implications for Immunity', *Leiden Journal International Law*, 18 (2005), 299–322. The idea that a different set of rules applied to international courts was also evident in the Pinochet case. For instance, Lords Slynn and Goff

Statute shall apply equally to all persons without any distinction based on official capacity. In particular, official capacity as a Head of State or Government, a member of a Government or parliament, an elected representative or a government official shall in no case exempt a person from criminal responsibility under this Statute, nor shall it, in and of itself, constitute a ground for reduction of sentence.[52]

The point is that in the issue of sovereign and diplomatic immunity we can identify different principles of solidarist international society and Kantian world society. In the former, the prosecuting authority is another particular community (i.e. another nation-state exercising universal jurisdiction) and therefore it has to be concerned about the impact it has on the norms that govern relations between particular communities (i.e. interstate law). As the *Yerodia* decision shows, when a national court acts in the universal interest it can put pressure on relations between states and because those take normative priority in international society, there is inevitably a limit to how far criminal justice can go to meet the universal interest. To be sure, good relations between states is a normative goal, but it is also an argument that allows tyrants to escape justice. Delegating authority to prosecute such individuals to a supranational and therefore impartial authority places less of a burden on interstate relations and therefore denies tyrants the refuge that a concern for 'international order' gives them. In short, where a solidarist international society is unstable because it asks states to intervene in the affairs of other states, a Kantian world society can go further in responding to the universal interests because it is less burdened by the impact it has on the relations between states.

argued against the decision to deny Pinochet immunity on the grounds that the practice cited to support that decision related to international and not national courts (see Chapter 3).

[52] Rome Statute, Article 27 (1). The fact that national courts are not allowed to exercise jurisdiction over foreign officials while they are in office may impact on the willingness of a state to cooperate with the ICC in such cases. The problem here is not with the ICC's jurisdiction, but with Article 98 of the Statute. This states that the Court 'may not proceed with a request for surrender or assistance which would require the requested State to act inconsistently with its obligations under international law with respect to the State or diplomatic immunity of a person or property of a third State, unless the Court can first obtain the cooperation of that third State for the waiver of the immunity.' This means that 'while a State party to the Statute cannot shelter its own head of State or foreign minister from prosecution by the International Criminal Court, the Court cannot request the State to cooperate in surrender or otherwise with respect to a third State.' Schabas, *An Introduction to the International Criminal Court*, 81. Or, as US Ambassador David Scheffer put it, 'a State Party that has present in its territory an alien who enjoys sovereign or diplomatic immunity under international law and against whom the ICC has issued an arrest warrant would honour such immunity to the extent that a third-State waiver were not obtained by the ICC.' David Scheffer, 'Article 98 (2) of the Rome Statute: America's Original Intent', *Journal of International Criminal Justice*, 3 (2005), 336–7. However, Dapo Akande argues that the ICC can expect a state party to ignore the claim to immunity if the visiting official is the national of a state party to the Rome Statute. See 'International Law Immunities and the International Criminal Court', *American Journal of International Law*, 98 (2004), 407–33.

It would, however, be naive to suggest that criminal justice is not a threat to international peace and security simply because it was being pursued by an international rather than national court. Indeed, the argument that the ICC's Prosecutor is a possible threat to international peace and security because he does not need the permission of the Security Council to launch an investigation is central to the US stance against the ICC. While that argument is ultimately an instrumentalist one designed to protect the privileged position that the United States occupies in the UN Security Council, the fact that 'justice' can clash with 'peace' makes it worth considering. Clearly, there are occasions when a national or an international court's pursuit of justice can complicate the move towards equally important goals such as peace or democratization. One might cite the indictment of Slobodan Milosevic at the height of the NATO bombing campaign, the indictment of the Liberian President Charles Taylor, which sabotaged the Accra peace conference, or as Chapter 3 suggested, the prosecution of Pinochet in the context of the amnesties granted by a democratizing Chile.[53] To suggest that the Rome Statute threatens international peace and security, however, is to overlook the fact that this problem was anticipated by the delegates at Rome and was addressed in Article 16 of the Statute. This codified the so-called 'Singapore Compromise', which allows the UN Security Council to postpone justice for a twelve-month period if nine of its members identify a genuine threat to international peace and security.[54]

The genius of this provision is that it upholds the separation of powers between the Prosecutor and the Security Council, but it allows the Security Council to maintain its role as the guardian of international peace and security. Article 16 does not affect the Prosecutor's ability to initiate an investigation, but it allows the Security Council to postpone that investigation for a renewable twelve-month period. In order to do this the Security Council has to pass a resolution, which requires the votes of nine members. The permanent member acting on its own, or indeed all five permanent members

---

[53] On the Court as a possible threat to the peaceful transition to democracy, see Ruth Wedgwood, who notes that 'the Rome Statute omits any direct account of the problem of amnesties, and the failure to acknowledge the legitimacy of considering local amnesties under the Statute may prove troublesome.' Ruth Wedgwood, 'The International Criminal Court: An American View', *European Journal of International Law*, 10 (1999), 96. While the issue of amnesties was discussed at Rome, no clear consensus developed. Sadat notes, however, that 'while the Statute does not condone the use of amnesties by its terms, presumably the Prosecutor has the power to accept them if doing so would be "in the interests of justice" [quoting Rome Statute Article 53 (1) (c)].' Sadat, *The International Criminal Court*, 67; Hafner et al. 'A Response to the American View', 109–13. Wedgwood is less than satisfied with this suggestion. 'One may question', she concludes (97), 'whether a judgement of high politics and prudence was best allocated to a prosecutor, rather than an international council of state.'

[54] Luigi Condorelli and Santiago Villalpando, 'Referral and Deferral by the Security Council', in Cassese, Gaeta, and Jones (eds.), *The Rome Statute*, 627–55.

acting together, cannot stop the Prosecutor from proceeding. The permanent member would need to persuade at least eight other states to vote for a resolution, which then can only request the Prosecutor to defer his investigation. This, of course, is radically different from the original draft of the Statute, which proposed that the only means of referring a situation to the Prosecutor was through a Security Council resolution. Under that proposal, a permanent member could veto such a resolution and an investigation would not even start. Should the permanent member veto an Article 16 resolution, however, they would only veto attempts to postpone justice. In such a case the Prosecutor, who has initiated the investigation himself, would be free to proceed. In this way the Statute maintains the Court's independence while providing the Security Council with a check on the Prosecutor so that a reasonable balance is struck between the pursuit of order and justice.

The Rome Statute therefore might offer a revolutionary vision of world society, but its real contribution is to articulate a new set of constitutive rules and to set up a new process of criminal justice that *complements* the society of states. In other words, the Rome Statute helps to constitute a world society along Kantian lines. There are two aspects to this. First, the Statute is obviously part of the legacy of Nuremberg and more immediately the UN ad hoc tribunals. As institutions of international criminal justice, these courts helped to sustain a common consciousness based on the principle of humanity even when that consciousness was so viciously assaulted during the Second World War and the mid-1990s. The ICC will continue in that tradition. However, and this is the second point, by changing the rules of global politics (i.e. by separating the institution of criminal justice from the society of states) the Statute helps constitute a society that is more inclusive than that, which gave rise to these previous courts. To the extent that this society is notionally universal (the qualification is explained below), then the Statute helps to constitute world society.

It is this second point that identifies the revolutionary quality of the Rome Statute. When criminal justice was restricted by the rules of international society (i.e. when it was contingent on the power of states and their concern for sovereignty, consent, immunity, comity, and international peace and security), it was selective. This inevitably limited, and in certain respects undermined, the social role that criminal justice played in (re)constructing a cosmopolitan consciousness. For instance, many victims of universal crimes have been denied their day in court because their status as victims was an inconvenience to the great powers. These people were often left wondering why their humanity was not recognized and why the inhumanity of their torturer was not punished. Criminal justice in other words can reaffirm a common consciousness based on humanity; yet if it is selective, it can simultaneously weaken that consciousness. The society of states, therefore, will not be able to respond to, nor will it be able to protect, a cosmopolitan consciousness based on humanity as long as the society of states defends those principles that encourage selectivity.

Unfortunately, the principles that encourage selectivity are also the principles (i.e. sovereignty, consent, immunity, and international comity) that help define the society of states. In this sense, there *is* an ontological tension between the society of states and world society. Yet, in an attempt to resolve that tension, the society of states, fully aware of its own limitations when it came to defending humanity, created the Office of the Independent Prosecutor and delegated the authority to exercise criminal justice to the ICC. The Court, in other words, was set up to address the problem of selective justice and thus to strengthen the social processes that (re)constitute humanity. To put it another way, it was set up to give a voice to those people whose claims to be part of humanity were being silenced because of the inability of states or the unwillingness of the Security Council to listen.[55] In this respect, the victims of acts that offend humanity can now call themselves citizens of a world society even if they felt excluded from national and international society.

THE COUNTER-REVOLUTION[56]

Revolutions are usually resisted by those who occupied a privileged position in the old order. Understanding this helps one to explain US opposition to an international court that is independent of the UN Security Council. The US government, for instance, strongly supported the work of the ICTY and

[55] As the head of the Argentine delegation Silvia A. Fernandez de Gurmendi noted, the need to give the victims of egregious human rights abuse a voice was the driving force behind the creation of an Independent Prosecutor. S. A. Fernandez de Gurmandi, 'The Role of the International Prosecutor', in Roy Lee (ed.), *The International Criminal Court*, 175–88; see also P. Kirsch, QC and D. Robinson, 'Initiation of Proceedings by the Prosecutor', in Cassese, Gaeta, and Jones (eds.), *The Rome Statute*, 662. The Statute actually refers to this in Section 3 of Article 15. Once the prosecutor has requested authority to investigate, victims may influence the Court's decision by making representations to the Pre-Trial Chamber. Article 68 is dedicated to the protection of victims and witnesses and their participation in proceedings. Section 3 permits their views and concerns to be presented and considered by the Court it is appropriate and in a manner which is not prejudicial to a fair and impartial trial. Furthermore, under Article 75 victims are entitled to seek from the Court reparations for the harm suffered by them. See Claude Jorda and Jérôme de Hemptinne, 'The Status and Role of the Victim', in Cassese, Gaeta, and Jones (eds.), *The Rome Statute*, 1387–419; Emily Haslam, 'Victim Participation at the International Criminal Court: A triumph of Hope over Experience?', in McGoldrick et al. (eds.), *The Permanent International Criminal Court*, 315–34.

[56] Sadat, *The International Criminal Court*, 8.

ICTR. Indeed William Schabas, a strong supporter of international criminal justice, describes the US commitment to the ICTY as 'an example to other states'.[57] Furthermore, under the Clinton administration the United States actively participated in the drafting of the Rome Statute and supported the creation of a permanent ICC.[58] Both the Clinton and the Bush administrations, however, have been unable to live with the Court's independence from the Security Council. In fact, the Bush administration argues that the Court's Independent Prosecutor represents a threat to international peace and security.[59] This overlooks the compromise contained in Article 16, which as noted above allows the Security Council to request the postponement of an investigation if nine of its members consider that investigation to be a threat to international peace and security and say so in a resolution. Given that other members of the Security Council have been able to accept this compromise, including the UK whose defection to the like-minded group of states was a pivotal moment in the Rome negotiations,[60] it is hard not to conclude that there is something else driving US policy.

It is important to recall in this regard that during the negotiations at Rome the United States did not oppose the creation of the ICC. Had the only means of referral been a Security Council resolution, which would of course have been subject to the permanent member veto, the Clinton administration would probably have voted in favour of the Statute at Rome and recommended that its signature of the Treaty of Rome be ratified by the Senate.[61] As it was, the Clinton administration did not succeed in limiting the means of referral exclusively to the Security Council. The Prosecutor can proceed independently and even though the Security Council can request deferral the United States cannot do this by itself. The United States now portrays this as a threat to international peace and security, but given the safeguards provided by

---

[57] William A. Schabas, 'United States Hostility to the International Criminal Court: It's All about the Security Council', *European Journal of International Law*, 15 (2004), 701–20.

[58] For an indication of this early support, see David Scheffer, 'International Judicial Intervention', *Foreign Policy*, 102 (1996), 34. Scheffer would lead the US delegation at Rome. For pre-Rome statements indicating the US position and guarded support, see David J. Scheffer, Address Before the Carter Center, Atlanta, Georgia, 13 November 1997; and Address before the Southern California Working Group on the International Criminal Court, Biltmore Hotel, Los Angeles, California, 26 February 1998. Schabas describes this early position as being 'well-disposed' to the initial ILC draft and describes US initiatives at Rome as 'positive and helpful', Schabas 'United States hostility', 712, 708.

[59] See, for instance, Marc Grossman, 'American Foreign Policy and the International Criminal Court', Remarks to the Center for Strategic and International Studies, Washington, DC, 6 May 2002. See also the work of John Bolton who was an early critic of the Court before becoming Under Secretary of State for Arms Control in the first Bush administration. 'Courting Danger: What's Wrong with the International Criminal Court', *The National Interest*, 54 (1998–9), 60–71.

[60] Sadat, *The International Criminal Court*, 7, 94.

[61] Schabas, 'United States', 710, 720.

Article 16 of the Statute this argument rings hollow. What the United States is truly concerned about is that it has lost the ability it had as a permanent member of the Security Council to determine when and where international criminal justice is done.

The second US concern is that the Independent Prosecutor will be inclined to pursue 'politicized' prosecutions that target US officials. The spectre of an 'untethered international Kenneth Starr', the Prosecutor who pursued President Clinton over his sexual misdemeanours in the White House, was held up by some as the nightmare scenario.[62] For instance, although John Bolton did not mention Starr by name, he did point out that America's 'depressing history argues overwhelmingly against international repetition'.[63] A part of that history that is often overlooked is the 1988 Supreme Court case *Morrison v. Olson*, which contested the constitutionality of the Ethics and Government Act 1978. Following the presidential abuses of the Watergate era, this Act created a special court and empowered the Attorney General to recommend to that court the appointment of an independent counsel to investigate and, if necessary prosecute, government officials for violations of federal criminal laws. In *Morrison v. Olson*, the Supreme Court upheld the Act's constitutionality, but in a dissenting opinion Justice Scalia anticipated contemporary concerns with the ICC. As Lessig puts it, Scalia argued that 'because individual liberty was at stake and because the temptation to use prosecution for political ends was so great, *a Prosecutor must be accountable to an actor who is himself democratically responsible*'.[64] This understanding of prosecution as a *political act* is central to understanding US opposition to the ICC, and it is explored in more detail in the following chapters.

At Rome, the US delegation argued that the Prosecutor would be overwhelmed by non-state referrals and the Security Council would be an appropriate 'filtering mechanism'.[65] The only means of guaranteeing the impartial application of justice that was also consistent with the normative priority accorded to international peace and security was, they argued, to restrict the means of referral to the UN Security Council. The irony of this kind of argument is not lost on America's critics. For instance, Samantha Power notes:

[62] Weschler, 'Exceptional Cases in Rome', 94–5.

[63] John Bolton, 'The Risks and Weaknesses of the International Criminal Court from America's Perspective', *Law and Contemporary Problems*, 64 (2001), 173; see also Jack Goldsmith and Stephen Krasner, 'The Limits of Idealism', *Daedalus*, 132 (2003), 54; see also Allison Marston Danner, 'Navigating Law and Politics. The Prosecutor of the International Criminal Court and the Independent Counsel', *Stanford Law Review*, 55 (2003), 1633–65.

[64] Lessig, '*Erie*-effects of Volume 110', 1799. Emphasis added.

[65] Giovanni Conso, 'The Basic Reasons for US Hostility to the ICC in Light of the Negotiating History of the Rome Statute', *Journal of International Criminal Justice*, 3 (2005), 320.

In saying that it wants to protect itself from a political ICC, the United States is seeking more than reasonable assurances about the Court's responsible execution of its mandate. The United States is reserving the right to define the term *political* in the context of the Court's actions. Of the 180 UN members who do not hold a veto on the Security Council, only some will share America's definition. Many deem the Security Council to be the epitome of a politically motivated institution and want an independent ICC precisely because they believe it will not be driven strictly by great power politics.[66]

The United States, however, has continued to play on its status as the sole superpower, arguing that UN peacekeeping will be threatened if exemptions from the Court's jurisdiction are not given to the soldiers of contributing states. More specifically, it argues that as the indispensable guarantor of international peace and security its servicemembers, state officials and even its citizens, should not be burdened with the threat of prosecution by the ICC.[67] This argument and the diplomatic confrontation it has caused is dealt with in detail in Chapter 6. The key point here is that the US attempt at the Rome Conference to limit the referral mechanisms failed. Non-governmental organizations *can* refer cases, and the Prosecutor *can* investigate without prior authorization of the Security Council. In a rearguard action, however, the United States and other states were able to limit the Court's independence by constructing what became known as the 'consent regime', which was eventually adopted as Article 12 of the Rome Statute.

The issue here was whether the Court would, as Germany argued, assume universal jurisdiction or whether, as the United States argued, states had to consent to the new legal regime.[68] It was decided at Rome that the Security Council could refer to a situation regardless of whether the states involved were party to the Treaty of Rome. This does not apply, however, when the Prosecutor exercises his *proprio motu* powers. In these instances, it was decided that a consent regime would apply. It was hoped that allowing states to consent to what is sometimes referred to as the Court's 'general jurisdiction' would ultimately be more beneficial in the long-term because it would increase political support among states.[69] The question that occupied the conference, however, was which states would be required to give their consent before the Court could exercise jurisdiction over a case that had been initiated *proprio*

---

[66] Samantha Power, 'The United States and Genocide Law', in Sewall and Kaysen (eds.), *The United States and the International Criminal Court*, 171.

[67] David J. Scheffer, 'Statement on Creating an International Criminal Court', Washington, DC, 31 August 1998; Scheffer, 'The United States and the International Criminal Court', 18.

[68] Kaul, 'Preconditions to the Exercise of Jurisdiction'.

[69] Michael Scharf, 'The ICC's Jurisdiction Over the Nationals of Non-Party States: A Critique of the U.S. Position', *Law and Contemporary Problems*, 64 (2001), 77.

motu by the Prosecutor. The United States argued that in this instance the Court could only exercise jurisdiction if the state where the accused was a national had consented to the Treaty of Rome.[70] Under this proposal, US nationals would not be prosecuted by the ICC if the United States withheld its consent from that treaty. For many delegations at Rome, however, this defeated the whole purpose of the Court. As the Republic of Korea (ROK) delegate put it, 'what applies to America also applies to [Saddam] Hussein; and simply by not signing, he could [under the American proposal] buy himself a pass'.[71]

In fact, the ROK delegation at Rome tabled the broadest proposal regarding non-universal jurisdiction. In order for the Court's Prosecutor to claim jurisdiction over any given case, one or more of the following four states would have to be party to the treaty or accept its jurisdiction on an ad hoc basis: the state where the crime took place, the state of nationality of the accused, the state that had custody of the accused, or the state of nationality of the victim.[72] As a compromise it was eventually agreed that the Court could assume automatic jurisdiction (i.e. state signatories would not need to 'opt-in' to specific jurisdictions) over those crimes where the accused was the national of a state party *or* those crimes that took place on territory of a state party. In a vain attempt to get its way, the United States proposed that the national and territorial criteria be conjunctive rather than disjunctive. In other words, the Prosecutor could only exercise jurisdiction if the alleged crime took place on the territory of a state party, *and* where the accused was a national of a state party.[73] Again, under this proposal Americans would be exempt from the Court's general jurisdiction if the United States withheld its consent from the Treaty of Rome. The conference rejected this in favour of what are the disjunctive criteria contained in Article 12.

This regime codified in this article obviously limits the freedom of the Independent Prosecutor. He may not need authorization from the Security Council to proceed, but his mandate is still contingent on the consent of states. Does this undermine the argument that the Rome Statute helps constitute world society? To the extent that 'world society' is universal then clearly it does; not all states are party to the Treaty of Rome. When the Court exercises

---

[70] Kaul, 'Preconditions to the Exercise of Jurisdiction', 600–1.

[71] Quoted in Weschler, 'Exceptional Cases in Rome', 101.

[72] Kaul, 'Preconditions to the Exercise of Jurisdiction', 599–600.

[73] Scheffer, 'The United States and the International Criminal Court', 20; Scheffer, 'Staying the Course', 72. As well as trying to limit Article 12 to nationals of state parties the United States proposed at Rome to 'exempt from the court's jurisdiction conduct that arises from the official actions of a nonparty state acknowledged as such by that nonparty'. David J. Scheffer, Twelfth Annual U.S. Pacific Command, International Military Operations and Law Conference, Honolulu, Hawaii, 23 February 1999.

universal jurisdiction, that is in cases referred by the Security Council, it is not independent. When it is independent, that is when the Prosecutor acts *proprio motu*, it does not have universal jurisdiction. It is possible, however, that the national of a state withholding its consent from the Treaty of Rome could still be prosecuted by the ICC. Thus, under Article 12 a situation involving crimes allegedly committed by a national of a non-party state which occurred on the territory of a state party could be investigated by the Independent Prosecutor without receiving the authorization of a state party or the UN Security Council. In this situation, the Court might be reliant on the fact that the territorial state is a state party, but after the point of ratification, the Court can determine whether that state is either willing or able to exercise jurisdiction. If it is not then the ICC can assume jurisdiction. It is this possibility that causes the United States to oppose the Court, which is the subject of Chapters 5 and 6.

CONCLUSION

It has been argued here that the Rome Statute helps to constitute world society. It sets up a permanent court that will continue to prosecute individuals for crimes that offend humanity and in so doing it offers a means of reaffirming a cosmopolitan consciousness at the moment it meets with opposition. In this respect, the Court contributes to the social process that existed prior to its formation and was advanced by national and international courts when they exercised jurisdiction over similar crimes. Their common task has been to restore 'faith in humanity' by prosecuting individuals who commit inhumane acts. Yet the ICC is different to its predecessors because the Rome Statute reconstitutes the relationship between the institution of criminal justice and nation-states. Prior to the Rome Statute, criminal justice was an institution of international society because it could not work without the state passing legislation authorizing national courts to prosecute universal crimes. The failure of states to do this meant international criminal justice was dependent on the UN Security Council and its willingness to create international tribunals. With the Rome Statute, however, a permanent court can exercise jurisdiction without prior authorization either from states or from the Security Council. In this respect the institution of criminal justice has been released from the rules of international society, and its sociological impact is no longer mediated by states. Criminal justice in other words is now an institution of world society.

This chapter also elaborated on the distinction introduced in Chapter 1 between a revolutionary conception of world society and a Kantian world society. Both visions exist within the Statute, but clearly the latter is more dominant for two sets of reasons. The first set of reasons has a normative character. The drafters of the Statute recognized the benefits of a world divided into nation-states, each acting as an agent of humanity, and the importance of comity between nation-states. In this respect, the organizing principle in this conception of world society is complementarity. In other words, states are free to govern as they please so long as they punish behaviour that violates the common values articulated in the Statute. Relations between states moreover can still be governed by the norms designed to facilitate good relations (e.g. non-intervention and diplomatic immunity) so long as these states accept that the ICC, as a disinterested party, can intervene to make sure those norms are not abused at the expense of humanity. This ability to recognize the normative benefits of international society is evident in Articles 17 and 16. The former recognizes that justice is often best served when it is done at the national level. For instance, it is probably easier to attain and to secure the evidence if a case is being handled by authorities local to the site of crime rather than a team of international investigators based in The Hague. Yet Article 17 also recognizes that national authorities are often unwilling or unable to conduct such investigations. By empowering the Court to act in these situations, rather than relying solely on national courts to act by exercising universal jurisdiction, the Statute offers a means of defending the values of world society without undermining the institutions that facilitate good relations between states. Where an overzealous Prosecutor does act in a way that threatens order then Article 16 recognizes the role played by the Security Council in maintaining international peace and security.

The second set of reasons why the Statute is not as revolutionary as it might have been is strategic in nature. In other words, the strategic calculations of states trying to defend their own particular interests forced those drafting the Statute to curtail the Court's independence. These concessions have weakened the Court, and their influence is most clearly felt in the restrictions placed on the Prosecutor by Article 12. The so-called 'consent regime' may have succeeded in encouraging support for the Court among states (although not the United States), but it has also served to create loopholes in the Court's jurisdiction that can be exploited by those whose actions threaten humanity.[74] For instance, by not including the custodial state in the list of consenting states where the Prosecutor can exercise his independence, the Statute may have inadvertently created a problem of 'travelling tyrants'.[75]

---

[74] In this respect, Article 12 is an example of the failings of positivist international law in general and this is explored in more detail in Chapter 7.

[75] Sadat, *The International Criminal Court*, 118.

Assuming such individuals are nationals of a state not party to the Statute and their crimes took place on the territory of a non-state party, they could still travel to a state party and escape the general jurisdiction of the ICC. The custodial state could try the defendant itself under its own national laws or extradite that individual to a jurisdiction that is willing and able to conduct such a trial. This, however, is extremely disappointing for those who campaigned for a strong Court because they do not trust states to take such action and because they are aware that international society continues to value sovereign and diplomatic immunity as demonstrated in *Yerodia*. In a situation where a state has custody over the accused but refuses to extradite or prosecute, the Security Council can of course authorize the ICC to intervene. This, however, is small consolation for those who sought to separate international justice from the political considerations of the Security Council.

These problems are a consequence of states unwilling to let go of the control they have exercised over the institution of international criminal justice when it was constrained by the rules of international society. It might be argued that states continue to exercise this kind of control because they are the ones who elect ICC officials and, perhaps most significantly, they are the ones who presently finance the Court. It is true that by opening up the creation and the management of the Court to a much wider collection of states (i.e. the Rome Conference, the PrepComm, and then the Assembly of State Parties), the institution of international criminal justice has been democratized; and it is true that the Prosecutor is independent and empowered to exercise jurisdiction over the citizens of states that have not consented to the Treaty of Rome. But have states really let go of the process? Can they not simply reassert total control by taking back what they have delegated to the Court? Ultimately, this is a question of politics and the balance of influence between cosmopolitan and (inter-)nationalist sentiments. Quite obviously, states can change their commitments and opt out of a regime as easily as they opt in. But the costs of doing so depend on how deeply embedded in the nation's political culture are the values advanced by the Court. For some governments, it might be impossible to withdraw from the Court if their national constituency shares the cosmopolitan consciousness that underpins the Court. For others, it might be politically costly not to oppose the Court if the nation sees itself as an exceptional and unique legal community. The point of this chapter, however, is that over time international criminal courts tend to strengthen the cosmopolitan consciousness simply by exposing and condemning inhumane actions. This in itself creates a loyalty to the idea of humanity and to the institutions of world society that put pressure on those loyalties that had once been exclusively reserved for the nation. This is something Hedley Bull was well aware could happen when he wrote of the changing loyalties that attended what he called 'new-medievalism'.[76] Bull also reminded us, however, that there was 'nothing historically inevitable' about this process and about the social construction of societies. This warning applies as much to the Kantian conception of world society as it does to the society of states.

[76] Bull, *The Anarchical Society*, 256.

5

Understanding US Opposition to the ICC

It was suggested in Chapter 4 that the United States might have ratified the Rome Statute if the only means of referring a situation to the Court was through a UN Security Council resolution. This will of course remain a 'what if' question. What is certain is that such a court would not have been as revolutionary as the one created by the Rome Statute, nor would it have been greeted as enthusiastically by other states. The fact that sixty states (the number needed to bring the Court into being) were willing to ratify the Rome Statute so quickly (by 11 April 2002) and way ahead of many expectations is symbolic of its appeal. The time needed to reach that point took US officials by surprise and caused the Bush administration to rethink the option of an anti-ratification campaign, the planning of which had been interrupted by the 9/11 attacks.[1] Since then states have continued to ratify the Rome Treaty despite intense US opposition to the ICC. A court tied to the Security Council may have gained US support but that statute would have been tainted by the charge of 'selective justice' and consequently it would not have been as popular. Nevertheless, the possibility that the United States could have supported a permanent if not independent court does suggest that Schabas is right when he writes that US opposition to the ICC is 'all about the Security Council'.[2]

To leave the analysis there, however, is to leave it incomplete. Clearly, the United States opposes the ICC because it cannot control when and where international criminal justice is done. The more penetrating question, however, is this: what is it about America that makes it demand such a privilege? This question takes on added salience when one compares the US position to that of its traditional democratic allies on the Security Council, the UK and France. As noted in Chapter 4, the UK played a pivotal role in the creation of an independent court. Its decision to join the like-minded group of states helped give the campaign for an independent court political credibility.[3] While

---

[1] Washington Working Group on the ICC, 'Status of ICC Legislation and Administration Review in the US, 2001 Year End Report'.

[2] Schabas, 'United States Hostility to the International Criminal Court', 701–20.

[3] Elizabeth Wilmshurst, 'Jurisdiction of the Court', in Roy Lee (ed.), *The International Criminal Court. The Making of the Rome Statute. Issues, Negotiations, Results* (The Hague: Kluwer Law International, 1999).

France might not be able to claim this kind of impact, it has nonetheless clearly accepted and supported the ICC.[4] Of course, the United States is by no means isolated among the permanent members of the Security Council, neither Russia nor China has (at the time of writing) ratified the treaty. Yet the US position is clearly at odds with that of the established democracies on the Security Council and with that of the society of democratic states more generally.[5] As institutions that promise to hold unchecked power accountable for human rights violations, one would expect all liberal democratic states to support the ICC. So why is the United States different?

Of course, the United States does not argue that it should be a great power's *privilege* to decide when and where international criminal justice can be done. Rather, it uses the idea of rights and responsibilities to justify its opposition to the ICC. It uses, in other words, the language of international society. It argues first that as the remaining great power in international society it has relatively greater responsibilities for maintaining international peace and security. As we saw in Chapter 4, this translates into policy in two ways. First, the United States argues that the sole means of referring a case to a permanent Court should be through the Security Council. Second, as the United States is the most likely provider of effective collective security or peacekeeping forces, it considers that its service personnel should be exempt from the Court's jurisdiction. The diplomacy surrounding this second claim is addressed in detail in Chapter 6, but it is worth pointing out here that America's contribution to these public goods is not as apparent as its rhetoric suggests. Of the 37,756 personnel serving in UN peace operations in December 2000 (i.e. well before the Court came into existence), 885 or just over 2 per cent were Americans.[6] In this respect, the United States did not carry greater responsibilities and did not therefore have the right to claim privileges before the law. The argument that the ICC prevented the United States from committing troops to UN missions

---

[4] France ratified the Rome Treaty on 9 June 2000. France, along with Colombia, took advantage of Article 124 of the Statute, which allows states to 'opt out' of the Court's jurisdiction over war crimes for the seven years after the Statute's entry into force. The fact that non-state parties do not have a comparable right is cited by the United States as one reason for opposing the treaty. On this and the 'correction' proposed by the Clinton administration, see Scheffer, 'Staying the Course', 80–1.

[5] Strong support for the Court was not limited to the world of developed democratic states either. At the time of writing, twenty-seven African states had ratified the Statute and several of these, notably Malawi, Lesotho, and South Africa, played a leading role in creating the Court. Nel, Philip, 'Between Counter-Hegemony and Post-Hegemony', 155. The important exception to support among developing democracies is India, see Usha Ramanathan, 'India and the ICC', *Journal of International Criminal Justice*, 3 (2005), 627–34.

[6] Figures taken from United Nations Department of Peacekeeping, www.un.org/Depts/dpko

was an excuse rather than a justification. A US reluctance to provide such troops predated the Court. Given that the Rwandan genocide was at least in part a consequence of that reluctance, one might also argue that a US *failure* to meet its international responsibilities actually helped create the need for a permanent ICC.

The United States is on stronger, although still contested, ground when it argues that it has the *right* to decide which laws govern its citizens. The central concern here is that the jurisdictional regime created by Article 12 of the Rome Statute is a violation of the principle of consent. Under this regime, the Prosecutor can proceed without Security Council authorization if, in the situation referred to him, the accused is the national of a state party or if the alleged crime took place on the territory of a state party. As Chapter 4 explained, the so-called 'consent regime' was a concession to the principle of state sovereignty designed to encourage as much support as possible across the society of states. At Rome, the US delegation tried to limit this regime to include only the nationals of state parties. Under this proposal, the Independent Prosecutor would not be able to investigate American citizens if the US Senate withheld the consent on the American people by refusing to ratify the treaty. The United States failed to achieve its aim at Rome and the Prosecutor can now investigate American citizens if their alleged crime took place on the territory of a state party despite the fact that the United States is not party to the Rome Treaty. For this reason, the Statute is seen as fundamentally undemocratic by opponents of the Court.

Even this argument, however, fails to explain why the United States differs from other liberal democratic states that seemingly have little trouble accepting the Court's jurisdiction by renegotiating their social contract. Again, why is the United States different? This chapter seeks to answer this question by highlighting the *cultural role* that consent plays in constituting the American nation and American nationalism. In this respect, the social contract codified by the US Constitution is not merely a legal document in the sense that it can be easily renegotiated. It is a potent symbol of a separate political community and a distinct American culture. To challenge the social contract by holding American citizens accountable to a law they, or their government on their behalf, have not consented to, is to challenge the very idea of America. In other words, the contractarian philosophy of Vattelian pluralists fuses with the communitarian mindset of American nationalists. Both hold fast to a stringent form of legal positivism to oppose the ICC. Where the former values America only as a negotiable means of achieving the social contract, however, the latter values the social contract as a means of realizing a non-negotiable conception of America.

This distinction is realized in the different attitudes of pluralists and nationalists towards the principle of sovereign equality. Vattelian pluralists do not discriminate between types of states. All states are equally sovereign regardless of their ideological make-up. Central to the nationalist's worldview, however, is not merely the independence of America and the sovereignty of the United States. The universal applicability of individual rights and democracy, and America's role in the promotion of these values, is another key aspect of the nationalist's story. American nationalists oppose the Court, in other words, because it challenges US sovereignty, but they do not accept the relativist approach to human suffering that is an implication of pluralist international society. Strictly speaking, then, they are 'Americanists' and not 'sovereigntists'.[7] They continue to promote the universal values that underpin the Rome Statute, but they do so by supporting international courts that receive a mandate from the UN Security Council or by conducting their own unilateral attempts at nation building. If the former policy is vulnerable to the familiar charge of 'selective justice', the latter is more easily identifiable as American imperialism.

The central argument of this chapter is that the United States opposes the Court because it threatens US interests *and* because it fundamentally challenges America's understanding of itself and the popular understanding of accountability. The second point is ultimately the more significant because an alternative understanding of what America *is* would automatically lead to an alternative conception of what American interests are. The central argument is made in four stages. The first section explains why the Clinton administration felt it necessary to sign the Treaty of Rome despite identifying 'significant flaws' in the Statute. It also explains how the Bush administration and Congress responded to this move. The second section returns to the specific legal arguments made for and against the Statute. It demonstrates the centrality of the Vienna Convention on the Law of Treaties to the US position and to its general conception of international society. The third section develops the idea that the US Constitution is more than just a legal document that embodies the social contract. It demonstrates how constitutionalism helps Americans construct a national identity that responds to a cultural need to be separate from the 'old world'. The final section further develops the theme of American exceptionalism by demonstrating how the universalism of enlightenment rationalism, which informs an important part of America's identity, means that the United States cannot turn its back on the victims of

---

[7] Peter J. Spiro, 'The New Sovereigntists. American Exceptionalism and Its False Prophets', *Foreign Affairs*, 79 (2000), 9–15. The term 'Americanist' is taken from John R. Bolton, 'Should We Take Global Governance Seriously?', *Chicago Journal of International Law*, 1 (2000), 205–21.

core crimes. It thus commits itself to the cause of international criminal justice while continuing to oppose the ICC.

SIGNING AND 'UNSIGNING' THE ROME TREATY

Despite its diplomatic defeat at Rome, the Clinton administration did not give up on the possibility of signing the Rome Treaty. It was reconciled to the Court being independent of the Security Council, and although the role given to the Security Council by Article 16 of the Statute was not what the United States had originally wanted, the Clinton administration 'supported that compromise as the best we could obtain under the circumstances'.[8] However, it continued to argue that the Court should not target the service personnel of 'responsible governments'. That, it further argued, would deter those governments from fulfilling their responsibility to maintain international peace and security. As Ambassador Scheffer put it:

In Rome, we indicated our willingness to be flexible as to how cases would be referred to the court, but we felt it was essential to recognize a government's right to assess the court's fairness and impartiality before allowing its people to come under the court's jurisdiction in the absence of a referral from the Security Council. This approach guaranteed the ability of responsible governments to undertake life-saving missions without fear that their troops would be dragged before a tribunal that had yet to stand the test of time.[9]

A series of post-Rome meetings of the Preparatory Commission or PrepCom, which was set up to prepare for the establishment of the Court, would provide Scheffer and the United States a further opportunity to address these concerns. The United States voted for the UN General Assembly Resolution to set up the PrepCom on 8 December 1998 and Scheffer believed that 'the problems in the treaty which prevent us from signing it' could be solved there.[10] There was, however, a pressing need to make some early progress in these meetings. Article 125 of the Rome Statute made 31 December 2000 the last possible day for the signature of the treaty. The treaty would of course remain open to accession by all states, but if the United States wished to remain engaged in the PrepCom process without ratification it had to sign the treaty

[8] Scheffer, 'Staying the Course', 70.

[9] Scheffer, 'Statement on Creating an International Criminal Court', Washington, DC, 31 August 1998.

[10] Scheffer, Twelfth Annual U.S. Pacific Command, International Military Operations and Law Conference, Honolulu, Hawaii, 23 February 1999; also Scheffer, 'The United States and the International Criminal Court', 21.

before that date. The crucial PrepCom meeting for Scheffer, therefore, was the November/December 2000 session. That meeting would have to address at least some of America's concerns if he was to recommend to the outgoing Clinton administration that the United States sign the Rome Treaty and remain engaged in the PrepCom process.[11]

The focus of Scheffer's strategy was a proposal to strengthen the complementarity regime. For opponents of the ICC, the worst-case scenario involved a Prosecutor that would ignore US attempts to maintain control over a case involving an American citizen. Scheffer personally recognized that this was highly unlikely. 'One would', he noted,

have to imagine the United States *not* using its authority under Article 18 (2) of the Statute to seize complete control of any investigation of a situation involving U.S. citizens, or of the United States *not* using its authority under Article 18 (4) to appeal an adverse ruling of the Pre-Trial Chamber to the Appeals Chamber, or of the United States *not* using its authority under Article 19 (2) (b) to challenge the admissibility of the case on the grounds of additional significant facts or significant change of circumstances in order to create the worst case scenario. . . . [12]

Politically, however, it was necessary for him to negotiate an additional safeguard. The vehicle for this would be the Relationship Agreement between the UN and the ICC, which was necessary under Article 2 of the Rome Statute. Attached to that would be yet another admissibility review *at the moment a suspect was being surrendered to the Court*. This, Scheffer argued at the PrepCom, 'will add greatly to the confidence of all States in the operation of the Court and it will strengthen the political will of States to contribute to UN peacekeeping and other international efforts to maintain or restore peace and security'.[13] The United States also tried, yet again, to exempt from the Court's general jurisdiction the nationals of non-party states who were engaging in official acts. The UN and the ICC would agree, according to the US proposal,

that the Court may seek the surrender or accept the custody of a national who acts within the overall direction of a UN Member State, and such directing State has so acknowledged, only in the event (a) the directing State is a State Party to the Statute, or the Court obtains the consent of the directing State, or (b) measures have been authorized pursuant to Chapter VII of the U.N. Charter against the directing State in relation to the situation or actions giving rise to the alleged crime or crimes, provided that in connection with such authorization the Security Council has determined that this subsection shall apply.[14]

---

[11] Scheffer, 'Staying the Course', 57.   [12] Scheffer, 'Staying the Course', 60–1.
[13] Scheffer, 'Staying the Course', 62.
[14] US proposed text for ICC supplemental document, quoted in Scheffer 'Staying the Course', 79; see also Scheffer, 'Article 98 (2) of the Rome Statute', 341–2.

The Relationship Agreement was adopted by the Preparatory Commission on 5 October 2001 *without* these specific proposals.[15] Although state parties and the NGO community were always sceptical towards the US proposal, Scheffer pins part of the blame on the Bush administration. Its 'short-sighted and anemic approach to the Preparatory Commission had the result of forfeiting opportunities well established by our negotiating initiatives in 2000, to strengthen protection of US interests'. In December 2000, however, Scheffer still hoped that US concerns could be addressed by the new administration. The prospect that the PrepCom process would produce positive results allowed him to argue that it was worthwhile signing the Rome Treaty in order to remain engaged.[16] The PrepCom process had reinforced Scheffer's general impression that signature of the treaty was in US interests, because, among other things, it would improve the prospect of negotiating exemptions from the Court's jurisdiction as well as help sustain 'its leadership on international justice issues'.[17] He therefore recommended to President Clinton that the United States sign the Rome Treaty, which the President did on 31 December 2000.

In the public statement explaining his decision, the President drew on Scheffer's reasoning. The US signature would help sustain a 'tradition of moral leadership' as well as keep the United States 'engaged in making the ICC an instrument of impartial and effective justice in years to come'.[18] Yet the President did not completely adopt Scheffer's view. In his statement on the 31 December, the President noted that:

[w]e are not abandoning our concerns about *significant flaws* in the Treaty. In particular, we are concerned that when the Court comes into existence, it will not only exercise authority over personnel of states that have ratified the Treaty, but also claim jurisdiction over personnel of States that have not. With signature, however, we will be in a position to influence the evolution of the Court. Without signature, we will not.[19]

---

[15] The agreement was approved by the Assembly of States Parties during its first session held in New York from 3 to 10 September 2002. On 4 October 2004, the Negotiated Relationship Agreement was signed by Judge Philippe Kirsch, President of the ICC and Kofi Annan, Secretary-General of the UN. The agreement entered into force upon signature. Press Release, Agreement Between the International Criminal Court and the United Nations, The Hague, 4 October 2004, at http://www.icc-cpi.int/

[16] Scheffer, 'Staying the Course', 63. For further discussion, including additional ways in which US concerns were addressed during the PrepCom process, see 'Staying the Course', 74–86.

[17] Scheffer, 'Staying the Course', 58.

[18] President Clinton, Statement on Signature of International Criminal Court Treaty, 31 December 2000, at www.amicc.org

[19] Clinton, Statement on the Signature, emphasis added.

Scheffer's account of the decision suggests that there was much debate about using the term 'significant flaws', and it is clear that he did not agree with this aspect of the President's statement. He may not have achieved 'the silver bullet of guaranteed protection that many officials within the Clinton administration had sought', but he rejected the President's description of the Treaty's flaws.[20] It was inaccurate and politically unhelpful. The term 'would only provide ammunition to the opponents of the ICC on Capitol Hill and elsewhere to recklessly bash the Treaty, using our own words to do so'.[21] This was compounded by the President's decision not to 'submit the Treaty to the Senate for advice and consent until our fundamental concerns are satisfied'.[22]

It did not take much foresight to recognize the accuracy of Scheffer's prediction. One merely needed to understand the intensity of opposition to the ICC on Capitol Hill. This had been building since the summer of 1998 when the United States failed to achieve its objectives at the Rome Conference.[23] The central focus of legislative opposition was the American Servicemembers Protection Act (ASPA), which had been introduced to Congress by chairman of the Senate Foreign Relations Committee, Senator Jesse Helms (R-NC), and by Representative Tom DeLay (R-TX) in the summer of 2000.[24] Among other things, this legislation prohibited cooperation with the ICC, restricted US involvement in UN missions unless US troops received exemptions from the Court's jurisdiction, placed restrictions on military assistance to supporters of the Court and authorized the President to use 'all necessary and appropriate means' to bring about the release of US citizens detained on behalf of the ICC. For this last reason, critics dubbed it the 'Hague invasion act'. ASPA was opposed by the Clinton administration, but many Democrats in Congress found it difficult to oppose such a patriotic sounding bill, particularly after the 9/11 terrorist attacks.[25]

---

[20] Scheffer, 'Staying the Course', 63.   [21] Scheffer, 'Staying the Course', 64.

[22] President Clinton, Statement on the Signature of the International Criminal Court Treaty.

[23] See e.g. S. Hrg, 105–724, 'Is a U.N. International Criminal Court in U.S. National Interests', Hearing Before the Subcommittee on International Operations of the Committee of Foreign Relations, United States Senate, 105th Cong. 2nd Sess. 23 July 1998.

[24] See J. Elsea, *US Policy Regarding the International Criminal Court*, Congressional Research Service Report RL31495 (2002), 8–19.

[25] On the Clinton administration's objections, see Ambassador David J. Scheffer, Ambassador-at-Large for War Crimes Issues and Head of the US delegation to the United Nations Preparatory Commission for the International Criminal Court, Statement before the House International Relations Committee, Washington, DC, 26 July 2000. On 10 May 2001, the House voted in favour of ASPA by 282 votes to 137. On the Bush administration's support for ASPA see the letter from Assistant Secretary of State Paul Kelly, which was placed on the Congressional Record, 26 September, 2001, S9856. On 7 December 2001, the Senate voted overwhelmingly in favour of ASPA by a margin of 78 to 22.

According to John Bolton, who had been a vocal critic of the Court while at the American Enterprise Institute,[26] President Clinton had signed the Treaty of Rome in order to tie President Bush's hands and to block the legislative path of ASPA.[27] His argument rested on a complex reading of the Vienna Convention on the Law of Treaties and a disparaging interpretation of the Clinton administration's approach to other international agreements. Regardless of the accuracy of this view, it nonetheless helps to explain why the Bush administration, which Bolton would join as Under Secretary of State for Arms Control and International Security, felt it necessary to respond to the political pressure for him to 'unsign' the Rome Treaty in May 2002.[28]

Under Article 18 (a) of the Vienna Convention,

a state is obliged to refrain from acts which would defeat the object and purpose of a treaty when it has signed the treaty or has exchanged instruments constituting the treaty subject to ratification, acceptance or approval, until it shall have made its intention clear not to become a party to the treaty.[29]

Bolton argued that the Clinton administration was aware of this rule and by signing the Treaty of Rome, the President had purposefully committed the United States to a policy of coexistence with the Court. The United States may not have been a state party but as a signatory state, it could do nothing to defeat the object and purpose of the treaty. President Bush, in other words, could not sign ASPA into law.

This interpretation of President Clinton's decision was heavily influenced by the earlier debate on the Comprehensive Test Ban Treaty (CTBT). On 13 October 1999, the Senate rejected that treaty by a vote of 51 to 48. Immediately after the Senate vote, however, the administration announced that it would continue its unilateral policy against testing. What annoyed Bolton was that instead of relying on the President's acknowledged constitutional power to do so under the commander-in-chief clause, the administration chose instead to rely on a provision in the Vienna Convention. He noted how Clinton's Secretary of State, Madeleine Albright, asserted to her foreign counterparts that despite the defeat in Congress the United States still intended to ratify the CTBT and under Article 18 of the Vienna Convention the United States would effectively be bound by that treaty. The Clinton administration, in other words, had looked to international law to legitimize a course of action

[26] See e.g. John R. Bolton, 'Courting Danger: What's Wrong with the International Criminal Court,' *The National Interest*, 54 (1998–9), 60–71.

[27] John R. Bolton, 'Unsign That Treaty,' *The Washington Post*, 4 January 2001.

[28] Senators Helms and Miller also publicly urged the President to unsign the treaty; see 'No Court Dates for America', *The Washington Times*, 11 April 2002.

[29] Vienna Convention on the Law of Treaties, 23 May 1969, UN Doc. A/Conf. 39/27.

that had been rejected by the American people. Rather than accept defeat on the CTBT President Clinton had, according to Bolton, tried to use the Vienna Convention as a means of restraining US policy without the consent of Congress. Bolton concluded that the Clinton administration's

zeal to find authority in an unratified international convention must surely be the high-watermark of Globalist achievements in the United States, truly snatching a victory out of the CTBT's ashes. The unrepentant Americanists in the Senate, however, did take due note of the President's preference for the Vienna Convention over the Constitution.[30]

Taking the 'Americanist' cause with him into the State Department, Bolton made sure that Clinton's CTBT strategy would not work with the ICC. On 6 May 2002, the Bush administration 'unsigned' the Treaty of Rome, which cleared the way for the President to sign a version of ASPA, which he did when he signed the Supplemental Defense Appropriations Act on 2 August 2002.[31] What was important to the administration, aside from the signal the act sent on the ICC, was that this draft of ASPA preserved presidential primacy in the making of foreign policy. Contained in the final version was a broad waiver that recognized the President's right to cooperate with the ICC or provide national security information to the Court if he determined it to be in America's national interest and was able to notify Congress. This is reinforced by a stipulation that no part of the bill may interfere with the President's constitutional authority to make foreign policy.[32]

Many observers expressed confusion as to the administration's purpose in taking this unprecedented and seemingly unnecessary act. To unsign a treaty was unheard of because it was commonly thought that a treaty was non-binding until it had been ratified.[33] Yet the decision can be understood when it is viewed from Bolton's perspective and the role it played in clearing the legislative path for ASPA. This account, however, does not fully explain why Bolton argued for unsigning the *Rome Treaty*. Why was he so concerned that by signing ASPA the President would violate Article 18 of the *Vienna Convention*? The fact that the United States had not ratified the Vienna Convention

[30] Bolton, 'Should We Take Global Governance Seriously?', 212.

[31] US Department of State, Letter to Kofi Annan from Under Secretary of State for Arms Control and International Security John R. Bolton, Washington, DC, 6 May 2002.

[32] American Servicemembers' Protection Act 2002, Public Law 107–206. For further commentary, see Konstantinos Magliveras and Dmitris Bourantonis, 'Rescinding the Signature of an International Treaty: The United States and the Rome Statute Establishing the International Criminal Court', *Diplomacy and Statecraft*, 14 (2003), 21–49.

[33] See, for instance, Statement by the Lawyers Committee for Human Rights, 'Un-signing the International Criminal Court Treaty is practically insignificant and politically counterproductive', 6 May 2002.

would surely have made it easy to ignore the Vienna Convention. Why was there a perceived need among Americanists to observe the Vienna Convention and to preserve its integrity? Indeed, why did the Bush administration go out of its way to point out that its actions were consistent with the Vienna Convention?[34] Answers to these questions lie in the fact that the Vienna Convention, in particular Article 34, is central to the US strategy of opposing the ICC and, more generally, to its conception of a society of states.

Before developing this point further in the following section, it is worth noting the way Americanists on Capitol Hill reacted to the administration's decision to unsign the treaty. They, of course, welcomed the decision, but what is interesting is that they too demonstrated their reliance on the Vienna Convention to justify the decision. For instance, chairman of the House International Relations Committee, Henry Hyde, defended the Bush administration's approach to international law. 'Champions of international law', he argued, 'should focus their fire on the Clinton administration for the dubious way in which they signed the Treaty'. 'International law', he concluded with implicit reference to Article 18 of the Vienna Convention, 'provides that signature [of a treaty] ... is seemed to represent political approval and at least a moral obligation to seek ratification.'[35] The clear message was that by rejecting the ICC the United States was well within its rights as defined by the society of states. It was acting consistently with the letter and spirit of international law when it unsigned the Rome Treaty and passed anti-ICC legislation. In fact, by opposing the ICC and acting according to the Vienna Convention the United States was, it was claimed, defending not just any kind of international law, but the kind that protected the principle of democratic accountability based on the nation-state.

DEFENDING THE SOCIETY OF STATES

Central to this claim has been the principled stand taken against the jurisdictional regime set up by Article 12 of the Rome Statute. As noted above, this article codified the so-called 'consent regime', which was considered by the Rome Conference to be a helpful way of increasing the level of support

---

[34] Transcript of Press Briefing by Ambassador-at-Large for War Crimes, Pierre Prosper, 6 May 2002, at http://fpc.state.gov/9965.htm; also Marc Grossman, 'American Foreign Policy and the International Criminal Court', Remarks to the Center for Strategic and International Studies, Washington, DC, 6 May, 2002.

[35] Hyde praises decision by Bush administration to unsign treaty establishing International Criminal Court, Committee of International Relations, US House of Representatives, at <http://www.house.gov/international_relations>

among states. Article 12 allows the Independent Prosecutor to initiate an investigation if the accused is the national of a state party or (and this is the controversial aspect) if the territory where the alleged crime took place is that of a state party. The United States opposed this compromise because an American citizen can conceivably be investigated and prosecuted by the Court if his or her alleged crime took place on the territory of a state party, despite the fact that the US government has withheld consent from the Treaty of Rome. Officials from the Clinton and Bush administrations, as well as academic commentators outside government, consider this a violation of the principle of sovereign consent.[36] This principle, moreover, is codified in contemporary international society by Article 34 of the Vienna Convention on the Law of Treaties. It states, in true Vattelian fashion, that '[a] treaty does not create either obligations or rights for a third State without its consent'.[37] From this perspective, therefore, the Rome Statute is inconsistent with international law.

Section 3 of Article 12 particularly annoyed the United States. This enabled non-party states to accept the jurisdiction of the Court on an ad hoc basis and for the purpose of investigating a particular case by lodging a declaration to that effect with the Court's registrar. For Scheffer, this exposed 'non-parties in ways that parties are not exposed'.[38] He used a hypothetical to explain US concerns:

with only the consent of a Saddam Hussein, even if Iraq does not join the treaty, the treaty text purports to provide the court with jurisdiction over American or other troops involved in international humanitarian action in northern Iraq, but the court could not on its own prosecute Saddam for massacring his own people.[39]

Even supporters of the Statute recognized this as 'an unfortunate bit of drafting'. It was, Scharf suggested, 'contrary to the original thrust of the statute, which, as conceived by the ILC, did not permit states the benefits of the statute without accepting the burden'.[40] This problem was also recognized, as Scharf anticipated, by the PrepCom, which did much to address US concerns by

---

[36] Scheffer, 'The United States and the International Criminal Court', 12–22; John R. Bolton, Under Secretary for Arms Control and International Security, 'American Justice and the International Criminal Court', Remarks at the American Enterprise Institute, Washington, DC, 3 November 2003; Madeline Morris, 'High Crimes and Misconceptions: The ICC and Non-Party States', *Law and Contemporary Problems*, 64 (2001), 13–66.

[37] Vienna Convention on the Law of Treaties, 23 May 1969, UN Doc. A/Conf. 39/27.

[38] Scheffer, 'The United States and the International Criminal Court', 18.

[39] Scheffer, Statement on creating an international criminal court, 31 August 1998. See also David J. Scheffer, Remarks before the 6th Committee of the 53rd General Assembly, New York, NY, 21 October 1998.

[40] Michael Scharf, 'The ICC's Jurisdiction over the Nationals of Non-Party States: A Critique of the US Position', *Law and Contemporary Problems*, 64 (2001), 78 note 56.

agreeing to Rule 44 (2) of the Rules of Procedure and Evidence. This states that the Court

requires that any non-State Party seeking to trigger an investigation would expose its own conduct to the full scrutiny of the ICC, thus discouraging politically-motivated charges and efforts to hold only one State accountable for alleged crimes within an overall situation.[41]

Yet this only addressed one aspect of US concerns. It did not remove the underlying complaint that Article 12 was inconsistent with the most fundamental aspect of treaty law, which held that states could not be bound without their consent. As Ambassador Scheffer put it,

The ICC is designed as a treaty-based court with the unique power to prosecute and sentence individuals, but also to impose obligations of cooperation upon the contracting states. A fundamental principle of international treaty law is that only states that are party to a treaty should be bound by its terms. Yet Article 12 of the ICC treaty reduces the need for ratification of the treaty by national governments by providing the court with jurisdiction over the nationals of a non-party state.[42]

This view of the relationship of Article 12 of the Rome Statute to Article 34 of the Vienna Convention on the Law of Treaties has, however, been strongly contested. For instance, Hans-Peter Kaul, who headed the German delegation at Rome, has argued that Article 12 of the Rome Statute imposes obligations not on third states as such but upon their nationals.[43] For instance, the Statute imposes obligations to arrest and surrender persons to the Court only if states are party to the Rome Treaty. Non-party states are under no such obligation.[44] The Statute is not therefore in breach of Article 34 of the Vienna Convention. From this perspective, individuals are already subject to a kind of law, that is customary international law, which allows states to exercise universal jurisdiction over the crimes contained in the Statute (see Chapters 2 and 3). The Rome Statute does nothing more than set up a new mechanism collectively to enforce this law. Kaul and other supporters of the Court also argue that territorial jurisdiction, on which part of Article 12 is based, is a long-established principle in the law between states. States have every right, they claim, to

---

[41] Scheffer, 'Staying the Course', 76.

[42] Scheffer, 'The United States and the International Criminal Court', 18. The footnoted reference to Article 34 of the Vienna Convention on the Law of Treaties contained in the original text is removed from the above quote.

[43] Kaul, 'Preconditions to the Exercise of Jurisdiction', 608–9; see also A. Pellet, 'Entry into Force and Amendment of the Statute', in Cassese, Gaeta, and Jones (eds.), *The Rome Statute*, 163–4; Gerhard Hafner et al. 'A Response to the American View', 117–8.

[44] Bert Swart, 'Arrest Proceedings in the Custodial State', in Cassese, Gaeta, and Jones (eds.), *The Rome Statute*, 1247–55.

delegate the exercise of territorial jurisdiction to a supranational organization like the ICC.[45] Michael Scharf, for instance, notes that such a move is
consistent with the legal principle established by the *Lotus Case*. It recognizes
that '[r]estrictions upon the independence of [s]tates cannot...be presumed'
and that international law leaves to states 'a wide measure of discretion which
is only limited in certain cases by prohibitive rules'.[46] From this perspective,
therefore, states have a right to delegate jurisdiction and conversely 'the state of
nationality has no right to exercise exclusive jurisdiction over acts committed
by its nationals abroad, whether they constitute official acts'. Indeed, Scharf
concludes that the American

suggestion that a state has a right of exclusive jurisdiction over its nationals concerning
acts committed abroad reflects a colonialist concept that was prevalent in earlier
centuries but has little relevance to modern practice.[47]

As one would expect, this counterclaim (that Article 12 of the Rome Statute
does not impose additional obligations on states and is therefore consistent
with the Vienna Convention) is not accepted by the US government. Nor
is it universally accepted across American academia. Madeline Morris, for
instance, identifies two types of cases that could come before the Court.

In addition to the cases that are concerned solely with individual culpability, there will
be ICC cases that focus on the lawfulness of official acts of states. Even while individuals, and not states, will be named in ICC indictments, there will be cases in which those
individuals are indicted for official acts taken pursuant to state policy and under state
authority. These official-act cases may well include cases in which an official state act
is characterized as criminal by the ICC Prosecutor (acting, very possibly, on a referral
from an aggrieved state), while the state whose national is being prosecuted maintains
that the act was lawful....In these sorts of ICC cases, notwithstanding the presence
of individual defendants in the dock, the cases will represent *bona fide* legal disputes
between states.[48]

As noted, the United States proposed at Rome (see Chapter 4) and during the
PrepCom (see above) to 'exempt from the court's jurisdiction conduct that
arises from the official actions of a non-party state acknowledged as such
by that non-party'.[49] The proposals were not accepted. As such, the Court
can exercise jurisdiction over US citizens even if they are acting in an official
capacity and given Morris's interpretation of this scenario as a '*bona fide* legal

[45] Kaul, 'Preconditions to the Exercise of Jurisdiction', 608–9.
[46] Scharf, 'The ICC's Jurisdiction', 75.   [47] Scharf, 'The ICC's Jurisdiction', 75.
[48] Morris, 'High Crimes and Misconceptions', 15; see also Wedgwood, 'The International
Criminal Court: An American View', 100.
[49] Scheffer, Twelfth Annual U.S. Pacific Command, 23 February 1999.

dispute between states', Article 34 of the Vienna Convention and the principle of sovereign consent remains at issue.

According to Morris, however, the official US position is not entirely accurate. Instead of arguing that the Rome Treaty illegally imposes additional *obligations* on states, the United States should argue that 'the ICC Treaty would abrogate the pre-existing *rights* of non-parties which, in turn, would violate the law of treaties'. These pre-existing rights include 'the right of a state to be free from the exercise of *exorbitant jurisdiction* over its nationals'.[50] These rights can be found in customary international law on jurisdiction. Morris recognizes that the *Lotus* decision cited by Scharf leaves states 'a wide measure of discretion', but she adds that this

must be read together with the other principles underlying and defining the customary law of jurisdiction. In short, the legitimacy of claimed new forms of jurisdiction must be determined, not assumed. The *Lotus* case places the burden of proof for this determination on the challenging state, but *Lotus* does not eliminate the necessity of making the determination of whether a claimed new form of jurisdiction is legitimate.[51]

The normative test for Morris is 'whether the conduct to be regulated is sufficiently linked to the legitimate interests of the state claiming jurisdiction to warrant recognition of jurisdiction'.[52] Customary international law recognizes that *states* have legitimate interests to be able to assert jurisdiction based on the national, territorial, passive personality, and (arguably) the universal principle. The issue raised by Article 12, however, involves the exercise of *delegated* territorial jurisdiction by a *non-state* body. Morris argues that this is legally flawed in two ways: first, there is no precedent for states delegating jurisdiction in this way;[53] and second, it constitutes 'a material alteration' of the customary understanding of territorial jurisdiction and should not therefore apply to states that choose to withhold their consent from the Rome Treaty.

---

[50] Morris, 'High Crimes and Misconceptions', 26. Emphasis added.

[51] Morris, 'High Crimes and Misconceptions', 49.

[52] Morris, 'High Crimes and Misconceptions', 49.

[53] Morris, 'High Crimes and Misconceptions', 50. Scharf and Morris disagree on the extent to which the International Military Tribunals at Nuremberg can be considered a precedent. Morris writes that 'the jurisdictional basis of the Nuremberg and Tokyo tribunals was not the collective exercise of universal jurisdiction but, rather, the consent of the defendants' state of nationality'. Morris, 'High Crimes and Misconceptions', 41. Whereas Scharf notes that 'in none of the judgments of the World War II international war crimes trials . . . do the judicial opinions cite the consent of Germany as the basis for the tribunals' jurisdiction'. As the sovereign German state did not exist at that time the Nuremberg Tribunals 'exercised the delegated territorial jurisdiction of its members without the consent of the state of the accused's nationality'. This, Scharf concludes, provides 'a strong historic foundation for the ICC's jurisdictional reach.' Scharf, 'The ICC's Jurisdiction', 105–6.

Morris advances several reasons why states might consent to universal and territorial jurisdiction exercised *by states* and object to it being exercised *by an international court.*

[T]he delegation of states' universal or territorial jurisdiction to an international court would materially increase the risk or burden imposed on a state whose national may be subject to prosecution for an international crime. This increased risk or burden arises, primarily in interstate-dispute type cases, from the elimination of states' discretion regarding methods of interstate dispute resolution, and from the potential practical, political, and precedential disadvantages that this loss of discretion implies. Applying the non-prejudice principle to the question whether states may delegate (or 'assign') jurisdiction to the ICC would lead to the conclusion that the delegation of jurisdiction from a state to the ICC is not permissible without the consent of what might be called the obligor state (the defendant's state of nationality) because it would materially increase the burden or risk imposed on that state.[54]

There is a lot to this analysis, but what Morris does not discuss is why the United States in particular prefers to preserve 'state discretion' and to maintain the possibility of resolving such disputes on a state-to-state basis. As the most powerful state in international society, it clearly has a particular interest in preserving rules that limit decisions on international criminal justice to states. As Chapter 3 showed, America's reaction to Belgian legislation demonstrates that it can better control the consequences of universal jurisdiction when it is exercised on an individual basis by states. It cannot so easily control these decisions when they are delegated to a supranational institution like the ICC. This might not be the purpose behind Morris's argument.[55] It is, however, a political consequence of her conclusion. The fact that the Clinton and Bush administrations found her arguments so convenient is clearly apparent from their appearance in public justifications of American policy. For instance, Ambassador Scheffer relied directly on Morris's article to argue that

customary international law does not *yet* entitle a state, whether as a Party or as a non-Party to the ICC Treaty, to *delegate to a treaty-based International Criminal Court* its own domestic authority to bring to justice individuals who commit crimes on its sovereign territory or otherwise under the principle of universal jurisdiction, without

---

[54] Morris, 'High Crimes and Misconceptions', 51.

[55] By quoting Arthur Rovine, who noted that 'weaker states derive an obvious advantage from legal settlement in disputes with more powerful opponents [...while...] the strong give up much of their leverage in a contest of legal briefs and argumentation', Morris is clearly aware of the power incentives at work. She does not, however, elaborate on the implications for assessing the US position. Morris, 'High Crimes and Misconceptions', 28.

first obtaining the consent of that individual's state of nationality either through ratification of the Rome Treaty or by special consent, or without referral of the situation by the Security Council.[56]

This argument—that the United States opposes the delegation of jurisdiction to a supranational court because it loses the influence it has when jurisdiction is exercised by states—reveals the political impact of the positivist approach adopted by Morris, Scheffer, and the US government generally. However, it does not silence the normative argument that sovereign consent is central to the democratic legitimacy of international law or their point that states should be free from the effects of treaty law if they withhold their consent. Some critics of the Court elaborate on this argument to great effect and their stance has clearly captured the attention of America's political elite. In his prepared statement to Congress, for instance, Lee Casey repeats the claim that under Article 34 of the Vienna Convention automatic application of the ICC treaty to the United States would be illegal.[57] Yet this is only the tip of the iceberg as far as Casey is concerned. His concern is not merely that the Court can claim jurisdiction over Americans without the consent of the US government. He is also concerned that the actual ratification of the Rome Treaty would itself undermine fundamental principles of constitutional democracy.

Casey argues, for instance, that any American brought before the ICC would be denied basic constitutional rights such as a trial by jury.[58] This particular argument has, however, been described as 'a red herring'.[59] Ruth Wedgwood, for instance, notes that

---

[56] Scheffer, 'Staying the Course', 65. Scheffer also used Morris's hypothetical example of France delegating territorial authority to Libya to prosecute an American citizen to illustrate their opposition to delegated jurisdiction. See Morris, 'High Crimes and Misconceptions', 46 and David J. Scheffer, 'International Criminal Court: The Challenge of Jurisdiction', Address to Annual Meeting of the American Society of International Law, Monarch Hotel, Washington, DC, 26 March 1999. This speech was informed by a reading of a draft of Morris's article; see Scharf, 'The ICC's jurisdiction', 70, 110. Scharf responds to Scheffer and Morris's hypothetical by noting 'the potential for abuse may be reduced where the jurisdiction is transferred not to an individual state [i.e. Libya] ... but rather to a collective court'. Scharf, 'The ICC's Jurisdiction', 112.

[57] Prepared Statement of Lee Casey, Hearing Before the Subcommittee on International Operations, 23 July 1998, 71.

[58] See Prepared Statement by Casey, 72. Congressional leaders have made much of the absence of trial by jury; see e.g. Prepared Statement by Senator Ashcroft, Hearing Before the Subcommittee on International Operations, 23 July 1998, 10.

[59] Mark Leonard, 'When Worlds Collide', *Foreign Policy*, 123 (2001), 72; Leonard's response is to the claim made by Marc A. Thiessen, in the same edition; see also Mariano-Florentino Cuellar, 'The International Criminal Court and the Political Economy of Anti-Treaty Discourse', *Stanford Law Review*, 55 (2003), 1607–12.

the offenses within the ICC's jurisdiction would otherwise ordinarily be handled through military courts-martial or through extradition of offenders to the foreign nation where an offense occurred. Thus, the detailed structure of American common law trial procedure would not ordinarily be applicable to these cases in any event.[60]

As both Scheffer and Wedgwood note, the United States worked hard at Rome and in the subsequent PrepComs to ensure that the court followed demanding standards of due process.[61] This has not gone completely unnoticed in Congress. For instance, Representative Delahunt has noted that the Statute 'contains perhaps the most extensive list of due process rights ever codified'. On that basis he has argued that American 'soldiers are at risk without this [the Rome] treaty. Today they can be prosecuted by any nation within its borders. The treaty corrects this by giving primary jurisdiction over American soldiers to American courts.' He concludes that 'we have nothing to fear from this treaty and everything to gain'.[62]

Yet the concern that the Rome Statute is inconsistent with the US Constitution runs much deeper than the issue of trial by jury and it once again focuses on the role of the Independent Prosecutor. Although US rhetoric on the ICC has expressed disquiet at the possibility of 'politicized' and 'anti-American' prosecutions, this in itself is somewhat of a red herring. As Justice Scalia noted in the *Morrison* v. *Olson* case (see Chapter 4), all prosecutions are in some sense political acts. Given this, a Prosecutor must be accountable to an actor who is himself democratically responsible.[63] The more significant concern therefore is that the ICC Prosecutor is not accountable to the American people. Again, the rhetoric of the US government tends to confuse the issue here. It does not hold back in charging that 'the Rome Statute creates a prosecutorial system of unchecked power',[64] but by not specifying the political community that is expected to hold the Prosecutor to account it creates the impression that US opposition to the ICC is easily addressed. For instance, supporters of the Court respond to this claim by listing the checks and balances contained within the Statute, many of which were proposed by the US delegation, including the creation of an Assembly of State Parties 'to oversee the management of the ICC and the prosecutor's work'.[65] Yet this is not the point for Americanists like Casey. He notes, for instance, that the Assembly

[60] Ruth Wedgwood, 'The Constitution and the ICC', in Sewall and Kaysen (eds.), *The United States and the International Criminal Court*, 121.

[61] See Scheffer's response in Additional Questions Submitted for the Record by the Committee, Hearing Before the Subcommittee on International Operations, 23 July 1998, 46; Wedgwood, 'The Constitution and the ICC', 123.

[62] Congressional Record, 10 May 2001, H 2097.

[63] *Morrison* v. *Olson*, 487, US 654 (1988) cited by Lessig, '*Erie*-effects of Volume 110', 1799.

[64] Grossman, 'American Foreign Policy and the International Criminal Court'.

[65] Scheffer, 'Staying the Course', 74.

of State Parties is open to all states regardless of their form of government. 'Given these facts', he concludes, 'the claims made by the Court's supporters that it will embody "American values", or that democratic accountability will be preserved through US representation in the Assembly of States, is nothing short of fantastic.'[66] To illustrate this point, the Court's opponents seized upon the May 2001 vote that removed the United States from the UN Commission on Human Rights.[67] Representative DeLay used the vote to illustrate how 'fickle' international institutions were, while his colleague Representative Hyde argued that the vote illustrated the dangers of a criminal justice system that could be influenced by the likes of China.[68] His point that the Assembly of State Parties includes non-democratic states was a valid one, even if his example was not. China was not a state party.

Supporters of the Court also note how the Prosecutor is in fact checked by the complementarity principle. With the passage of the 1996 War Crimes Act and the 1997 Genocide Convention Implementation Act, for instance, the proper execution of *American* law would likely cause the ICC to drop its interest in cases involving US citizens.[69] Once more however, this safeguard does not satisfy critics like Casey. The Rome Statute, he notes, only provides national courts with *primary*, not *exclusive* jurisdiction. This, he argues, is fundamentally inconsistent with Article 3 of the US Constitution, which states that 'the judicial power of the United States is vested in the Supreme Court, and in lower federal courts as may be established by Congress. This power, he concludes, 'cannot be exercised by any body or institution that is not a court of the United States'.[70] It might be unlikely that the Prosecutor will ever be interested in the actions of American service personnel. It is even less likely that the Court would second-guess a US Court and assert jurisdiction over a situation after ruling that the United States was 'unwilling' genuinely to carry out an investigation or prosecution. For American opponents of the Court, however, the *theoretical possibility* of ICC involvement is highly significant. As Casey puts it, the Treaty of Rome's 'constitutionality must be assessed based upon the nature and scope of the power it vests in that court, not upon the likelihood that this power will be used in any particular manner.'[71] In these terms, the issue is one of possibilities and not probabilities. It might be unlikely

[66] Lee A. Casey, 'The Case Against the International Criminal Court', *Fordham International Law Journal*, 25 (2002), 843–4.

[67] Barbara Crossette, 'For the First Time, U.S. Is Excluded from UN Human Rights Panel', *New York Times*, 4 May 2001.

[68] Congressional Record, 8 May 2001, H2124. See also Thiessen, 'When Worlds Collide', 66.

[69] Robinson O. Everrett, 'American Servicemembers and the ICC', in Sewall and Kaysen (eds.), *The United States and the International Criminal Court*, 143–4.

[70] Prepared Statement of Lee Casey, 65.   [71] Prepared Statement of Lee Casey, 68.

that the ICC would second-guess a US court, but the legal possibility means that the Rome Statute

transfers the ultimate authority to judge the policies adopted and implemented by the elected officials of the United States...away from the American people and to the ICC's prosecutor and judicial bench. This would violate the first principle of democracy—the American people have an inherent right to choose, directly and indirectly, the men and women who will exercise power over them, and to hold those individuals accountable for the exercise of power.[72]

In this sense, US opponents of the ICC are motivated not only by the fact that the Assembly of State Parties contains non-democratic states that may influence the Court. Even if democratic states continued to dominate the Assembly of State Parties, it is likely that US sovereigntists would still complain that the ICC threatens *American* democracy by placing it within the jurisdiction of officials that are neither appointed by, nor indirectly accountable to, *the American people*. In this respect, Casey's position illustrates the earlier point that an international society which unites around liberal democracy (what Buzan calls a Convergence interstate society) does not necessarily surrender sovereignty as an organizing principle. States only come under pressure to do this when the Kantian complaint (i.e. that democratic states do not always behave democratically in international society) becomes politically significant. This, however, is neither a consideration nor a concern for Casey's position, which is essentially a nationalist one.

UNDERSTANDING THE US POSITION: THE CULTURAL ROLE OF DEMOCRACY

US opposition to the ICC thus operates on two levels. The first concerns international criminal justice as a tool of statecraft. The United States has been able more or less to control when and where justice of this kind is done. The United States fears losing that control because the ICC is independent of the Security Council and presumably resistant to US pressure in a way small states like Belgium are not. The United States advances a conception of international society based on statehood therefore, because it is in that kind of a society that the United States can maximize its power and more easily pursue its particular interests. The popularity of the Rome Statute, however, did force the Clinton administration onto the defensive. It had to accept an independent Court as a reality, and it had to reduce its policy aims to finding pragmatic solutions

---

[72] Casey, 'The Case Against', 843–4.

to the jurisdictional regime that exposed American citizens. For some, like Morris, the Clinton administration was wrong to compromise on a matter of legal principle. This criticism reveals a second level of US opposition. Having initially argued that the United States could not sign the Rome Treaty because 'fundamental principles of treaty law still matter and we are loath to ignore them',[73] the United States, at least according to Morris, 'undermined its own legal position' by then engaging with the Court and seeking exemptions for US officials.[74] This 'strictly purist perspective' is rejected by Scheffer, who argues that 'practical solutions must be found' otherwise 'the Court's universality and effectiveness will suffer'.[75]

There is then a sense in which US policy on the ICC is divided between reconcilables like Scheffer who support the Court so long as US citizens are exempt from it and irreconcilables, like Casey, who argue that the Court is inconsistent with the principle of sovereign consent and constitutional democracy based on the nation-state. The irreconcilable position has been, as some of the contributions to the debate on ASPA indicate, politically significant in Congress. Compare, for instance, Casey's position to that of Representative Tom DeLay. 'The framers of the Constitution', he states,

would reject this peculiar foreign legal system as a form of tyranny. The notion that our citizens, men and women in uniform, would be subject to the whims of a foreign court [sic] is anathema to the principles of the American founding. American citizens and their military personnel should never be subject to laws not created by the American people.[76]

It also finds expression in the Bush administration's public position. As noted, Under Secretary of State for Political Affairs, Marc Grossman, appealed to the founders' wisdom to justify the decision to unsign the Rome Treaty. The Statute, he argued, created a prosecutorial system that is an unchecked power and he warned, recalling the words of the Founding Father John Adams, that 'power must never be trusted without check'.[77] A determination to preserve the vision of the American Republic as conceived by the founders is clear. The US ambassador to the UN, John Negroponte, for example, was insistent.

Our Declaration of Independence states that ... 'governments are instituted among men, deriving their just powers from ... the consent of the governed' ... We have built up in our two centuries of constitutional history a dense web of restraints on

---

[73] Scheffer, 'The United States and the International Criminal Court', 18.

[74] Morris, 'Universal Jurisdiction in a Divided World', 350.

[75] Scheffer, 'Staying the Course', 66 n. 69.

[76] Congressional Record, 10 May 2001, H2124. The ICC is an international not a foreign court.

[77] Grossman, 'American Foreign Policy and the International Criminal Court'.

government, and of guarantees and protections for our citizens.... The history of American law is very largely the history of that balance between the power of the government and the rights of the people. We will not permit that balance to be overturned by the imposition on our citizens of a novel legal system they have never accepted or approved, and which their government has explicitly rejected.[78]

It is in this light that the connection between US foreign policy and the positivist conception of international law, which evolved out of Vattel's own brand of republicanism, becomes obvious. Vattel's influence on the founding fathers has already been noted in Chapter 2. His view that laws derive their legitimacy from the consent of those they govern obviously reinforced those already disposed to the contract theory of those who clearly influenced the founders like Locke.[79]

Put in this way, it is not surprising that the United States sees the ICC as a threat. The Court grew out of a consensus across international society and it arguably violates the principle of consent that was at the heart of the American Revolution. Set alongside the position of the European states, however, the US accusation that the Court is a threat to democracy becomes problematic. From this perspective, the US concern for democratic account-ability might be considered a mere cover for the national interest, which also influences its policy. If European states can support the Court without feeling that their democracies are being undermined, then surely the democracy argument cannot explain US policy. Yet this interpretation underestimates the argument of those democrats who oppose the ICC. The fact that India also stresses the value of democratic accountability within the borders of sovereign states suggests that the US argument is not simply a rhetorical diversion. Of course, India and the United States share a post-colonial culture, which sensitizes them to issues involving their sovereignty. Yet it is the particular role played by the social contract in constituting American independence and its sense of being exceptional, which helps to explain why the United States has been unable to follow the lead of its European allies and support the ICC.

America might be regarded as different to European states in the sense that it has lacked the ethnic, religious, or even linguistic bonds around which people could unite. However, the *idea* that sovereignty rested with 'the people', and that a constitution would provide a legal framework in which the people could exercise sovereignty without impinging on certain inalienable rights,

---

[78] Explanation of Vote and Remarks by Ambassador John D. Negroponte, United States Permanent Representative to the United Nations, 12 July 2002.

[79] On the influence of the writings of enlightenment rationalism, see Bernard Bailyn, *The Ideological Origins of the American Revolution* (Cambridge and London: Harvard University Press, 1992), 26–30.

has provided Americans with a unifying civic identity.[80] This has generally been referred to as the American Creed, which sees American identity solely in terms of political principles. It is said to act as 'the cement in the structure' of a disparate nation.[81] Admittedly, the role played by this idea in constituting America as a nation is contested. Compare, for instance, Richard Hofstadter's well-known claim that '[i]t has been our fate as a nation not to have ideologies but to be one', with Michael Lind's claim that a 'nation may be *dedicated* to a proposition, but it cannot *be* a proposition'.[82] From Lind's perspective, American nationalism has 'more to do with family neighbourhood, customs and historical memories than with constitutions or political philosophies'.[83] Yet even if one can recognize America as a nation, which exists independently of political ideas, there is no denying that its *political* culture is largely dominated if not determined by the Creed or a 'liberal tradition'.[84] Lind in fact does not deny its influence. It is the essential element in a liberal or civic conception of American nationalism, which is often locked in a cultural battle against the less inclusive, nativist, or Jacksonian perspectives.[85]

The political idea that government rests on the consent of the people and that the people are themselves checked by a higher form of constitutional law has therefore played a specific cultural role in American society. The Constitution has done more than just set up a system of government. It has helped to identify a particular community. It not only provided the means through which a government of the people, by the people, and for the people was created, it actually helped to define who 'the people' were. It is, as Michael Foley notes, 'far from being simply a legal charter'.[86]

[80] Michael Foley, 'The Democratic Imperative', in Anthony McGrew (ed.), *Empire. The United States in the Twentieth Century* (London: Hodder and Stoughton in association with Open University Press, 1984).

[81] Gunnar Myrdal, *An American Dilemma: The Negro Problem and Modern Democracy* (New York: HarperCollins, 1962), 3.

[82] Quoted in Anatol Lieven, *America Right or Wrong. An Anatomy of American Nationalism* (London, HarperCollins, 2004), 49; Michael Lind, *The Next American Nation. The New Nationalism and the Fourth American Revolution* (New York: Free Press, 1995), 5.

[83] Lind, *The Next American Nation*, 7; see also Samuel Huntington, *Who Are We? America's Great Debate* (London: Free Press, 2004). Huntington argues that 'the core of their [American] identity is the culture that the settlers created, which generations of immigrants have absorbed, and which gave birth to the American Creed. At the heart of that culture has been Protestantism' (62).

[84] Louis Hartz, *The Liberal Tradition in America: An Interpretation of American Political Thought since the Revolution*, 2nd edn. (San Diego, CA: Harcourt Brace Jovanovich, 1991).

[85] For the 'liberal-nativist' debate, see Lind, *The Next American Nation*, 7–10; for the 'civic—Jacksonian' debate see Lieven, *America Right or Wrong*. Lieven's use of the label Jacksonian is taken from Walter Russell Mead's, *Special Providence. American Foreign Policy and How It Changed the World* (New York: Alfred Knopf, 2001), 218–63.

[86] Michael Foley, *American Political Ideas. Tradition and Usages* (Manchester and New York: Manchester University Press, 1991), 195–6.

The Constitution not only marked the creation of the American republic, it has also defined the character of its subsequent history and political ethos. As a result, the American nation is conceived in constitutional terms while American nationalism is seen as the derivative of American constitutionalism. National crises are therefore equated with constitutional crises; and American victories are identified as occasions when the Constitution has prevailed over adversity.[87]

This realization helps one to understand why the United States opposes the ICC when other democracies based on similar social contracts can support it. Where other democracies can renegotiate their social contract and accept the Court's jurisdiction because it is not considered a threat to their national identity, American nationalists feel threatened by the ICC because of the political role that the Constitution and the rule of law plays in defining America. This is *especially* the case for liberal or civic nationalists. This may be surprising given that liberals are often considered internationalists, but it is a feature of the debate on the ICC that the traditional dichotomies used to describe US foreign policy are redundant. Liberals *and* Realists; internationalists *and* isolationists; unilateralists *and* multilateralists, all oppose the Court because it goes beyond familiar concepts such as an international society of independent states. This point becomes even clearer when one considers that Wilsonian liberal internationalists, who might be expected to support the Court, only envisage international institutions making the world safe for democratic *states*. Supranational institutions have not been considered as a means of enforcing IHL that complements states and even if this were considered, it would run up against the other Wilsonian priorities such as the collective security of states and possibly national self-determination. It is worth noting, in this regard, that Wilson himself opposed the trial of Kaiser Wilhelm after the First World War, although this was perhaps inspired more by the possibility that Bolshevism would profit from German discontent than any consideration of ideological inconsistency. Even with that qualification, however, it is clear from the way Wilson's Secretary of State Robert Lansing defended the principle of sovereign immunity that the society of states was a central component of Wilsonianism. According to him

The essence of sovereignty was the absence of responsibility. When the people confided it to a monarch or other head of State, it was legally speaking to them only that he was responsible, although there might be a moral obligation to mankind. Legally, however, there was no super-sovereignty.[88]

[87] Foley, *American Political Ideas*, 196.
[88] Quoted by Peter MaGuire, *Law and War. An American Story* (New York: Columbia University Press, 2001), 77. On US attitudes to the trial of the German Kaiser, see Gary Jonathan Bass, *Stay the Hand of Vengeance. The Politics of War Crimes Tribunals* (Princeton, NJ and Oxford: Princeton University Press, 2000), 58–105.

All of the mainstream traditions in US foreign policy thinking, therefore, are seemingly opposed to the Court as matters of principle and practice. The argument that the Court threatens democracy may be more important to liberal or civic nationalists than it is to the Jacksonian nationalists who appeal to nativist conceptions of America as a folk community independent of political ideas such as the social contract, but this is too fine a distinction to have any real impact on the debate. The key point is that the idea of the social contract between the nation and the state is fundamental to America's conception of itself and that idea is seen as being theoretically inconsistent with the cosmopolitanism of the Court, ergo the United States must oppose the ICC.

THE US ALTERNATIVE

All states are ' "imagined communities", devoid of ontological being apart from the many practices that constitute their reality', but America, it seems, 'is peculiarly dependent on representational practices for its being'. America is 'the imagined community par excellence'.[89] US opposition to the ICC is in this respect an extension of the Declaration of Independence or the daily Pledge of Allegiance. It is a representational practice designed to instantiate a particular image of America. Just as the act of international criminal justice is a means of constituting a cosmopolitan consciousness, so the act of opposing international criminal justice is a means of reaffirming a national consciousness. What we are witnessing, in other words, is an ideological battle between nationalists and cosmopolitans as each seek to define the rules that help construct social realities.

US opposition to the ICC, therefore, is not just about the Security Council and it is not simply about democracy. These certainly play a role, but primarily US opposition to the ICC is about boundaries. More specifically, it is about boundaries that identify distinctive democratic communities who look to America as the shining example of democratic governance. The cultural need to be exceptional and to be held up as an example to others predates the political revolution of 1776. It can be found in the theories of New England Puritanism. Between 1630 and 1660, some 20,000 Puritans were driven from 'old' England by the efforts to 'purify' the Church of England.[90] Against this background, their colonization of British America came to be seen as 'an event

---

[89] David Campbell, *Writing Security: United States Foreign Policy and the Politics of Identity* (Manchester, UK: Manchester University Press, 1998), 91. Benedict Anderson, *Imagined Communities. Reflections on the Origins and Spread of Nationalism* (London: Verso, 1991).

[90] Campbell, *Writing Security*, 107.

designed by the hand of God to satisfy his ultimate aims'.[91] To be certain, Puritanism was not the driving force behind the Revolution. This was seventeenth century radicalism, which helped to harmonize 'Enlightenment abstraction, common law precedents, covenant theology, and classical analogy'.[92] Yet to the extent that enlightenment rationalism, classical analogy, and certainly common law precedent did not necessarily demand separation from England, Puritanism did much to advance the idea that the Revolution and the political and cultural system that followed was part of 'the new world' and an example that the old world would do well to follow.[93]

This 'exemplarism' influenced what Mead has called the 'Jeffersonian tradition' of US foreign policy thinking.[94] As John Quincy Adams put it on 4 July 1821, the United States would not go abroad 'in search of monsters to destroy'. It would be, according to this tradition, 'the well-wisher to the freedom and independence of all. She is the champion and vindicator only of her own.'[95] Unfortunately, the shining light of American constitutional democracy, based as it is on the state, now illuminates a pathway that is increasingly being called into question by the continuing problems of decolonization and seemingly irreversible processes of globalization. Democracy and accountability at the level of the state have been difficult, if not impossible for certain communities to achieve. Supporters of the ICC offer a cosmopolitan response to this problem. For them, the idea that power should be held accountable for its abuse of fundamental human values need not be dependent on sovereign statehood. Yet because the idea of 'America' does depend on the idea of statehood to instantiate its exceptional identity, the United States cannot support the ICC. The cosmopolitan's failure to heed the American example is interpreted by Americanists not as a search for more appropriate solutions to the problem of accountability in global politics; rather, it is portrayed as a threat to the United States and to democracy.

The views of American nationalists and American sovereigntists, however, are not identical. Sovereignty is simply a legal means of articulating US opposition to the Court, but it should be made clear that the principle the

[91] Bailyn, *The Ideological Origins*, 32.   [92] Bailyn, *The Ideological Origins*, 54.

[93] On America's 'civil religion', which was formed by a blending of religious and political exceptionalism, see Huntington, *Who are We?*, 103–6.

[94] Mead, *Special Providence*, 174–217. The term 'exemplarism' is used by H. W. Brands *What America Owes the World. The Struggle for the Soul of Foreign Policy* (Cambridge: Cambridge University Press, 1998); for an analysis using a similar framework, see Walter A. McDougall, *Promised Land, Crusader State: The American Encounter with the World since 1776* (Boston, MA: Houghton Mifflin, 1997).

[95] John Quincy Adams, 'An Address Delivered at the Request of the Committee of Arrangements for Celebrating the Anniversary of Independence, at the City of Washington on the Fourth of July 1821 upon the Occasion of Reading the Declaration of Independence', quoted by Mead, *Special Providence*, 193.

United States emphasizes is sovereign consent and not the sovereign equality of states. There is a significant difference. Where the latter does not discriminate between states, the Americanist understanding of the former is that 'the people' are ultimately the sovereign authority in any state. Unlike sovereigntists and Vattelian pluralists, therefore, Americanists do distinguish between democratic and non-democratic as well as failed states. The ideas of Vattel and other enlightenment rationalists may have supported the idea of an independent and sovereign United States based on a social contract with the people of America, but those ideas also rested on the assumption that certain rights are universal. To forget this would be as un-American as ratifying the Rome Statute. US nationalists, therefore, cannot turn their backs on the victims of crimes against humanity by accepting the relativist implications of sovereign equality. Proposing an alternative to the ICC is therefore culturally necessary.

This is evident in the historical evolution of the Wilsonian position. Where it supported sovereign immunity at the end of the First World War, it advocated the trial of Nazi leaders at the end of the Second World War, although the fear that Bolshevism would exploit German discontent again tempered this commitment to criminal prosecutions.[96] It is also evident in the Bush administration's policy statements on the ICC. For instance, when Under Secretary of State Marc Grossman explained why the Bush administration unsigned the Rome Treaty he reiterated the belief that 'those who commit the most serious crimes of concern to the international community should be punished' and that 'the best way to combat these serious offences is to build domestic judicial systems'. Under the heading 'Our Philosophy', he continued:

While we oppose the ICC we share a common goal with its supporters —the promotion of the rule of law. Our differences are in approach and philosophy. In order for the rule of law to have true meaning, societies must accept their responsibilities and be able to direct their future and come to terms with their past. An unchecked international body should not be able to interfere in this delicate process. . . . The existence of credible domestic legal systems is vital to ensuring conditions do not deteriorate to the point that the international community is required to intercede. *In situations where violations are grave and the political will of the sovereign state is weak, we should work, using any influence we have, to strengthen that will.* In situations where violations are so grave as to amount to a breach of international peace and security, and the political will to address these violations is non-existent, the international community may, and if necessary should, intercede through the UN Security Council as we did in Bosnia and Rwanda.[97]

---

[96] On the political pressure to end the Nuremberg trials see MaGuire, *Law and War*, 203–34.

[97] Grossman, 'American Foreign Policy and the International Criminal Court', Emphasis added.

This commitment to 'nation building' may have sounded strange coming from an administration that had attacked its predecessor for engaging in similar practices.[98] Taking on the role of vindicator as opposed to exemplarist, Wilsonian as opposed to Jeffersonian, is, however, a predictable response to the ICC, particularly when one considers the politics of identity that are operating here. American nationalists not only see the United States as an independent state, they also see it as the leader of a society of other independent states. Its own example of constitutional democracy, however, has lacked persuasive power, and its failure to prevent crimes against humanity in the past has given rise to a cosmopolitan alternative (i.e. the ICC). Faced with this alternative vision of global democracy, one that offers a cosmopolitan vision of world society as opposed to international society of states, American nationalists respond in two ways. First, they portray the alternative vision as a threat (rather than a complement) to democracy; and second, they seek to reconstitute their preferred image of America by committing themselves to an internationalist agenda. Both responses can be seen as representational acts driven by the need to perpetuate a particular image of the United States.

CONCLUSION

It is difficult for supporters of the ICC to accept that the Rome Statute is philosophically distinct from, and in opposition to, those enlightenment values that helped constitute the United States. They cannot understand why the Statute, which promises that the Court will complement rather than supersede American law, is not acceptable to the American government. This confusion is symptomatic of a wider dissonance within democratic theory and across democratic societies. There may be agreement on the need for supranational institutions to derive legitimacy from democratic states. As Armin von Bogdandy puts it commenting on Jürgen Habermas's proposal for the constitutionalization of international law, '[n]either the participation of NGOs nor that of the global parliamentarian institutions appear to be possible sources of proper legitimacy for global institutions'. But where cosmopolitan democrats like Habermas run up against American exceptionalism is where they argue that supranational institutions can govern in 'fields that require little democratic legitimacy' such as the enforcement of 'principles that enjoy broad legitimacy throughout the world, as proven by global moral indignation

---

[98] Condoleezza Rice, 'Promoting the National Interest', *Foreign Affairs*, 79 (2000), 45–62.

on occasions of serious infringement.'[99] This approach, which von Bogdandy notes is consistent with the liberal tradition of judicial review, may legitimize the actions of an independent international Prosecutor, but it does not get past a view that is deeply embedded in American culture, which is that the judiciary plays a political role. As the American law professor, Paul Kahn, puts it:

because our constitutionalism is a matter of political identity rather than an elaboration of an abstract logic of rights, American legal scholarship—unlike those of virtually everywhere else—is quite comfortable speaking of the political role of the courts. Our law bears a political burden quite uncharacteristic of the function of law elsewhere.[100]

Thus, in contrast to the Habermasian view that world law 'can operate in fields that require little democratic legitimacy' the American view demands that Prosecutors must, as Lessig put it, 'be accountable to an actor who is himself democratically responsible'.[101] According to this latter view, the ICC must be opposed because its Prosecutor cannot be held accountable to a national community and it is at that level that democracy and accountability operate.

Whether the Rome Statute and the US Constitution are reconcilable is therefore somewhat beside the point. That question is contingent on the politics of identity that is driving US opposition to the Court. In their attempts to persuade their opponents, advocates of the Court argue that the Rome Statute actually complements American democracy, but in certain respects, this line of argument is self-defeating. The argument that the ICC *complements* American democracy is inevitably a threat to nationalists who want to preserve the image of America as an *exceptional* democracy. David Campbell captures this in his book *Writing Security*. He writes

The mere existence of an alternative mode of being, the presence of which exemplifies that different identities are possible and thus denaturalizes the claim of a particular identity to be *the* true identity, is sometimes enough to produce the understanding of threat.[102]

There are certainly occasions when the ICC is portrayed as America's 'Other'. For instance, Marc Thiessen describes advocates of the Court as impulsively

---

[99] Armin von Bogdandy, 'Constitutionalism in International Law. Comment on a Proposal from Germany', *Harvard International Law Journal*, 47 (2006), 238–9; commenting on Habermas's 'Does the Constitutionalization of International Law Still Have a Chance?', in Jürgen Habermas, *The Divided West*, forthcoming.

[100] Paul W. Kahn, 'American Exceptionalism, Popular Sovereignty, and the Rule of Law', in Michael Ignatieff (ed.), *American Exceptionalism and Human Rights* (Princeton, NJ and Oxford: Princeton University Press, 2005), 206–7.

[101] Lessig, 'Erie-effects of Volume 110', 1799.   [102] Campbell, *Writing Security*, 3.

'dictatorial'.[103] Likewise, Senator Helms, whom Thiessen worked for, uses the Court to reinforce a preferred image of America's founding. He noted how advocates of the Court accused him of 'eighteenth-century thinking'. 'I find that a compliment' he said.

It was the eighteenth century that gave us our Constitution and the fundamental protections of our Bill of Rights. I'll gladly stand with James Madison and the rest of our Founding Fathers over that collection of ne'er-do-wells in Rome any day.[104]

There is, however, an underlying irony to the nationalist position. It appeals to positivist conceptions of and to the pluralist institutions of international society in order to protect a system of government that is based on the consent of the American people. The processes that created the ICC, like those that create customary international law, are considered a threat to democracy because they are considered to bind nations that have not necessarily given their consent. Yet if America's founding fathers had been as attached to this stringent form of legal positivism as the nationalists of today are it is possible that the American Revolution would not have taken place. Legal positivism did not help to conceive the United States. For instance, Sir Ernest Barker notes that

[h]owever much the colonists had sought to base themselves on actual law and actual rights—whether they alleged their own charters or compacts, or the legal rights of all English subjects, or the legal limits of the sovereignty of parliament (either in content or in extent) under the English constitution—they had all along been ultimately driven from each of the grounds they alleged to the final ground of natural law and their natural rights.[105]

Furthermore, the concern that sovereigntists today express over the possibility that the customary law of nations is nothing more than what legal scholars say it is did not seem to worry America's founders. Fundamentally,

the appeal they made to natural law and natural rights was the appeal *to their own ideas of what ought to be law and what ought to be rights*—no matter what law might actually be or what rights actually were. Jefferson once said to Patrick Henry, who refused to trust in charters, that once he 'drew all natural rights from a purer source—the

---

[103] Thiessen, 'When Worlds Collide', 65.

[104] Quoted by Weschler, 'Exceptional Cases in Rome', 111.

[105] Sir Ernest Barker, 'Natural Law and the American Revolution', in *Traditions of Civility. Eight Essays* (Cambridge: Cambridge University Press, 1948), 307. See also Ruggie, who argues that the 'narrow and formalistic position' of the nationalists 'would require us to sacrifice the values of justice to a particular normative preference as to how law should be made—one for which there is no basis in the Constitution itself'. Ruggie, 'American Exceptionalism', 329.

feelings in his own heart.' The feelings in their own hearts about what ought to be were the inspiration of the colonists generally.[106]

Put like this, the irony of America's policy is obvious. It now clings to legal positivism as a means of opposing an international legal development that is based on a consensus of what international society ought to be. The United States now occupies the privileged position in international society, and it now resists revolutions based on appeals to non-positivist legal doctrines. It opposes demands for what solidarists and cosmopolitans see as just change. It does this by appealing to the example it sets as a democratic state based on enlightenment ideas, but unfortunately that example has been neither pure nor powerful enough to prevent a culture of impunity from evolving within the kind of international society that it demands. As a Kantian solution to this problem, the ICC is by no means a product of *post*-enlightenment thinking. Supporters of the Court can, like Helms, go back to the eighteenth century to find support for their arguments. It does, however, demand what has been called a post-Westphalian conception of statehood and this is at present seemingly beyond contemporary understandings of 'America'. How these post-Westphalian states interact with the United States is the subject of Chapter 6.

[106] Barker, 'Natural Law', Quoting J. C. Miller, *Origins of the American Revolution*, 128.

6

Europe, the United States, and the International Criminal Court

Previous chapters have attempted to understand recent developments in international criminal justice through the interpretive framework provided by the English School approach to IR. These chapters argued that the Statute helps to constitute what English School scholars have tentatively called world society by articulating a set of core crimes and setting up a system of justice that is independent of the society of states. Chapter 5 sought to explain why the United States opposes this development. In contrast to other democratic states, the United States sees the Court as a threat to its autonomy and to its democracy. This perception of 'threat' is driven by nationalists who see in the policy of opposing the Court an opportunity to reaffirm an exceptional American identity. Chapter 5 also identified a division between irreconcilables, who oppose the Court as a matter of principle and those who can be reconciled with the Court as long as American citizens are not subject to its jurisdiction. The irreconcilable position is now largely academic. The United States was not able to prevent other states from ratifying the Rome Statute and while the lack of American support certainly limits the Court's effectiveness, it has not stopped the Prosecutor from conducting investigations.[1] The United States, in other words, has been forced to live with the Court and to do this it has continued to search for ways to exempt US citizens from the Court's jurisdiction.

Where the Clinton administration tried to do this within the ICC framework—as Chapter 5 noted, it signed the Rome Statute in order to guarantee a US presence at the PrepCom meetings—the Bush administration chose to ignore the PrepCom process. Instead, the Bush administration

---

[1] Since taking office on 16 June 2003, the Independent Prosecutor Luis Moreno-Ocampo has begun to investigate situations in Uganda, the DRC, and Sudan. The first two were self-referrals, which according to certain commentators was not anticipated by the Statute and the Prosecutor's decision to investigate is considered to be in breach of the complementarity principle. See Claus Kress, ' "Self-Referrals" and "Waivers of Complementarity" Some Considerations in Law and Policy', and Paola Gaeta, 'Is the Practice of "Self-Referrals" a Sound Start for the ICC?', *Journal of International Criminal Justice*, 2 (2004), 944–8 and 949–52. The situation in Darfur was referred to the Prosecutor by the UN Security Council. This is discussed in detail below.

pursued two strategies. First, and in line with the 'alternative' policy discussed in Chapter 5, the United States supported (in Iraq), or at least advocated (in Sudan), ad hoc national or regional courts with jurisdictions that excluded US citizens. Second, it sought to negotiate exemptions from the ICC's jurisdiction through its bilateral relations with other states and through the United Nations Security Council. These two policies reinforce a central theme, which is that the United States maximizes its power and more effectively advances its particular interests through the institutions of the society of states. In this kind of society, the United States can claim that it has the right to negotiate 'bilateral non-surrender agreements' with other states.[2] It can also claim that the exemptions it seeks are not only in America's interests. They are, it claims, in the interests of international society as a whole. If, in other words, international society is to demand that the United States meets its responsibility as a great power and commits armed forces to international peace-enforcement and peacekeeping operations, then international society should not add to America's burden by subjecting its servicemembers to the jurisdiction of the ICC.

These strategies have posed dilemmas for those states committed to the success of the ICC. For instance, states on the UN Security Council have had to consider whether they should stick to the principle that those acting in an official capacity are not immune from criminal prosecution and thereby risk US support for peacekeeping operations; or whether they should support the United States and thereby risk the integrity and appeal of the Rome Statute. Likewise, America's proposal that the Security Council create another ad hoc Court to investigate the situation in the Darfur region of Sudan has further tested the commitment of states to the ICC. Where the crimes of Saddam Hussein fell outside the temporal jurisdiction of the ICC, the atrocities in Darfur took place after 1 July 2002 and could therefore be investigated by the Court. As Sudan was not a state party to the Treaty of Rome, however, the Prosecutor required Security Council authorization before he could proceed. Given the expectation that the United States would veto any such resolution, states were faced with another dilemma. Either they bypass the ICC and cooperate with the US proposal to set up an ad hoc court or they insist on the ICC as the most appropriate forum at the risk of paralyzing the international community's response to the atrocities in Darfur.

---

[2] These agreements have been called 'bilateral immunity agreements' by NGOs. See generally the Coalition for the International Criminal Court www.iccnow.org/usandtheicc.html. However, the agreements provide that the custodial state will surrender any American suspect to the United States rather than to the ICC. They do not grant the suspect immunity per se and the assumption is that he or she will face judicial proceedings in American courts. Scheffer, 'Article 98 (2) of the Rome Statute', 335.

These dilemmas were particularly acute for European governments. They were the driving force behind the successful establishment of the Court, yet they were also keenly aware of the contribution America made to peacekeeping, not least in Europe itself. Their response is the focus of this chapter. It not only offers insight into the state of transatlantic relations, it also acts as a significant case study on European identity. Recent European history suggests a cultural and political trajectory in the opposite direction to the United States. Where US opposition to the ICC indicates a determination not to yield sovereignty for the wider purpose of humankind, European states have become the ultimate expression of a post-Westphalian association.[3] Of course, this experiment has been regionally focused and it is by no means certain that the EU will submit to global associations in the same way it expects member states to submit to it. How the EU relates to non-European states and to citizens of world society will of course help to decide whether the EU is simply a reconfigured Westphalian superstate or whether it is indeed a new kind of political association. One might look to the European policy on the ICC for part of the answer to this question. As noted, the ICC articulates the post-Westphalian idea of world society. How the EU and its member states relate to it and how they relate to other societies, 'which do not find the vision of post-Westphalian community especially congenial',[4] should give some indication as to the identity of that regional association.

EUROPE, THE ICC, AND A POST-WESTPHALIAN FOREIGN POLICY

In many respects, the EU and the ICC share the same philosophical underpinnings. Both seek to broaden the conception of political community and to include in the decisions of that community those individuals and groups that would otherwise have been excluded by a more limited conception of citizenship. Obviously, the depth of these communities varies greatly. Citizens of the EU not only have a form of legal redress through the European Court of Human Rights; they can also elect members of the European Parliament.[5] Citizenship in world society is much more limited, but by offering a form of legal redress under international humanitarian and human rights law, the ICC does seek to provide some kind of protection to those who

---

[3] The idea of post-Westphalian statehood is associated with the work of Andrew Linklater. See Andrew Linklater, *The Transformation of Political Community. Ethical Foundation of the Post-Westphalian Era* (Oxford: Polity Press, 1998).

[4] Linklater, *The Transformation*, 183.   [5] Linklater, *The Transformation*, 198–203.

would otherwise lack any citizenship rights. Given these shared philosophical goals, one would expect the EU and its member states to support the ICC. There is always a possibility, however, that despite its post-Westphalian promise, the EU will repeat the American experience and evolve into a kind of Westphalian superstate. As Linklater notes, the challenge for the EU 'is to link this experiment in close political cooperation in Europe with the larger project of increasing autonomy across the world. . . . Adding transnational citizenship to national forms which already exist is an important reason for regional cooperation, but it is incomplete without larger efforts to promote the ideals of cosmopolitan citizenship.'[6] This requires, he continues, 'international joint action to ameliorate the condition of the most vulnerable in world society'.[7]

Clearly, there is concern that the EU will turn into a 'fortress' and pursue a version of European citizenship that is in conflict with a version of cosmopolitan citizenship. An example of this is the impact that the European common agricultural policy has on the interests of farmers in the developing world. With regard to European policy towards the ICC, however, that concern seems misplaced. European governments have not allowed a regional identity or particular interests to stand in the way of the creation of a Court that seeks to advance a conception of world citizenship. Indeed, virtually all the European states, with the notable exception of France, were members of the 'Like-Minded Group' (LMG). This was a group of over sixty states with a shared commitment to an independent and effective Court chaired by Canada during the preparatory negotiations and Australia during the Rome Conference.[8] In fact, the group had been formed during the preparatory stages by a number of European and Latin American states that were frustrated by the opposition of the great powers to the establishment of the ICC. Germany played a key role in this group. Along with Argentina, for instance, it pushed for a Prosecutor that was independent of the Security Council. It was considered a 'major development' when the UK formally joined the group during the preparatory negotiations.[9] Its decision, which was a consequence of the New Labour government's attempt to push foreign policy in a more 'ethical' direction, was crucial in establishing the Court's independence. With the UK supporting the idea of an Independent Prosecutor, the unanimity of the permanent five on the Security Council was broken. In fact, on this particular issue it is clear that the Europeans acted as a counterweight to US power. As Sadat notes, 'strong

  [6] Linklater, *The Transformation*, 204.   [7] Linklater, *The Transformation*, 206.
  [8] For a list of states see Schabas, *An Introduction*, 16.
  [9] Kirsch and Robinson, 'Reaching Agreement at the Rome Conference', in Cassese, Gaeta, and Jones (eds.), *The Rome Statute*, 70; Schabas, *An Introduction*, 16–17.

support from many European countries and other traditional US allies rallied the West behind the Court despite the opposition of the United States.'[10]

The strong support for the Court continued after the Rome Statute was adopted for ratification. By the summer of 2005, all member states of the EU, including those that joined in 2004, had signed the Rome Statute. Only the Czech Republic had yet to ratify it. Indeed, European states had been instrumental in creating the impetus behind the process of ratification leading to the early creation of the Court. Of the 25 member states, 20 had ratified before the 60th ratification was deposited on 11 April 2002. Greece, Latvia, Lithuania, and Malta all ratified soon after.[11] The support of EU member states was matched by the EU itself. In June 2001, for instance, the EU adopted a common position on the ICC. It stated that the 'principles of the Rome Statute...are fully in line with the principles and objectives of the Union....The effective establishment of the Court and implementation of the Statute requires practical measures that the EU and its Members should fully support'. At that point, only thirty-two states had ratified the Rome Treaty but the common position committed the EU and its member states

to further this process by raising the issue of the widest possible ratification, acceptance, approval or accession to the Rome Statute and the implementation of the Statute in negotiations or political dialogues with third States, groups of States or relevant regional organisations, wherever appropriate.[12]

Towards this end, the EU made diplomatic approaches to more than sixty countries, including a visit to Japan in December 2004.[13] It also funded an ICC ratification campaign.[14] Once the Court became a reality with the 60th ratification, the EU committed member states to 'contribute to the worldwide ratification and implementation of the Statute'.[15]

---

[10] Sadat, *The International Criminal Court*, 7.

[11] This pattern of support is reflected in wider Europe with forty-two out of the forty-five members of the Council of Europe signing the Statute. The exceptions are Armenia, Azerbaijan, and Turkey. Thirty-eight of the forty-two signatories have ratified. See http://www.coe.int.

[12] Common Position 2001/443/CFSP of 11 June 2001, Official Journal of the European Communities, L 155/19.

[13] As of February 2005, sources indicated that the Japanese government planned to accede to the Rome Statute and had begun drafting legislation. This process is expected to be completed by July 2007. Japan would replace Germany as the state making the largest financial contribution to the ICC. www.iccnow.org

[14] McGoldrick, 'Political and Legal Responses to the ICC', 391.

[15] Common Position 2002/474/CFSP of 20 June 2002, Official Journal of the European Communities, L 164/1.

BILATERAL NON-SURRENDER AGREEMENTS AND
THE (AB)USE OF ARTICLE 98

Shortly after the Bush administration unsigned the Rome Statute, it committed itself to the ambitious policy of signing bilateral non-surrender agreements with every single sovereign state.[16] Although this policy was portrayed by NGOs as another attempt to undermine the Court, the administration claimed that its actions were fully consistent with Article 98 (2) of the Rome Statute.[17] This states that the Court

may not proceed with a request for surrender which would require the requested State to act inconsistently with its obligations under international agreements pursuant to which the consent of a sending State is required to surrender a person of that State to the Court, unless the Court can first obtain the cooperation of the sending State for the giving of consent for the surrender.[18]

This article had been included in the Statute to preserve so-called 'status of forces agreements' (SOFAs), which are used to make sure that those troops stationed abroad and who commit offences as part of their official duties are not subject to a foreign jurisdiction.[19] NGOs complained that Article 98 (2) related only to agreements signed *before* the creation of the ICC, but both the Clinton and Bush administrations insisted that new non-surrender agreements could be consistent with the Statute.[20] The fact that such agreements had been considered by the Clinton administration is clear from Ambassador Scheffer's comments on the issue. His recollection of the US position at the PrepCom meetings suggests that had Al Gore won the 2000 election US strategy would not have differed greatly from that under George Bush. Although a concerted effort to negotiate non-surrender agreements was not started until the summer of 2002, Scheffer notes how the Clinton administration also considered new Article 98 agreements as a means of protecting American service personnel. Indeed, Scheffer had recommended signing the

---

[16] 'U.S. to Seek Bilateral Deals on ICC', *Wall Street Journal*, 15 July 2002.

[17] See Human Rights Watch, 'United States Efforts to Undermine International Criminal Court', at www.iccnow.org/documents; for the US response see John R. Bolton, Under Secretary for Arms Control and International Security, Remarks to the Federalist Society, Washington, DC, 14 November 2002.

[18] Rome Statute, Article 98 (2).

[19] See Wedgwood, 'The Constitution and the ICC', 123–7.

[20] Scheffer, 'Article 98 (2) of the Rome Statute', 340. This view is supported by James Crawford SC, Philippe Sands QC, and Ralph Wilde, *Joint Opinion, In the Matter of the Statute of the International Criminal Court and in the Matter of Bilateral Agreements Sought by the United States under Article 98 (2) of the Statute*, 5 June 2003, 18; and by the Dutch government, see William A. Schabas, First Report of the International Law Association, Berlin Conference (2004), International Criminal Court, 14, 20.

Rome Treaty because he believed it improved the prospect of negotiating such agreements.[21] He also recommended that Washington should make it clear to any government objecting to a special Article 98 (2) agreement that it would 'suffer in its bilateral relationship with the United States'.[22] Although Scheffer argued that the United States should only negotiate Article 98 (2) agreements with 'targeted governments', rather than all governments as was the policy of the Bush administration, his recommendation nevertheless resembled the thinking that underpinned Republican policy. 'The United States', he argued,

should negotiate Article 98 (2) agreements with targeted governments (particularly if we conclude they are not adequately covered by Status of Forces Agreements), thus protecting U.S. personnel from surrender to the ICC from those countries. *This would enable the United States to use its bilateral leverage to accomplish its multilateral objective.* In the context of the campaign against terrorism, the United States should use its leverage with coalition members to achieve this protection. The United States would stipulate that it will not ratify the ICC Treaty until a 'critical mass' (defined reasonably) of such Article 98 (2) agreements have been concluded.[23]

It is unlikely that a new Democrat administration would have been as forceful in its pursuit of such agreements as the Bush administration, but this is somewhat beside the point. Unwilling to accept the outcome of multilateral negotiations, both Republicans and Democrats considered it appropriate that the United States achieve its national objectives through coercion. The additional point is that once the issue was put in a bilateral rather than multilateral context, the United States was more able to achieve its objective.

The Bush administration certainly took a hard line when negotiating bilateral non-surrender agreements. For some critics, the diplomatic pressure that was employed was out of all proportion to what was at stake. For instance, in July 2003 the administration suspended military aid to thirty-five states that refused to sign such agreements. This hard-line approach was partly driven by the ASPA, which set 1 July 2003 (the Court's first anniversary) as a deadline for the recipients of US aid to sign non-surrender agreements.[24] During the negotiations on ASPA, however, the Bush administration had always insisted on a clause that allowed the President to waive conditionality if he determined that US national interests were at stake. It was the President therefore who received most criticism when the United States suspended the military assistance packages.[25] A *Washington Post* editorial summarized the feeling among

---

[21] Scheffer, 'Staying the Course', 58.   [22] Scheffer, 'Staying the Course', 98.

[23] Scheffer, 'Staying the Course', 99. Emphasis added.

[24] Scheffer, 'Article 98 (2) of the Rome Statute', 350–1.

[25] Of the states that had yet to conclude an agreement Afghanistan, DRC, Djibouti, East Timor, Ghana, Honduras, and Romania received Presidential waivers until November 2003, while Albania, Bosnia, Botswana, Macedonia, Mauritius, Nigeria, Panama, and Uganda received

the administration's critics. The President, it concluded, had erred in making what was essentially 'a gratuitous ideological point'. It had

needlessly offended some of the governments that have most supported his foreign policies at a moment when sympathy for those policies around the world is dangerously weak. Once again the administration has broadcast the message that its own ideological agenda is more important than its global alliances and that bullying is the best means to get its way. And once again, U.S. prestige will be weakened.[26]

Despite this criticism, the US Congress continued to link aid to non-surrender agreements. For instance, the so-called Nethercutt Amendment, which was introduced to the Foreign Operations Appropriations Bill in July 2004 by Rep. George Nethercutt, a Republican from Washington state, linked the Economic Support Fund to Article 98 agreements.[27] This aid was intended to help allies promote democracy, fight terrorism and corruption, resolve conflict and even, in the case of the Caribbean, coordinate disaster response programmes. As a result, a key ally in the Middle East, Jordan, stood to lose $250 million in aid unless it signed a non-surrender agreement.[28] Even Republicans in Congress began to question the administration's priorities. For instance, Jim Kolbe (R-AZ) described the measure as 'a very, very heavy hand ... At a time when we are fighting the war on terrorism, reducing this tool of diplomatic influence is not a good idea.'[29] Despite this opposition, the House voted for the amendment by a margin of 241 to 166 on 15 July 2004. Once the Appropriation Bill cleared

waivers until January 2004. Presidential Determination No. 2003-27, 1 July 2003. Some of these countries had waivers extended indefinitely once they concluded non-surrender agreements. See Presidential Determination No. 2003-28, 29 July 2003 (Albania, Bosnia, Djibouti, Mauritius, and Zambia); Presidential Determination No. 2003-40, 25 September 2003 (Afghanistan, DRC, Georgia, and Honduras); Presidential Determination No. 2004-03, 6 October 2003 (Colombia); and Presidential Determination No. 2004-07, 1 November 2003 (Antigua, Botswana, East Timor, Ghana, Malawi, Nigeria, and Uganda). Romania was granted a six-month extension. Presidential Determination No. 2004-09, 21 November 2003 (Bulgaria, Estonia, Latvia, Lithuania, Slovakia, and Slovenia) with regard to specific projects related to US operations in Afghanistan and Iraq. All documents at www.iccnow.org

[26] Editorial, 'Pointless Punishment', Washington Post, 6 July 2003. This kind of criticism was not limited to the liberal press. On the frustration within the military, see Victoria K. Holt and Elisabeth W. Dallas, On Trial: The US Military and the International Criminal Court, Report No. 55, The Henry L. Stimson Center, March 2006, 56–9. See also the Quadrennial Defense Review Report, 6 February 2006, for an indication that these frustrations were beginning to have an impact on policy. It urged consideration of 'whether the restrictions [of] the American Servicemembers Protection Act (ASPA) on IMET and other foreign assistance programs pertaining to security and the war on terror necessitate adjustment as we continue to advance the aims of the ASPA.'

[27] Text available at www.iccnow.org

[28] Human Rights Watch, 'US: Congress Tries to Undermine War Crimes Court', 8 December 2004.

[29] Congressional Record, 15 July 2004, H5882.

the Senate the President signed it and the Nethercutt Amendment into law the following December. The same month Jordan signed a non-surrender agreement and the President waived the restriction that had been imposed by the Nethercutt Amendment.[30]

The Bush administration has clearly been willing to risk other foreign policy objectives in order to secure non-surrender agreements. Those states that saw the suspension of US military aid included key allies in the fight against illegal drug trafficking. For instance, Ecuador and even Colombia (the third largest recipient of US military aid) saw assistance packages suspended despite their centrality to America's 'war on drugs'.[31] The policy also impacted on those governments in Eastern Europe that were hopeful of joining NATO. For example, Bulgaria, Croatia, Estonia, Latvia, Lithuania, Serbia and Montenegro, Slovakia, and Slovenia all saw their aid suspended when they refused to sign a non-surrender agreement, although most of these would ultimately receive presidential waivers. The notable country missing from this list was Romania. It had escaped the fate of its neighbours by being one of the first states to sign a bilateral agreement with the United States.[32] Yet Romania's eagerness to please the United States, which was heavily influenced by its desire to enter the NATO alliance, put it in an extremely difficult position with the EU. It had agreed to the US proposed pact before European governments had formulated a common position and unfortunately for Romania, who also had ambitions of joining the EU, the common position would oppose the non-surrender agreements proposed by the Bush administration.[33] Ultimately, Romania bridged the divide by noting that it had not ratified the July 2002 agreement.[34] This solution had been recommended by the Parliamentary Assembly of the Council of Europe in 2002, which also stated its 'support for those member and observer states of the Council of Europe that have resisted entering into bilateral immunity agreements'.[35] Evidence that such a stance was acting as a counterweight to US pressure can be seen in the fact that

---

[30] CICC, Country Positions on Bilateral Immunity Agreements, www.iccnow.org

[31] Editorial 'Bungling Bully: Strong-Arm Diplomacy Is Damaging US Interests Abroad', *Financial Times*, 3 July 2003.

[32] Nicholas Kralev, 'NATO Hopeful Vows to Aid U.S. on World Court', *Washington Times*, 26 July 2002.

[33] EU Guiding Principles concerning arrangements between a state party to the Rome Statute of the International Criminal Court and the United States regarding the conditions to Surrender of Persons to the Court, 30 September 2002, www.iccnow.org

[34] CICC, Country Positions on Bilateral Immunity Agreements, www.iccnow.org

[35] Council of Europe, Parliamentary Assembly Resolution 1300 adopted 25 September 2002 and Report of the Committee on Legal Affairs and Human Rights of the Council of Europe, Threats to the International Criminal Court, 24 June 2003, assembly.coe.int

Bulgaria was about to sign an Article 98 agreement only to change its mind when it became a candidate member of the EU.[36]

At one level, the European position may have been interpreted as inconsistent. America's intention to sign Article 98 agreements had reportedly received 'private encouragement' from certain European allies.[37] It was clear by September 2002, however, that the Council of the EU actually opposed the proposed non-surrender agreements. The key sticking point for the Europeans was the fact that the Bush administration intended Article 98 agreements to cover all US citizens and not just American service personnel. The American template for agreements, which was made available to NGOs in July 2002, prevented states from surrendering to the ICC or to a third party with the intention of eventual transfer to the ICC 'current or former government officials, employees (including contractors), or military personnel *or nationals*' of the United States.[38] In its 'Guiding Principles' on the matter, however, the EU made clear that member states should not enter into this kind of agreement. It stated that the act of

entering into US agreements—as presently drafted—would be inconsistent with ICC States Parties' obligations with regard to the ICC Statute and may be inconsistent with other international agreements to which ICC State Parties are Parties.[39]

It did not rule out the possibility of member states signing non-surrender agreements with the United States but noted in the Guiding Principles that 'any solution should cover only persons present on the territory of a requested State because they have been sent by a sending State, cf. Article 98 paragraph 2 of the Rome Statute'. In addition, any agreement needed to 'include appropriate operative provisions ensuring that persons who have committed crimes falling within the jurisdiction of the Court do not enjoy impunity'.[40]

The European position, therefore, was that state parties could only promise not to surrender Americans to the Court if they had been 'sent' to that state on official business. Obviously, this did not include all US nationals. To sign the agreement as drafted by the United States would be a violation of a state party's obligations to the Rome Statute. A state that had signed but not ratified the Rome Treaty, moreover, would be in breach of Article 18 of the Vienna Convention on the Law of Treaties, which, as noted in previous chapters,

[36]   Schabas, First Report, 12.
[37]   Lincoln P. Bloomfield, Jr., Assistant Secretary for Political-Military Affairs 'The US Government and the International Criminal Court', Remarks to the Parliamentarians for Global Action, Consultative Assembly of Parliamentarians for the International Criminal Court and the Rule of Law, United Nations, New York, 12 September 2003.
[38]   CICC, Proposed Text of Article 98 Agreements with the United States, July 2002, emphasis added, www.iccnow.org
[39]   EU Guiding Principles.   [40]   EU Guiding Principles.

prevents states from doing anything to undermine the purpose of the treaty they had signed. This conclusion was supported by academic opinion.[41] For instance, Crawford, Sands, and Wilde noted that non-surrender agreements under Article 98 only applied to persons who were on the territory of requested states 'as a result of an act of a sending State (e.g. in sending to the requested State a diplomat or as a member of a visiting military force pursuant to a SOFA). On this basis', they conclude,

> it is not sufficient for such a person to be a national of the State concerned. As a matter of ordinary meaning, a tourist or a contractor is not a 'sent' person, any more than would be a foreign minister visiting a State Party in a private capacity....In this way the agreements being sought by the US go well beyond the scope of the agreements envisaged by Article 98 (2). We endorse the approach taken by the EU Guidelines....[42]

Significantly, this interpretation was echoed by David Scheffer, who had of course negotiated the Rome Statute, including Article 98, on behalf of the Clinton administration. As noted above, Scheffer had recommended an Article 98 strategy but his proposal was not merely quantitatively different—he did not consider the need for universal coverage—it was qualitatively different to that adopted by the Bush administration. According to Scheffer, the United States need only target certain states and, more importantly, it should only seek non-surrender agreements for US citizens engaged in official acts. In pointing out this difference, Scheffer also argued that the Bush administration's policy was inconsistent with Article 98 (2) of the Statute. It was, moreover, inconsistent with the original intent of those drafting the Statute, *including the American delegation*. Like Crawford, Sands, and Wilde, whose analysis he described as 'one of the most accurate interpretations of Article 98 (2)', his dispute with the Bush administration rested on the interpretation of the term 'sending state' as it appears in Article 98 (2). He writes

> Though, as a government official, I often spoke of the grave risk of politically motivated prosecutions against American officials and military personnel, neither I nor other top US officials in the Clinton Administration aligned such concerns, in the context of the ICC, with the fate of strictly private citizens abroad. The original intent behind Article 98 (2) was relegated to persons acting at the *direction* of the 'sending State'. Whatever their arguable merit, the extraordinary leaps into the private sector, as demonstrated by Bush Administration officials, were never contemplated during the long years of negotiation that preceded and immediately followed adoption of Article 98 (2).[43]

---

[41] See Harmen Van Der Wilt, 'Bilateral Agreements between the United States and States Parties to the Rome Statute: Are They Compatible with the Object and Purpose of the Statute?', *Leiden Journal of International Law*, 18 (2005), 104–5.

[42] Crawford, Sands, and Wilde, *In the Matter of the Statute*, 20.

[43] Scheffer, 'Article 98 (2)', 346.

Despite these arguments, the Bush administration has continued to insist that their policy is consistent with Article 98 (2) of the Statute. For instance, Assistant Secretary of State Lincoln Bloomfield, Jr. defended the policy by stating that the Europeans had backtracked on its initial encouragement and that their new stance did 'not serve the interests of Europe, the EU, or the states of Europe'. Bloomfield also implied European hypocrisy, noting that some European governments 'have required very broad, if ambiguous, immunity from exposure to any tribunal of persons related in any way to their peace-keeping deployments to Afghanistan'.[44] As these agreements related to service personnel 'sent' by states and not citizens travelling in a private capacity, however, the Europeans could argue that they were consistent with Article 98 (2) of the Rome Statute.[45] Aside from this, however, Bloomfield argued that State Department lawyers could find support for the United States position 'in the usage found in other conventions such as the Vienna Convention on Consular Relations [VCCR], whose use of the term "sending state" refers to all persons who are nationals of the sending state.'[46] Finally, Bloomfield argued that the United States position was wholly justified because

The United States is a nation of immigrants; we have familial ties to localities all over the world. Our national interests know no bounds: we have diplomatic representation almost everywhere, and our private businesses and educational institutions are similarly represented far and wide.

This astonishing position took a flawed argument even further. As noted in previous chapters, the United States has consistently argued that a great power's responsibilities demand unique rights, in this case the right for its service personnel to be exempt from the Court's jurisdiction. Here Bloomfield seemed to argue that America's business interests made a unique contribution to the global capitalist system and US citizens should thus be exempt from the Court's jurisdiction. If the US insistence that it have exclusive jurisdiction over its nationals concerning acts committed abroad is 'a colonialist concept',[47] then this is surely is the clearest expression of that.

The United States has continued to pursue the Article 98 strategy and states have continued to sign the non-surrender agreements. On 2 May 2005, for instance, Angola signed an agreement to ensure that Americans would not be surrendered to the ICC without US consent. It was the 100th bilateral

---

[44] Bloomfield, 'The US Government and the International Criminal Court'.
[45] See comments by the Dutch representative in Schabas, First Report, 15.
[46] Bloomfield, 'The US Government and the International Criminal Court'. This claim is flatly contradicted by Scheffer in 'Article 98 (2) of the Rome Statute', 347.
[47] Scharf, 'The ICC's Jurisdiction', 75.

non-surrender agreement signed by the United States.[48] Of these forty-two are party to the Rome Statute and, at least according to the European position, in breach of their obligations to the ICC. For the most part, European governments have observed the EU guidelines and refused to sign the non-surrender agreements proposed by the United States. Among those states that are part of wider Europe and party to the Rome Statute only Albania, Bosnia-Hercegovina, Macedonia, and Romania have signed. As noted above, Romania has refused to ratify the agreement. This suggests that, in answer to the question posed at the outset of the chapter, European governments remain committed to the Rome Statute and to a post-Westphalian conception of a European identity. What is equally apparent, however, is that the transatlantic division on the question of non-surrender agreements has put many states in the position of having to choose between the Rome Statute and their own particular interests in terms of their relationship with the United States. This kind of dilemma was also experienced by those states that had seats on the UN Security Council during the summer of 2002 and 2003.

UN PEACEKEEPING AND THE (AB)USE OF ARTICLE 16

Following the Rome Conference, the United States argued that the Statute 'could inhibit the ability of the United States to use its military to ... participate in multilateral operations.'[49] Moreover, the Clinton administration had sought to gain exemptions for those involved in UN authorized military deployments during the March and June 2000 PrepComm meetings.[50] That suggestion had met with little support and the possibility that US troops could fall under the general jurisdiction of the Court if they were serving in a UN mission on the territory of a state party to the Rome Statute continued to alarm the US government as President Bush entered the White House. His administration decided to bring the matter to a head in the summer of 2002 when the Security Council was charged with renewing the mandate of the United Nations in Bosnia-Hercegovina (UNIMBH), including the International Police Task Force (IPTF). Bosnia was one of the celebrated states to ratify the Rome Statute on 11 April 2002 and thereby bring the Court into existence. A crime that was alleged to have been committed on its territory, therefore, could fall under

[48] Richard Boucher, US signs 100th Article 98 Agreement, Press Statement, 3 May 2005.
[49] D. Scheffer, Head of the US Delegation to the UN Diplomatic Conference on the Establishment of a Permanent International Criminal Court, Testimony Before the Senate Foreign Relations Committee, 23 July 1998.
[50] Scheffer, 'Staying the Course', 78–80.

the general jurisdiction of the Court. Theoretically, then, American members of UNIMBH could be prosecuted by the Court even though the United States was not party to the Rome Statute. In response, the US proposed a Chapter VII resolution on 19 June 2002, which decided

that persons of or from contributing states . . . shall enjoy in the territory of all Member States other than the contributing State immunity from arrest, detention, and prosecution with respect to all acts arising out of the operation and that this immunity shall continue after termination of their participation in the operation for all such acts.[51]

The US threat to withdraw its contribution to the IPTF was obvious. A month earlier US diplomats had tried to insert immunity guarantees into a resolution authorizing a similar mission in East Timor. After the Security Council rejected the proposal, the US withdrew three military observers and seventy-five civilian police from the mission.[52] Despite Secretary of Defense Donald Rumsfeld's denials that this move had anything to do with the ICC, it was later confirmed by senior Defense Department officials that 'the added risks created by the ICC necessitate our withdrawing the US peacekeepers from the East Timor mission'.[53] On Bosnia, however, there were implicit but ultimately much more significant dangers. First, a failure to pass the resolution might prompt America to withdraw its 8,000 troops from the Balkans; and second, a US decision to veto this and subsequent peacekeeping resolutions would pose particular problems for states like Germany and Ireland. For legal and political reasons, they could only deploy forces if they had a UN mandate.[54]

The American position was attacked by a coalition of like-minded states, NGOs, and the UN Secretary-General. For them, the American policy was unjustified but neither the supporters of the Court on the Security Council nor the United States wanted to jeopardize the peacekeeping mission. Thus, on 21 June, the date by which the mandate was supposed to be renewed, the Security Council adopted resolution 1418 (2002), which extended the provision through to 30 June. As a reminder of America's resolve, however, a draft resolution extending the UN mandate in Bosnia to 31 December was subsequently defeated by a vote of thirteen in favour, one against (United

[51] US Draft Resolution, 19 June 2002. Cited by Carsten Stahn, 'The Ambiguities of Security Council Resolution 1422 (2002)', *European Journal of International Law*, 14 (2003), 91.

[52] Colum Lynch, 'U.S. Seeks Court Immunity for E. Timor Peacekeepers', *Washington Post*, 16 May 2002.

[53] Colum Lynch 'Bush Promises to Try to Save Bosnia Mission. U.S. Immunity to War Court Is Key', *Washington Post*, 3 July 2002.

[54] McGoldrick, 'Political and Legal Responses', 417.

States) and one abstention (Bulgaria).[55] At the urging of National Security Adviser Condoleezza Rice, President Bush agreed to further resolutions (1420 and 1421) extending the deadline to 3 July and then 10 July respectively and it was during this period that the United States, working with the UK, circulated the draft of a resolution that would ultimately deliver a compromise.[56] The United States now attempted to make its position consistent with the Rome Statute. Acting under Chapter VII of the UN Charter, it requested

consistent with the provision of Article 16 of the Rome Statute, that the ICC for a twelve-month period shall not commence or proceed with any investigations or prosecutions involving current or former officials or personnel from a contributing State not a Party to the Rome Statute for acts or omissions relating to UN established or authorized operations.[57]

Also included in this draft was an automatic extension of the exemption unless the Security Council decided otherwise.

As noted in Chapter 4, Article 16 allowed the Security Council to postpone a prosecution for one year if nine of its members identified it to be a threat to international peace and security. This particular proposal, however, came under intense criticism from the UN Secretary-General, the Coalition for the ICC and states party to the Rome Statute. For instance, UN Secretary-General Kofi Annan wrote to Secretary of State Colin Powell objecting to the use of Article 16 to achieve a blanket exemption of a particular group prior to the identification of a threat to international peace and security. Article 16, Annan wrote, was 'meant for a completely different situation'. These situations were to be considered on a case-by-case basis and according to their particular merits. Article 16 could not be made to apply to a blanket exemption for a particular category of individuals. In this respect, the draft resolution envisaged a reinterpretation of the Rome Statute. Consequently, Annan concluded, the draft resolution 'flies in the face of treaty law since it would force States that have ratified the Rome Statute to accept a resolution that literally amends the treaty'. The US proposal moreover was contrary to the wording of Article 16, which prescribed that such resolutions were renewable after a twelve-month period and could not be automatically prolonged.[58] In addition, the draft resolution was said to violate Article 27 of the Rome Statute which states

[55] Warren Hodge, 'Bosnia Veto by the U.S. Is Condemned by Britain', *New York Times*, 2 July 2002.

[56] Jess Bravin, 'U.S. Fails to Solve ICC Dispute over Peacekeeping Forces', *Wall Street Journal*, 5 July 2002.

[57] Stahn, 'The Ambiguities of Security Council Resolution 1422', 92. Emphasis added.

[58] Letter from UN Secretary-General Kofi Annan to US Secretary of State Colin Powell of 3 July 2002, www.iccnow.org. Ambassador Scheffer has also called the US position 'highly unorthodox and not at all what the framers of the Rome Statute, including the US delegation, had in mind when Article 16 was negotiated.' Scheffer, 'Article 98 (2)', 351.

that 'immunities or special procedural rules which may attach to the official capacity of a person, whether under national or international law, shall not bar the Court from exercising its jurisdiction over such a person.'[59]

A NEW HIERARCHY OF RESPONSIBILITIES?

The debate that followed provides an important insight into the troubled relationship between the international society of states and world society. In seeking exemptions from the Court's jurisdiction for UN peacekeepers, the United States was in effect extending (and probably exploiting) the pluralist logic behind the kind of immunities discussed in Chapter 3. The demand of world society, that no individual be above international humanitarian or human rights law and that states cooperate with the ICC on that basis, was deemed to be in conflict with the 'smooth working' of international society, in this case the ability of states to fulfil a duty to provide peacekeepers. For many, including the UN Secretary-General, however, the trade-off between international justice and peacekeeping was unfounded. Given the historical record of UN missions and the safeguards in the Rome Statute, including the principle of complementarity, it was, he argued, 'highly improbable' that a peacekeeper would appear before the ICC. It was unreasonable, therefore, for the United States to put at risk the whole system of United Nations peacekeeping operations.[60]

At the Security Council meeting on 10 July, Canada reiterated many of the Secretary-General's points. It argued that for the Security Council to invoke Chapter VII was, in this particular situation, to exceed its mandate and this would do great damage to its credibility. The resolution itself would send the message that peacekeepers were above the law and would promote what New Zealand called an 'unconscionable double standard'. Along with France, Canada also noted how America's specific concern over the status of their personnel in Bosnia overlooked the fact that the ICTY had primacy over jurisdictional questions in that area.[61] The United States had not raised these concerns regarding the ICTY when in fact the danger to US servicemembers was, if anything, greater given the absence of a complementarity provision in

---

[59] CICC, Open Letter to Members of the UN Security Council, 2 July 2002.

[60] Letter from UN Secretary-General Kofi Annan to US Secretary of State Colin Powell of 3 July 2002, www.iccnow.org

[61] UN Security Council, 4568 mtg., U.N. Doc. S/PV.4568 (2002).

the Charter of the ICTY.[62] The Coalition for the ICC went even further. 'In every peacekeeping mission' they noted

the US either has no personnel in the mission, the host state is not a party to the ICC, or the ICTY has primacy. Thus, total exposure to the ICC is zero in every case.... Given this, it appears that the intention is not to protect its own peacekeepers, but to undermine the court.[63]

Canada also picked up Annan's concern that the resolution would set a precedent in relation to the sovereign right of states to make treaties. For Canada the resolution would 'set a negative precedent under which the Security Council could change the negotiated terms of any treaty it wished—for example the Non-Proliferation Treaty.... The proposed draft resolution would thereby undermine the treaty-making process.'[64]

Marc Weller supported the Canadian position. He wrote, for instance, that the resolution

was probably unlawful in terms of the UN Charter. Chapter VII of the Charter is not available as a means of legislation or super-legislation at the behest of the one or other state. The superior powers of Chapter VII can only be deployed in response to a concrete and actual threat to international peace and security. The possible loss of the US as a force-contributing state cannot conceivably be invoked as such a threat.[65]

Yet academic opinion is by no means united on this. For instance, Bryan MacPherson notes that critics may 'contend that increased reluctance by a few states to contribute to peacekeeping operations is hardly the type of threat to the peace contemplated by Article 39 [of the Charter]', but ultimately the Security Council is 'its own judge when it interprets its powers under the Charter'.[66] Salvatore Zappalà echoes this when he contends that the US threat to veto UN peacekeeping missions was an abuse of its great power status,

---

[62] See also Sir Jeremy Greenstock, then British Ambassador to the United Nations, 'America Is Not So Special that She Can Be Allowed to Shirk Her Obligations', *The Independent*, 2 July 2002.

[63] CICC, 'Zero US Exposure to ICC', 11 July 2002, www.iccnow.org

[64] UN Security Council, 4568 mtg., U.N. Doc. S/PV.4568 (2002). Most if not all of these points were supported by New Zealand, Jordan, Germany, Ireland, Liechtenstein, Malaysia, France, Iran, Switzerland, Colombia, Mexico, and Samoa. Speaking on behalf of the African Union, the Rio Group and the European Union, South Africa, Costa Rica, and Denmark respectively also made statements that supported Canada's position. Only India supported the US, although Singapore explicitly stated their support for using Article 16 as a means of finding a compromise.

[65] Marc Weller, 'Undoing the Global Constitution: UN Security Council Action on the International Criminal Court', *International Affairs*, 78 (2002), 708; see also Jain, Neha, 'A Separate Law for Peacekeepers: The Clash between the Security Council and the International Criminal Court', *European Journal of International Law*, 16 (2005), 244.

[66] Bryan MacPherson, 'Authority of the Security Council to Exempt Peacekeepers from International Criminal Court Proceedings', *ASIL Insights*, July 2002. See also Stahn, 'The Ambiguities of Security Council Resolution 1422', 87.

but 'there is nothing illegal in a permanent member announcing that it will vote against certain classes of SC [Security Council] resolutions. Therefore, it is difficult to maintain that there was no basis to act under Chapter VII, particularly since it is generally recognized that the Council enjoys very broad discretion in determining which situations amount to a "threat to peace".'[67] Likewise Carsten Stahn is critical of the invocation of Chapter VII in this situation, but the determination of a threat to peace, he concludes, 'remains in substance a political decision which lies at the heart of the Council's discretion and should not be subject to review by individual UN Member States'.[68]

MacPherson also notes that there is nothing in the Charter to suggest that the Security Council cannot, where it has identified a threat to the peace, take an action inconsistent with treaty or customary international law. On the contrary, the Charter implies that such actions might be necessary. Article 2 (7) prohibits the UN from intervening in matters within the domestic jurisdiction of any state but indicates that the prohibition does not apply in the case of enforcement measures taken under Chapter VII.[69] The Charter further provides in Article 103 that in the event of a conflict between a state's obligations under an international agreement and the UN Charter, the obligations under the Charter shall prevail.[70] Indeed, Singapore referred to this in the Security Council debate.[71] Many Chapter VII resolutions have required modification or suspension of trade or mutual defence agreements. Thus, the obligation to comply with a Security Council decision made under Chapter VII would prevail over the obligation that a state acquires as a party to the Rome Treaty. This did not mean that the proposed Security Council resolution 'amended' the Statute, as Annan and others feared, but that in every treaty it is implicit that its terms are subject to overriding UN obligations.[72] If the

---

[67] Salvatore Zappalà, 'The Reaction of the US to the Entry into Force of the ICC Statute: Comments on the UN SC Resolution 1422 (2002) and Article 98 Agreements', *International Journal of Criminal Justice*, 1 (2003), 119; see also Roberto Lavalle, 'A Vicious Storm in a Teacup: The Action by the United Nations Security Council to Narrow the Jurisdiction of the International Criminal Court', *Criminal Law Forum*, 14 (2003), 203. As Lavalle puts it: 'Strictly speaking, article 16 is unnecessary: if it did not exist the Council nonetheless could, in the lawful and proper exercise of its powers under article 41, impose on the ICC the obligation to suspend investigations or prosecutions as provided in article 16 (or differently).'

[68] Stahn, 'The Ambiguities of Security Council Resolution 1422', 98.

[69] MacPherson, 'Authority of the Security Council'; see also Stahn, 'The Ambiguities of Security Council Resolution 1422', 99.

[70] John Murphy refers to this as a 'supernorm'. Murphy, *The United States*, 21.

[71] UN Security Council, 4568 mtg., U.N. Doc. S/PV.4568 (2002), 23–4.

[72] MacPherson, 'Authority of the Security Council'. For a contrary argument, which states that Article 103 does not apply when resolutions are passed contrary to the intent of the UN Charter, see Jain, 'A Separate Law for Peacekeepers', 250–1. In a similar vein, Zappalà argues that on this particular occasion the Security Council renounced invoking the primacy of obligations arising

Security Council passed America's draft resolution, then a state party to the Rome Treaty was, as a member of the UN, obligated to observe the resolution even though it might have been considered to be inconsistent with Article 16 and therefore contrary to their obligation to uphold the integrity of that Statute.[73] In this respect, one might argue that as far as states are concerned the demands of international society and the UN Charter will always prevail over the demands of world society and the Rome Statute when they are in competition.

To leave the argument there, however, is to misunderstand the complexity of the Canadian argument. For Canada and many other delegations, the proposed draft resolution was indeed a distortion of Article 16 of the Rome Statute. Following on from a point made in the Secretary-General's letter of 3 July, Canada argued that the draft resolution was 'Lewis-Carroll-like' for standing the meaning of Article 16 on its head. The negotiating history made clear that recourse to Article 16 could only be on a case-by-case basis, where a particular situation—for example the dynamic of a peace negotiation—warrants a twelve-month deferral. 'The Council', Canada concluded, 'should not purport to alter that fundamental provision'. As noted above, the UN Charter enables the Security Council to determine threats to international peace and security under Article 39 and to pass a resolution that binds states given that under Article 103 of the Charter a Security Council resolution prevails over any other form of international law. Yet a Security Council resolution can only prevail in these circumstances if it is passed, which of course requires nine members to vote for it; and in deciding which way to vote on the draft resolution *the individual states themselves* are bound by their treaty obligations. Thus Canada, which was not at that time a voting member of the UN Security Council, reminded states party to the Rome Statute of their obligations.[74] It concluded that '[t]hose states that have pledged to uphold the integrity of the [Rome] Statute—*especially the six States Parties in the*

---

from the UN Charter under Article 103, preferring to ground its resolution in the ICC Statute. Having done so the ICC itself could, he argued, rule that the resolution was not binding and ignore the Security Council's request to defer an investigation or prosecution. Zappalà, 'Reaction of the US', 119–21.

[73] For an argument that seeks to strengthen the Court's independence from international society by noting Article 103 of the Charter binds states but not the ICC itself, see Dan Sarooshi, 'The Peace and Justice Paradox: The International Criminal Court and the UN Security Council', in Dominic McGoldrick, Rowe, and Donnelly (eds.), *The Permanent International Criminal Court*, 107–8; see also Zappalà, 'Reaction of the US', 119–22 and Stahn, 'The Ambiguities of Security Council Resolution 1422', 101–3.

[74] Article 26 of the Vienna Convention on the Law of Treaties provides that: 'Every treaty in force is binding upon the parties to it and must be performed in good faith.'

[*Security*] *Council*—have a special responsibility in this regard'.[75] In other words, parties to the Rome Statute could not vote for the proposed resolution at the UN Security Council if they wished to preserve the integrity of the Rome Statute.

Such a calculation illuminates how the creation of the ICC influences the perspective on what was referred to in Chapter 3 as good international citizenship. Prior to the formation of the Court a good international citizen might be expected to maintain international order by respecting and where possible protecting the rule of pluralist international society. Given the evidence of a consensus on universal values (e.g. human rights) the state might be expected to encourage the evolution of a solidarist international society by advancing rules that legitimize state behaviour when they advance those values. By pooling their sovereignty to set up an institution like the ICC, however, post-Westphalian states go one stage further in their efforts to protect universal values. Having done that, they are then, as the Canadians pointed out in July 2002, expected to preserve the integrity of the Rome Statute. The difficulty with this position, of course, is that not all states support the Court and there remains value in cooperating with those 'Westphalian' states to preserve the institutions of international society such as peacekeeping. Whether the establishment of the ICC seriously threatened peacekeeping making it prudent for post-Westphalian states to compromise on their commitment to the integrity of the Rome Statute is what was being debated in the summer of 2002. As is demonstrated in the following section, the post-Westphalian states of the EU came to very different conclusions on how to answer this question and how best to relate to the United States.

THE DEBATE OVER UN SECURITY COUNCIL RESOLUTIONS 1422 (2002) AND 1487 (2003)

Canada's opposition to America's draft resolution was echoed by the German statement at the debate on 10 July. Like Canada, Germany was speaking as a non-voting member of the Security Council. It argued that the draft resolution was not consistent with Article 16, which the founders only envisaged invoking on a case-by-case basis. Voting for the resolution, therefore, would be 'doing the world community a disservice'.[76] This was repeated by Denmark.

---

[75] UN Security Council, 4568 mtg., 10 July 2002, U.N. Doc. S/PV.4568 (2002), 4, emphasis added; see also Stahn, 'The Ambiguities of Security Council Resolution 1422', 100–1.

[76] 4568th Meeting of the UN Security Council, 10 July 2002, S/PV.4568 (Resumption 1) 9.

Speaking on behalf of the EU, it reminded the Security Council of the European commitment to the Court. It also repeated Kofi Annan's argument that it was highly improbable that a peacekeeper would be under suspicion of committing a core crime and should that suspicion exist the Rome Statute contained plenty of safeguards to ensure he or she would be dealt with by national jurisdictions. On the other hand, Denmark recognized the important contribution made by the United States to UN peacekeeping and expressed its desire to see the UN mandate for the mission in Bosnia renewed. Summarizing the dilemma faced by post-Westphalian states it concluded: 'We strongly urge all members of the Security Council to do their utmost to achieve a solution that does not harm the integrity of the Rome Statute ... and which ensures the uninterrupted continuation of United Nations peacekeeping.'[77]

Despite the concerns expressed in the statements of Security Council members the US draft resolution passed by a unanimous vote on 12 July. Resolution 1422 (2002) requested the ICC to refrain from initiating investigations and prosecutions with respect to personnel of UN missions that belonged to states not party to the Statute. The United States had dropped the demand that the resolution be renewed automatically.[78] To the relief of many, the Security Council quickly passed resolution 1423 (2002), which extended the mandate of UNMIBH.[79] The Europeans were as relieved as most; however, Germany's Justice Minister Herta Dýubler-Gmelin best captured the mood when she argued that 'special rules for strong countries, particularly when the issue at stake is the global pursuit of the worst human rights violations, are inappropriate and not compatible with the principles of the rule of law.' She concluded that it was good that peacekeeping would not be blocked, 'but a sour aftertaste remains'.[80]

The six state parties that voted for resolution 1422 (2002) and, according to the Canadian argument, reneged on their obligations to uphold the integrity of the Statute were Bulgaria, France, Ireland, Mauritius, Norway, and the UK.[81] It might also be argued that France, Ireland, and the UK also reneged on an obligation to the European Common Foreign and Security Policy, although the explicit statement that 'it is eminently important that the integrity of the Rome Statute be preserved' was only added to the Common Position in

---

[77] 4568th Meeting of the UN Security Council, 10 July 2002, S/PV.4568, 9.
[78] UN Document S/Res 1422, 12 July 2002.   [79] UN Document S/Res 1423, 12 July 2002.
[80] Judy Dempsey, 'Little Applause on Criminal Court Deal', *Financial Times*, 15 July 2002.
[81] 4572nd Meeting of the UN Security Council, 12 July 2002, S/PV.4572. The other states voting in favour were Cameroon, China, Colombia, Guinea, Mexico, Russia, Syria, Singapore, and the United States. Colombia and Guinea became state parties on 5 August 2002 and 14 July 2003 respectively after resolution 1422 (2002) was passed.

June of 2003.[82] Indeed, when the resolution came up for renewal in July of 2003 Germany, which was then a voting member of the UN Security Council, took a very different position to the Europeans who had voted for resolution 1422 (2002). The arguments against exempting UN peacekeepers had not changed. The Secretary-General again argued that the trade-off between peacekeeping and justice was groundless and Germany noted that if anything the ICC played an important role in protecting peacekeepers from attack. Germany concluded that 'justice is, and must remain, indivisible'.[83] Rather than, as it saw it, violate its obligation to uphold the integrity of the Rome Statute, Germany abstained from the vote on what became resolution 1487 (2003). France and Syria also abstained with the twelve remaining members of the Council voting for it.[84] Of these Bulgaria, Spain, and the UK might have been considered to be in violation of their obligations to the Rome Statute.

In response, the UK sought to reconcile the competing demands of international and world society by explaining the position it had taken. On the one hand, it associated itself fully with the position of the EU and distanced itself from the concerns of the United States. On the other, it rejected the argument that resolutions 1422 (2002) and 1487 (2003) were inconsistent with the Rome Statute and welcomed the fact that they enabled the United States to contribute to UN peacekeeping and other missions. It stressed that the compromise was an exceptional measure and that it was not renewable without further scrutiny in the Council.[85] From this perspective, the UK, Bulgaria, and Spain had not reneged on their obligation to the Rome Statute; rather, they had realized the importance of the United States to the success of international peacekeeping and recognized the possibility of a compromise by using Article 16 the Statute and Chapter VII of the Charter.

Academic analysis, however, tends to disagree with the British position. Carsten Stahn, for instance, noted that resolution 1422

---

[82] Common Position 2003/444/CFSP on 16 June 2003, Official Journal of the European Union, L 150/67. Resolution 1336 (2003) of the Parliamentary Assembly of the Council of Europe described UN Security Council resolution 1442 (2002) and its renewal as 'a legally questionable and politically damaging interference with the functioning of the International Criminal Court'.

[83] 4772nd Meeting of the UN Security Council, 12 June 2003, 25.

[84] Angola, Bulgaria, Cameroon, Chile, China, Guinea, Mexico, Pakistan, Russia, Spain, the UK, and the United States voted in favour of renewal. 4772nd Meeting of the UN Security Council, 12 June 2003, 22.

[85] 4772nd Meeting of the UN Security Council, 12 June 2003, 22–3. If the compromise was exceptional it was not unique, see resolution 1497 (2003) on Liberia, UN Document S/Res/1497 (2003), 1 August 2003.

may be compatible with the wording of Article 16, which simply states that no investigation or prosecution may be commenced or proceeded with after a deferral request, without spelling out when such a request may be made. But it is hard to reconcile with the purpose of the provision and its systematic position in the Statute. . . . The purpose of this provision is quite clear. It was negotiated to enable the Council to delay the exercise of jurisdiction by the ICC in situations in which the resolution of a specific conflict warrants a deferral of prosecution. Perhaps the most classic example is the suspension or omission of proceedings that might destabilize peace negotiations. But Article 16 was certainly not meant to provide a basis for the immunity of a whole group of actors in advance and irrespective of any concrete risk of indictment or prosecution.[86]

From this perspective, the UK's interpretation of Article 16 was too imaginative. Even if one accepted this criticism, however, one might still argue that the UK's decision was prudent. Had the Security Council followed Germany's lead and abstained from supporting the compromise important UN missions would have been put at risk. One might also argue that the UK's strategy of engaging the United States through Article 16 was vindicated when the United States did not seek to renew resolution 1487 (2003). However, this decision was not a consequence of America's changing attitude towards the Court. Rather, it was a reflection of the fact that the Security Council was increasingly losing patience with the United States after the invasion of Iraq and the Abu-Ghraib prisoner abuse scandal.

'GENOCIDE' IN SUDAN AND UN SECURITY COUNCIL RESOLUTION 1593 (2005)

The British argument that by continuing to engage the United States the Europeans will be able to persuade the United States to alter its course has been somewhat discredited by the diplomacy surrounding the Iraq War. Yet, on the issue of the ICC, there is further evidence that a policy of compromise is beginning to erode US opposition. On 31 March 2005, the Security Council unexpectedly passed resolution 1593 and referred the situation in the Darfur region of Sudan to the ICC.[87] The referral was unexpected because it had for so long been taken for granted that the United States would veto any such move, particularly given its opposition to the mere mention of the ICC in the previous resolutions. This opposition had persisted, even after the International Commission of Inquiry on Darfur had recommended an ICC referral in its Report to the Secretary-General of 25 January 2005. Ironically, that inquiry had not gone as far as the US government in describing the human rights

---

[86] Stahn, 'The Ambiguities', 88–9.   [87] S/Res/1593 (2005), 31 March 2005.

abuses in Darfur as 'genocide', but it had compiled a dossier of information on crimes against humanity, which would form the basis of the referral to the ICC.[88] Rather than accept the International Commission's recommendation, however, the US government had proposed alternative means of securing accountability. It did not, in the words of the US Ambassador-at-Large for War Crimes Issues Pierre Prosper, 'want to be party to legitimizing the ICC' through a UN referral.[89] In fact, the idea of ICC involvement was described by an unnamed State Department official as 'a total non-starter'.[90]

In certain respects, the administration's line on Darfur was taken from Congress. For instance, Colin Powell's use of the word 'genocide' on 9 September 2004 was significant, but it was also an echo of the Congressional resolution two days earlier.[91] Being sensitive to the administration's policy on the ICC, however, Congress responded to the International Commission's report by introducing in March 2005 The Darfur Accountability Act. This avoided reference to the ICC but called on the UN Security Council to take steps 'to ensure prompt prosecution and adjudication of those named ... *in a competent international court of justice'.*[92] This was consistent with the administration's intention either to create a new ad hoc court or to expand the Rwandan Tribunal's jurisdiction. The objection to an ICC referral was again cast in normative, or as Prosper put it, 'philosophical' terms. These were familiar to anyone following US policy since Under Secretary of State Grossman had explained why the US government had chosen to unsign the Rome Treaty. Grossman had then argued that justice had to be done at the local level if the rule of law was to mean anything. Now Prosper argued that the ICC was too far removed from the problem in Sudan and that the people of Africa would not see justice being administered.[93]

If this position satisfied the philosophical concerns of those communitarians suspicious of cosmopolitan institutions like the ICC, it did not satisfy those in Congress who were concerned about the cost of such an alternative. Human Rights Watch had put the cost of the United States proposal at $30 million in the first 6–8 months, rising to $100 million annually. This was

---

[88] For discussion see William A. Schabas, 'Darfur and the "Odious Scourge": The Commission of Inquiry's Findings on Genocide', *Leiden Journal of International Law*, 18 (2005), 871–85.

[89] Mark Turner, 'UN Divided after Bombardment of Village in Darfur', *Financial Times*, 28 January 2005.

[90] Nicholas Kralev, 'US Balks at Global Court Use for Darfur', *Washington Times*, 21 January 2005.

[91] H.Con.Res.467 also called for US intervention to stop the atrocities. The resolution is available at <http://savedarfur.org/>

[92] The Darfur Accountability Act 109th Congress 1st Session S.495. Emphasis added.

[93] Remarks by Ambassador Prosper, Darfur, War Crimes, The ICC and the Quest for Justice, The Brookings Institute, 22 February 2005.

compared to the overall budget of $88 million for the ICC, which would not require additional start-up costs.[94] These figures were picked up by Senator Dodd who also noted the 'irony' of the administration's position, which had previously been critical of the Rwandan Tribunal because of its perceived inefficiency.[95] Senator Leahy put a similar point to the new Secretary of State Condoleezza Rice. Why, he asked, could the United States not agree to give the victims in Darfur a chance to have their cases heard in a court that was already up and running? At that stage, however, Rice was sticking to the administration's line, which held that the ICC was a flawed institution because it could hold citizens of non-state parties 'to an unaccountable and potentially politically motivated prosecution.'[96]

At the Security Council, the US position found support at the UN among the Chinese and Algerians.[97] European governments, however, had embraced the International Commission's recommendation of a referral to the ICC. They knew, moreover, that unlike the issue of peacekeeping forces in Bosnia the United States was in a relatively weaker position should the question of a referral to the ICC come to the Security Council. Having declared the situation in Darfur to be 'genocide', and with the possibility that the Congress and Security Council would not support another ad hoc tribunal, the Bush administration could not veto a resolution referring the situation to the ICC without upsetting many of its own supporters. Indeed much of the pressure for accountability in Darfur came from evangelical Christian groups who had long been aiding civilians caught up in Sudan's civil war. The Bush administration's political dilemma translated into a European and more specifically a British opportunity, a fact that was articulated most clearly by the former British Foreign Secretary Robin Cook. '[British] Ministers tell us', he noted, 'they are looking for a way forward, but that will only be possible through agreement in the security council—in other words, with the US. But do they really believe that the Bush administration would have the gall to cast a US veto to block Darfur being committed to the international criminal court?'[98] Indeed, US commentators predicted that 'the Bush administration would be too ashamed to exercise its veto and might abstain instead'.[99]

[94] Human Rights Watch, 'EU Should Push for the ICC Referral of Darfur during Rice Visit', 10 February 2005.

[95] Hearing of the Senate Foreign Relations Committee on the Subject of the Nomination of Robert Zoellick to the Deputy Secretary of State, 15 February 2005.

[96] Hearing of the Senate Appropriation Committee on Fiscal Year 2005 Emergency Supplemental, 17 February 2005.

[97] See 5125th Meeting of the UN Security Council, 16 February 2005.

[98] Robin Cook, 'If Not Darfur, Then Where? US Hostility to the International Criminal Court Knows No Bounds', 11 February 2005.

[99] Nicholas Kristof, 'Why Should We Shield the Killers?', *New York Times*, 2 February 2005.

On this occasion the British government's position was sympathetic to Cook's reasoning. By supporting the French proposal to refer the matter to the ICC through a Security Council resolution, it put the Bush administration in a difficult position. Like the exemptions for peacekeepers in Bosnia, however, the British government also led the attempts to find a compromise that would allow the United States to support the resolution. For some, the British were seen to be wavering in their support for the ICC and next to the enthusiasm of the Canadians and New Zealanders, it is easy to see how the British concern for 'consensus' might have been interpreted as a concern for the Bush administration's predicament.[100] Ultimately, a compromise similar to resolution 1422 was struck. The United States agreed to abstain on the vote on the Sudan referral because resolution 1593 would not impinge on the legal status of those personnel that were part of the UN mission in Sudan, which had been set up by resolution 1591 (2005) to help foster peace in Darfur. Resolution 1593 stated explicitly that nationals of states not party to the Rome Statute other than those from Sudan 'shall be subject to the exclusive jurisdiction of that contributing State'. Understandably, the Sudanese complained of 'double standards',[101] a fact which was not lost on the Washington press corps. The United States was left having to explain why, as an anonymous questioner put it to the State Department spokesman,

the US government believes that citizens of Sudan, which signed the Rome Statute but has not ratified it and, therefore, is not a state party to it, should be subject to its jurisdiction when the crux of the American argument is that US citizens should not be subject to its jurisdiction because the United States is not a state party to it.[102]

US officials could respond only by stating that this was (again) an 'extraordinary situation' and that because the UN Security Council had spoken, Sudan was obliged to cooperate with the ICC even though it was not a party to the Rome Treaty.[103]

---

[100] Anne Penketh, 'Britain Accused of Siding with US on Darfur Killings', *The Independent*, 2 February 2005; Judy Dempsey, 'UK Caught between US and EU over Sudan', *International Herald Tribune*, 2 February 2005.

[101] See statements by Sudanese officials in Colum Lynch, 'UN Council's Resolution on Atrocities in Sudan Is Passed', *Washington Post*, 1 April 2005.

[102] US State Department Press Briefing, 1 April 2005.

[103] US State Department Press Briefing, Under Secretary of State for Political Affairs, Nicholas Burns, 1 April 2005. As for the cooperation of other states see Luigi Condorelli and Annalisa Ciampi, who emphasize the fact that section 2 of resolution 1593 (2004) merely 'urges' states to cooperate with the court rather than 'demand.' 'Comments on the Security Council Referral of the Situation in Darfur to the ICC', *Journal of International Criminal Justice*, 3 (2005), 590–9.

CONCLUSION

For some commentators the US decision to abstain on Resolution 1593 (2005) marked 'a significant diplomatic change of course'.[104] Before accepting this conclusion, however, two mitigating factors must be taken into account. First, the United States had always supported the idea of a permanent international court if the sole means of referral was through the Security Council. That way the United States could control when and where international justice was done by vetoing any resolution that clashed with its national interests. To this extent, the US support for the Sudan referral was not inconsistent with its policy on the ICC and indeed this argument had been anticipated by staunch opponents of the Rome Statute.[105] Second, because the United States was able to influence the debate in the Security Council it was again able to negotiate exemptions from the Court's jurisdiction. This was not the original intention of the drafters of the Statute and it once again illustrates, along with the analysis of the Article 98 agreements and exemptions for peacekeepers in Bosnia, that the United States is able better to advance its interests through the institutions of international society. On the issues of peacekeeping and genocide in Darfur, the Security Council was ultimately willing to compromise with the United States for the sake of the greater good. These compromises have normative value, but they are not without costs. They detract from the legitimacy of the ICC's investigation, particularly in the eyes of those being investigated. Contrary to the US intention that the international community send 'a direct signal' to those committing atrocities in Darfur, US policy on the ICC continues to send mixed messages.

Given this conclusion, should the Europeans have appeased US demands at the Security Council or should they have stood firm and opposed the US policy as they have done on Article 98 agreements? It should be noted that the United States was not the only permanent member on the Security Council that might have vetoed resolution 1593. China had its own policy towards the Court and its own interests in Sudan to think about. It is possible that the Europeans had to meet US demands in order to isolate China and prevent it from exercising its veto. Furthermore, one should not underestimate the significance of the precedent created by the Security Council

---

[104] Warren Hoge, 'UN Votes to Send Any Sudan War Crime Suspects to World Court', *New York Times*, 1 April 2005; see also Philippe Sands, 'International Law: Alive and Kicking', *The Guardian*, 17 May 2005.
[105] See, for instance, comments by former Assistant Attorney General Jack Goldsmith, 'Support War Crimes Trials for Darfur', *Washington Post*, 23 January 2005; also comments by Lee A. Casey in Colum Lynch, 'US, Europe Debate Venue for Darfur Trials', *Washington Post*, 20 January 2005.

referral to the ICC. While the Bush administration continues to oppose the ICC, it has nonetheless inadvertently recognized the ICC as, in the words of the Darfur Accountability Act, 'a competent international tribunal'. Thus, instead of passing anti-ICC legislation, the House of Representatives calls on the President to 'render assistance to the efforts of the ICC to bring to justice persons accused of genocide, war crimes or crimes against humanity in Darfur'.[106] Indeed, US officials now reportedly concede that they cannot delegitimize the court, and Assistant Secretary of State for African Affairs Jendayi Frazer has suggested it is policy to cooperate with the Court if it requests US assistance.[107]

In this respect, the Darfur case has exposed the political vulnerability of those who oppose the Court. The republican concern for checks and balances and national sovereignty strongly influences the US debate on the Court, but it is clear that the liberal concern for universal human rights is not absent from that debate. When the US alternative to the ICC—that is workable national courts or a new ad hoc international court—was unachievable, Americanists in the US government could not bring themselves to vote against the defence of universal justice even if it was done through a Court that challenged fundamental principles of state sovereignty. Any US politician uncertain of the balance between the principles of sovereign consent and international justice only had to look at the opinion polls on the issue. The American people it seems were overwhelmingly in favour of referring the issue to the ICC. In a March 2005 poll, for instance, 60 per cent of those asked favoured sending the cases to the ICC, while only 29 per cent favoured sending them to a temporary tribunal.[108] Two months later a separate poll found that 91 per cent of those asked felt that the United States should cooperate with the ICC.[109] The cost of

[106] Darfur Peace and Accountability Act, 2005, House Resolution 3127, 109th Congress, 1st Session, 29 June 2005. Unfortunately for supporters of the Court, the call for cooperation by the House of Representatives was not contained in the Senate version of the bill, which passed on 19 November 2005. See Darfur Peace and Accountability Act, 2005, Senate Resolution 1642, and Darfur Peace and Accountability Act (H.R. 3127), which passed the House on 6 April 2006.

[107] Jess Bravin, 'US Warms to Hague Tribunal', *Wall Street Journal*, 14 June 2006; Testimony by Assistant Secretary Jendayi E. Frazer, Bureau of African Affairs, 'Prospects for Peace in Darfur', House International Relations Committee, 18 May 2006.

[108] Chicago Council on Foreign Relations and the Program on International Policy Attitudes at the University of Maryland, www.pipa.org/

[109] Poll by the International Crisis Group and Zogby International, www.amicc.org/; see also Program on International Policy Attitudes, 'Americans on International Courts and Their Jurisdiction over the US', 11 May 2006, which stated that a 'majority [of Americans] favours giving international bodies the power to judge individuals charged with extreme violations of human rights if a national government is not performing this function. A large majority favours US participation in the International Criminal Court even after hearing US government objections.' www.worldpublicopinion.org/pipa/

US opposition to the ICC therefore is not only material, something that is also apparent in the US support for the Iraqi Special Tribunal. There is seemingly a profound ideological cost. The lesson for European supporters of the Court is that they are on the right side of the argument and that they should be patient and stick to their post-Westphalian principles, even if at times this means making prudent compromises that satisfy the US government.

7

International Society and America's War on Terrorism

The evidence presented in Chapter 6 contributes to the general argument that the United States prefers an international society of states because it is in this kind of society that it can preserve the preferred image of itself and advance its particular interests. The United States was able to gain through its bilateral relationships with weaker states, and through the UN Security Council, the kind of guarantees that it was unable to gain from the ICC and its supporters. This chapter advances that argument one stage further by focusing on the US response to a postmodern challenge of a very different kind, al-Qaeda. The terrorist attacks of 9/11 were clearly crimes against humanity and for some commentators an appropriate response would have been the creation of a special international court. An ad hoc arrangement such as this would have been required because the attacks fell outside the temporal jurisdiction of the ICC.[1] It is clear, however, that the Bush administration's suspicion of international criminal justice was not the only factor preventing such a move. The perception existed that the terrorist threat had developed because the law, particularly under the Clinton administration, had hamstrung US policy.[2] After 9/11, the United States would interpret the terrorist threat through the prism of 'war' rather than 'crime' and the President would claim broad executive powers including the ability to determine when international law could restrain US actions. As is explained below this response has been contested in US courts. This is significant to the extent that the Bush administration's perception of international law is not necessarily representative, but this is not the focus of this chapter. The purpose of this chapter is instead to demonstrate how in their response to the threat posed by violent non-state actors, US

---

[1] Roy S. Lee, 'An Assessment of the ICC Statute', *Fordham International Law Journal*, 25 (2002), 756–7; Geoffrey Robertson, 'Lynch Mob Justice or a Proper Trial', *The Guardian*, 5 October 2001; see also 'There Is a Legal Way Out of This', *The Guardian*, 14 September 2001; 'Kangaroo Courts Can't Give Justice. We Need an International Tribunal for Terrorist Suspects', *The Guardian*, 5 December 2001; Imran Khan, 'Terrorists Should Be Tried in Court', *The Guardian*, 12 October 2001.

[2] See, e.g. Ruth Wedgwood, 'The Law of War: How Osama Slipped Away', *National Interest*, 66 (2001–2), 69–75.

policymakers have defended and then exploited the institutions of international society, most notably the state's exclusive right to violence, sovereignty, and sovereign consent. It does this in three sections.

The first section provides historical context by examining the Reagan administration's rejection of the 1977 Protocol Additional to the Geneva Conventions. By recognizing the right to lawful belligerency of certain non-state actors (i.e. national liberation movements), the Protocol threatened, at least according to the Reagan administration, an international order based on the state's exclusive right to violence. While this was not the only US concern with the Protocol, and while the Reagan administration was not consistent in its opposition to armed non-state groups, the argument does indicate the way in which the norms of international society have been used to advance US interests. The refusal to apply all aspects of IHL to America's war on terrorism has parallels with this earlier debate. To extend certain aspects of IHL to the war against al-Qaeda would have suggested that as a non-state actor al-Qaeda could engage in lawful belligerency if it met those specific criteria informed by the general principles of discrimination and proportionality. Given al-Qaeda's terrorist tactics this was, of course, highly unlikely. This argument, however, does demonstrate how a particular application of the laws of war can pose a radical threat to an international society based on statehood. Where the national liberation movements protected under the 1977 Protocol actually reinforced international society by at least aspiring to statehood, applying the laws of war to al-Qaeda was revolutionary because this movement was a stateless network inspired by universal religious imperatives.[3] Accepting the possibility that transnational actors (TNAs) that did not even aspire to statehood could nonetheless engage in lawful belligerency would have been a radical alteration of the role that the laws of war play in helping to constitute international society. Indeed, it would help constitute something where the adjective 'international' would no longer apply.

As the second section notes, however, the US refusal to apply the laws of war after 9/11 was itself driven by a radical policy that sought to create the legal space for a much more aggressive approach to combating terrorism. What made this policy radical was the fact that solidarist norms—that is norms that protect the individual from abuse in a time of war—were deeply embedded in international society. Practices such as torture or cruel and degrading treatment were obviously banned under international law. Despite this, certain US lawyers sought to overturn this common understanding and they did this by

---

[3] Barak Mendelsohn, 'Sovereignty under Attack: The International Society Meets al-Qaeda Network', *Review of International Studies*, 31 (2005), 45–68; see also Charles A. Jones, 'War in the Twenty-first Century: An Institution in Crisis', in Richard Little and John Williams (eds.), *The Anarchical Society in a Globalized World* (Basingstoke, UK: Palgrave Macmillan, 2006), 170.

evoking the constitutive rules of the society of states, namely sovereignty and sovereign consent. According to this view, which would ultimately inform US policy, detainees in the war on terrorism did not have rights because they were fighting on behalf of a non-state actor (al-Qaeda) which could not engage in lawful belligerency and could not consent to the Geneva Conventions. Human rights, in other words, were linked to citizenship and citizenship was linked not to a society of humankind but to a society of sovereign states. In such a society, combatants had rights if they fought for states that had consented to the Geneva Conventions. The war on terrorism was not a war between sovereign states and therefore the rights granted by the laws of war did not apply, at least according to the Bush administration. Of course, the detainees at Guantánamo Bay *were* citizens of states and those states protested against their detention, but as soon as the issue was placed in an interstate setting the US government could use the relative power it had in its bilateral relationships in order to secure its own interests. Dealing with terrorism through the society of states, therefore, not only provided additional normative criteria for delegitimizing the non-state actor, it also advanced US interests by putting the issue in a legal and political setting that it can more or less dictate. Moreover, as the third section of the chapter demonstrates, the institution of sovereignty initially provided the Bush administration with a means of escaping the oversight of the US judiciary. The Guantánamo Bay interrogation facility, they argued, was not within the jurisdiction of US courts because it was on Cuban sovereign territory. Again, the lawyers for the Bush administration chose to apply a law where state sovereignty was central because it is in the space between sovereign states that American power, and indeed presidential power, works most effectively. Their arguments were—to reverse Justice Jackson's famous description of the Nuremberg trials—one of the most significant tributes that reason has ever paid to power.

INTERNATIONAL SOCIETY AND LAWFUL COMBATANCY

The laws of war (or IHL) recognize the right of a limited number of individuals to kill. As Hedley Bull notes, this is one of the ways that international society restricts the right to make war. These laws legitimize organized deadly violence when it is conducted on behalf of states. The second limitation, which because it is concerned with humanity rather than the state might be understood as a solidarist development, is the restriction on the way in which war is conducted.[4] Individuals can kill as long as that action is part of a state

---

[4] Bull, *Anarchical Society*, 182.

policy that is deemed to be discriminatory (i.e. it does not target civilians) and proportional (i.e. it cannot be expected to cause incidental loss of life, which is excessive to the military advantage anticipated).[5] The question of whether international society recognized the right of non-state military forces to engage in legitimate combat and to qualify as prisoners-of-war (POWs) if captured was addressed by Article 4 of the Third Geneva Convention. To claim the privileges entitled to POWs, which included immunity from prosecution as well as protections against mistreatment, non-state combatants had to fulfil the following conditions:

(a) That of being commanded by a person responsible for his subordinates;
(b) That of having a fixed distinctive sign recognizable at a distance;
(c) That of carrying arms openly;
(d) That of conducting their operations in accordance with the laws and customs of war.

It is easy see how these conditions are consistent with and seek to advance fundamental principles of IHL. Combatants could not be allowed to jeopardize the protected status of civilians by failing to distinguish themselves as military personnel. Neither could the common criminal, that is someone who acted in a private capacity, claim immunity from prosecution because he claimed to be fighting a 'war'. To be entitled to that privilege a person had to be part of a group with a command structure that resembled the army of a state. A violent act by a person who did not fulfil any of these conditions was not necessarily considered a war crime because that person had no right to claim combatant status. International society could not therefore exercise universal jurisdiction over the offence. However, such acts were considered unlawful (i.e. crimes *in* war), and they were to be prosecuted under national legislation.[6] The fact that so many states had in their past called upon their citizens to resist an occupying enemy is one reason why international society was at the time reluctant to make such an offence a criminal act that carried universal jurisdiction.[7]

The problem these conditions posed for the legal status of resistance movements and citizen armies was recognized by Richard Baxter, who would eventually lead the American delegation at the negotiations on the Additional

---

[5] These principles are perhaps best articulated by Rules 1 and 14 of the ICRC's statement on customary international humanitarian law. See Henckaerts and Doswald-Beck, *Customary International Humanitarian Law*, 3–8 and 46–50.

[6] Richard R. Baxter, 'So-called "Unprivileged Belligerency": Spies, Guerrillas and Saboteurs', *The British Yearbook of International Law*, 28 (1951), 338.

[7] Baxter, 'So-called "Unprivileged Belligerency"', 335.

Protocols in the mid-1970s.[8] Writing over twenty years earlier Baxter challenged the usefulness of the Article 4 criteria. They would not encompass the kind of guerrilla tactics that 'the realities of modern warfare' were encouraging and neither could they be reconciled with significant political ideologies. 'Only a rigid legal formalism', he noted,

could lead to the characterization of the resistance conducted against Germany, Italy and Japan as a violation of international law. Patriotism, nationalism, allegiance to some sort of political authority have replaced the desire for loot, which has traditionally been attributed to the guerrilla, in motivating civilians to take an active part in warfare. And finally, it must not be forgotten that in the Marxist view of the 'people's war', to which a considerable number of important military powers subscribe, popular resistance, including guerrilla warfare, is regarded as a necessary and proper means of defence.[9]

The implication was that the regime codified by the 1949 Geneva Convention was an anachronism. Playing on words that drew attention to the precarious nature of laws that 'hang on the type of clothes worn', Baxter concluded that 'it is possible to envisage a day when the law will be so retailored as to place all belligerents, however garbed, in a protected status.'[10]

Baxter's point was not to condone guerrilla tactics, but to recognize that many groups who were intent on violent resistance had little or no incentive to abide by the laws of war because the law did not recognize their potential as lawful combatants. If their attacks on legitimate targets were deemed criminal simply because of the clothes they wore, then they had little incentive to avoid other criminal acts such as the targeting of civilians. In order to create such an incentive, Additional Protocol I changed the criteria for irregular (non-state) forces.[11] Article 43 defined privileged belligerents as armed forces that are under a command responsible to a party involved in the conflict. This removed the clothing requirement of the 1949 conditions but still separated the guerrilla force from the common criminal who committed illegitimate acts of violence. Article 44 reaffirmed the principle of discrimination by demanding that the guerrilla distinguish himself from the civilian population when he was preparing and when he was actually committing the act of violence against his enemy. The fact that he was at other times likely to be indistinguishable from the civilian population did not, under these new criteria, automatically make him an unlawful combatant; neither did it deny him the protection of

---

[8] Hans-Peter Gasser, 'Agora: Protocol I to the Geneva Convention. An Appeal for Ratification by the United States', *The American Journal of International Law*, 81 (1987), 916.

[9] Baxter, 'So-called "Unprivileged Belligerency"', 335.

[10] Baxter, 'So-called "Unprivileged Belligerency"', 343.

[11] Aldrich, 'New Life for the Laws of War', 704.

POW status if he was captured. Of course, if he was found by a competent tribunal to have failed to distinguish himself from the civilian population in the preparation and conduct of the attack he could still be prosecuted for unlawful belligerency. Likewise, if he engaged in terrorist acts by intentionally attacking civilians or other personnel protected by the Geneva Conventions, then he could be prosecuted.[12]

President Carter signed Protocols I and II, which supplemented common Article 3 of the 1949 Geneva Conventions relating to armed conflict of a non-international character, on 12 December 1978. On 29 January 1987, however, President Reagan wrote to the US Senate stating that his administration would not seek ratification of Protocol I, because it was 'fundamentally and irreconcilably flawed'.[13] There were several reasons for reaching this conclusion. The first was the opposition voiced by the military. A focus in this regard was the prohibition placed on reprisals against the civilian population or civilian objects by Articles 51 and 52, respectively.[14] It was argued that the removal of what was considered a right of reprisal placed 'further respect for the rule of law in jeopardy'. As W. Hays Parks who contributed to the military review of the Protocol noted:

Because a reprisal involves an illegal act—accomplished for the limited purpose of forcing the enemy to cease certain illegal acts—it is politically sensitive, particularly in a democracy with a history of respect for the rule of law. But reprisals or the threat thereof have proved necessary and effective in preventing violations of the law of war, and the US government was opposed to a broadening of restrictions on reprisals at the Diplomatic Conference. The American delegation was unwilling to break consensus on this matter ... Nonetheless, the American military review recognized the historic pattern of abuse of U.S. and allied prisoners of war by their enemies, and concluded that a broad reservation to the prohibition on reprisals contained in articles 51 and 52 of Protocol I was essential as a legitimate mechanism in order to ensure respect for the law of war.[15]

While US military opposition was presented as a concern for the rule of law, it was clearly motivated by a perception that the Protocol had created what

---

[12] Aldrich, 'New Life for the Laws of War', 773; see also Yves Sandoz, Christophe Swinarski, and Bruno Zimmerman (eds.), *Commentary on the Additional Protocols of 8 June 1977 to the Geneva Conventions of 12 August 1949* (Geneva: Martinus Nijhoff Publishers for the International Committee of the Red Cross, 1987), 522–5.

[13] Reagan, Letter of Transmittal, The White House, 29 January 1987. Reprinted in 'Agora: The US Decision Not to Ratify Protocol I to the Geneva Conventions on the Protection of War Victims', *American Journal of International Law*, 81 (1987), 910–2.

[14] The Position of the United States on Current Law of War Agreements: Remarks of Judge Abraham D. Sofaer, Legal Adviser, United States Department of State, 22 January 1987, *American University Journal of International Law and Policy*, 2 (1987), 468–9.

[15] W. Hays Parks, 'Air War and the Law of War', *Air Force Law Review*, 32 (1990), 95–7.

one observer later called 'a gentlemanly handicap', whereby the technologically advanced powers would limit their capacity to respond to guerrilla attacks.[16] If that was not the intention of those who negotiated the Protocol, it nevertheless persuaded the US military to oppose ratification. As the legal adviser to the State Department, Abraham Sofaer explained:

Before ratifying any agreement that deals with U.S. national security, we must be satisfied that the terms of agreement are reasonable and that they can be implemented without undue consequences in terms of U.S. casualties. Our Joint Chiefs of Staff have unanimously concluded that this is clearly not the case with respect to Protocol I. U.S. soldiers would have to pay the price for such unreasonable limitations through unnecessary casualties and charges of criminal activity.[17]

These military objections by themselves, however, were insufficient reason for refusing to ratify the Protocol. As defenders of the agreement noted, close US allies like the UK had become a party to Protocol I by reserving the right of reprisal and as the above quote suggested this path was open to the United States.[18] What strengthened the case for rejecting Protocol I, however, was a normative concern that international order relied on laws that restricted the right to wage war to the sovereign state. The focus here was Article 1 (4), which stated that IHL applied not only to those referred to in common Article 2 of the Geneva Conventions (i.e. 'armed conflict between two or more of the High Contracting Parties [states]') but also to

...armed conflicts which *peoples* are fighting against colonial domination and alien occupation and against racist regimes in the exercise of their right of self-determination, as enshrined in the Charter of the United Nations and the Declaration on Principles of International Law concerning Friendly Relations and Co-operation among States in accordance with the Charter of the United Nations.[19]

To the Reagan administration, which saw no reason to challenge what was perceived to be the objective and apolitical character of the laws that governed war between sovereign states, this statement unduly politicized international law by introducing 'vague' and 'subjective' standards to issues concerning

[16] Jeremy Rabkin, 'The Politics of the Geneva Conventions: Disturbing Background to the ICC Debate', *Virginia Journal of International Law*, 44 (2003), 182.

[17] Abraham Sofaer, 'Agora: The US Decision Not to Ratify Protocol I to the Geneva Conventions on the Protection of War Victims (cont'd)', *The American Journal of International Law*, 82 (1988), 785.

[18] Theodore Meron, 'The Time Has Come for the United States to Ratify Geneva Protocol I', *The American Journal of International Law*, 88 (1994), 682–4.

[19] Protocol Additional to the Geneva Conventions of 12 August 1949, and relating to the Protection of Victims of International Armed Conflicts (Protocol I), 8 June 1977. Emphasis added.

the applicability of IHL.[20] It argued that the 'political neutrality' of the 1949 Geneva Conventions was being jeopardized. Certain benefits might be derived from reform, but 'these would likely prove fleeting' in a world where the neutrality and thus moral force of the law was damaged.[21] Moreover, the Protocol elevated

the international legal status of self described 'national liberation' groups that make a practice of terrorism. This would undermine the principle that the rights and duties of international law attach principally to *entities that have those elements of sovereignty* that allow them to be held accountable for their actions and the resources to fulfil their obligations.[22]

Non-state groups, Sofaer went on to explain, lacked the resources and oftentimes the will to provide adequate protection for prisoners of war.[23] In this respect, Protocol I had, at least according to Deputy Assistant Secretary of Defense for Negotiations Douglas Feith, 'robbed civilian Peter to pay terrorist Paul'.[24] If international society were to treat national liberation movements as lawful combatants, then it would enhance their political status. To the extent that they could claim immunity from prosecution, it also enhanced their legal status vis-à-vis the sovereign state. It was, however, naive to expect that non-state groups would reciprocate by acting more responsibly. The decision to create new criteria for lawful belligerency in Articles 43 and 44 was dismissed in these terms. 'The changes', Sofaer argued, 'undermine the notion that the Protocol has secured an advantage for humanitarian law by granting terrorist groups protection as combatants.'[25] Under the old regime, a 'terrorist' could be prosecuted for hiding among civilians; now, at least according to Sofaer, the 'terrorist' could claim immunity from prosecution as a prisoner of war even though he had not made a sufficient effort to distinguish himself from the civilian population. This put at risk civilians by confusing the combatant–non-combatant distinction that was so clear in the 1949 Geneva Conventions.[26] While supporters of the Protocol responded by noting that members of national liberation movements who committed terrorist acts could still be prosecuted for war crimes, others questioned whether national liberation

---

[20] Reagan, Letter of Transmittal, 911.

[21] Douglas J. Feith, 'International Responses', in Uri Ra'anan et al. (eds.), *Hydra of Carnage. International Linkages of Terrorism. The Witnesses Speak* (Lexington, KY: Lexington Books, 1986), 272.

[22] The Position of the United States, 465. Emphasis added.

[23] The Position of the United States, 465; see also Feith, 'International Responses', 270.

[24] Feith, 'International Responses', 277.   [25] The Position of the United States, 467.

[26] Feith, 'International Responses', 278–9.

movements had the legislative and judicial capacity to do this.[27] This created a situation where certain 'causes' (i.e. those fighting racism, colonialism, and alien occupation) could claim the right of lawful belligerency without any prospect that the movements on their behalf would fulfil the duties expected of responsible actors in international society. In this regard, the Protocol threatened to repeat 'the long story of evils done in the name of "just war" '.[28] Supporters of Protocol I were therefore accused of being 'more concerned about protecting "national-liberation" fighters than they were about protecting civilians'.[29] The treaty was, Feith concluded, a 'law in the service of terror'.[30]

The Reagan administration further argued that international order, which was based on the state's exclusive right to violence, was threatened by this change to the laws of war. Thus, Sofaer warned that the provision in Article 1 (4) was a recipe for chaos. It

obliterated the traditional distinction between international and non-international armed conflicts. Any group within a national boundary, claiming to be fighting against colonial domination, alien occupation, or a racist regime, can now argue that it is protected by the laws of war, and that its members are entitled to POW status for their otherwise criminal acts. Members of radical groups in the United States have already done so in our own federal courts.[31]

What Sofaer did not make explicit, however, was the fact that the cases he had in mind were all examples of US courts rejecting the claim of criminal groups to POW status. The argument that Protocol I weakened the state's claim to hold an exclusive right to use legitimate force was nevertheless central to the US approach to IHL. In fact, it can help explain why the Reagan administration was willing to ratify amendments to common Article 3 of the Geneva Conventions, which related to the activities of non-state groups in non-international armed conflict. These were written into Protocol II, which extended humanitarian protections to 'dissident armed forces and other organized groups which under responsible command exercise such control over a part of its territory' (Article 1).[32] Crucially, however, it did not change that

---

[27] G. I. A. D. Draper, 'Wars of National Liberation and War Criminality', in Michael Howard (ed.), *Restraints on War. Studies in the Limitation of Armed Conflict* (Oxford: Oxford University Press, 1979), 154–5.

[28] Draper, 'Wars of National Liberation', 158.

[29] Douglas J. Feith, 'Protocol I: Moving Humanitarian Law Backwards', *Akron Law Review*, 19 (1986), 534.

[30] Douglas J. Feith, 'Law in the Service of Terror—The Strange Case of the Additional Protocol', *National Interest*, 1 (1985), 36–47.

[31] The Position of the United States, 465; see also Abraham Sofaer, 'Terrorism and the Law', *Foreign Affairs*, 64 (1986), 913.

[32] Protocol Additional to the Geneva Conventions of 12 August 1949, and relating to the Protection of Victims of Non-International Armed Conflicts (Protocol II), 8 June 1977.

aspect of common Article 3, which stated that the application of humanitarian protections 'shall not interfere with the legal status of the Parties to the conflict'.[33] In fact, Protocol II reaffirmed the state's sovereign right 'to maintain or re-establish law and order' (Article 3) by outlawing rebel groups and prosecuting their members through impartial courts (Article 6).[34] In contrast, Protocol I extended POW status and immunity from prosecution to national liberation movements and thus weakened the state's claim to have a monopoly on lawful violence. It undermined the sovereignty of states and, the US argued, their ability to maintain international order and combat terrorism.

As well as these military and normative concerns, the Reagan administration's rejection of Protocol I can also be understood in overtly political terms. For instance, much was made of the fact that the PLO had attended the negotiations and that its delegation had celebrated Protocol I because in their eyes it reaffirmed the legitimacy of their struggle.[35] Likewise, the PLO embraced what they saw as the protections accorded to their combatants by Article 44.[36] Supporters of the Protocol rejected any notion that national liberation movements like the PLO necessarily gained political and legal legitimacy or military advantage, and they argued that there was no need for the United States to buy into the PLO's rhetoric. It is clear, however, that the Reagan administration did listen to the PLO, and they were loath to hand this victory to Israel's enemy.[37] Israel was in fact the only state to vote against Article 1 (4) and it refused even to sign Protocol I. Handing the PLO a victory such as this would, Feith argued, enhance its ability 'to win support in the West—to raise funds and win diplomatic backing'.[38] He lambasted the Carter administration for signing the Protocol and for following an international consensus that was dominated by socialist and third world states. The United States, he argued, should have resisted the will of the majority and stood up for a policy where principle coincided with the interests of the United States and its allies.[39] As well as the military and normative concerns, therefore, one can also understand the rejection of Protocol I in terms of a nationalist administration's refusal to accept the consequences of Carter's 'consensus-mongering'.[40]

---

[33] Common Article 3, Geneva Conventions, 12 August 1949.
[34] Protocol II Additional to the Geneva Conventions.
[35] The United States Position, 467.   [36] Feith, 'International Responses', 276.
[37] See e.g. Feith, 'International Responses', 280.
[38] Feith, 'Moving Humanitarian Law Backwards', 534.
[39] Feith, 'International Responses', 272–4; Feith, 'Law in the Service of Terror', 43.
[40] Feith, 'International Responses', 280.

STATE SOVEREIGNTY AND THE WAR ON TERRORISM

One might argue that the threat to order posed by extending the right of lawful combatancy to non-state actors was exaggerated by the United States in order to complement its support for allies who were fighting national liberation movements, notably Israel. This does not mean that the sole reason for the United States refusing to ratify the Protocol was its policy towards Israel. In fact, Feith's focus was the defence of any state that was fighting the national liberation movements that were supported by the Soviet Union.[41] Rather, it simply means that the Protocol's recognition of the right of national liberation movements to engage in lawful combat was not necessarily the threat to the society of states that US rhetoric made out. In fact, one might argue that by only recognizing the right to lawful belligerency of those groups that aspired to statehood (i.e. national liberation movements) the Protocol actually reinforced the idea of a society of states.[42] The problem posed by the declaration of the war against al-Qaeda, however, is that it clearly did challenge the idea of a society of states by implying that war is an activity not merely of states or state-like actors but of transnational actors that do not even aspire to statehood. This of course was not the intention of the US government when it declared 'war' on al-Qaeda. That declaration, however, did pose a legal dilemma, particularly if one accepted the Reagan administration's concern that by extending the laws of war to non-state groups one 'enhances their stature' by treating them as soldiers.[43] The presence of Reagan appointees in the Bush administration, notably Douglas Feith who heavily influenced US thinking on Protocol I, suggests that such an argument might have influenced policy.[44] Furthermore, if one examines the documentary evidence that is now available, it is clear that US government lawyers sought to perpetuate a conception of international society that limited the right to wage war to states.

There is no denying that the Bush administration understood the 'war on terrorism' not simply as a rhetorical expression of resolve but as a declaration with profound legal effect. Indeed, Department of Justice (DOJ) lawyers made much of the fact that the President had been legally authorized by Congress 'to use all necessary and appropriate force' and that the UN Security Council had recognized America's right to defend itself against terrorist attacks.[45] Yet

---

[41] See generally Feith, 'Moving Humanitarian Law Backwards'.

[42] To reiterate the arguments of those that supported Protocol I, this in no way legitimized the manner in which national liberation movements chose to fight their war. The Protocol continued to outlaw terrorist tactics and individuals who implemented those tactics were liable for prosecution under national and international law.

[43] Sofaer, 'Agora: The US Decision Not to Ratify Protocol I', 786.

[44] Feith served as Under Secretary of Defense for Policy from July 2001 to August 2005.

[45] S.J.Res. 23, 14 September 2001, 107th Cong. 1st Sess.

they also made clear that the 'war on terrorism' was a different kind of war because Congress had authorized the use of force not only against 'nations', but also against '*organizations,* or *persons* he [the President] determined planned, authorized, committed, or aided the terrorist attacks'.[46] Implicit in this declaration was the threat to international order identified by the Reagan administration. If organizations or even individuals could wage war, then presumably they could claim POW status and avoid prosecution for violent acts that did not violate the laws of war. This weakened the state's monopoly on violence and the role it played in maintaining order. To avoid this problem and to avoid handing al-Qaeda a legal tool in the subsequent war, US lawyers recalled the category of unlawful belligerency.

According to the administration's interpretation of international society, those acting on behalf of states had an exclusive right to engage in lawful combat. Any 'organization' or 'person' pursuing violent acts against the state in a time of war were therefore 'unlawful combatants' that could be prosecuted by military commissions. This argument suited a dual purpose. First, by declaring 'war', this strategy concentrated power around the President and it guaranteed immunity from prosecution for American leaders as state actors. Second, by declaring that non-state actors were not lawful combatants it had the normative purpose of confining the right to wage war to representatives of sovereign states. Although it might sound counter-intuitive given the level of international opposition to America's legal strategy in the war on terrorism, it is clear that such a strategy was working *within* a concept of international society. The United States was in fact defending the state's exclusive right to wage war and it was in this sense seeking to reconstitute a pluralist conception of the society of states.

The US decision to apply those aspects of the laws of war that limit the right of belligerency to states was thus consistent with a narrow (pluralist) conception of international society. Its decision not to apply other aspects of the Geneva Conventions, however, clearly demonstrates a reluctance to abide by those broader (solidarist) conceptions of international society that place limits on the way war is conducted. It is argued here, however, that this move was not an outright rejection of international society; rather it too was grounded in a pluralist conception of international society based on state sovereignty. For instance, lawyers at the DOJ argued that the Third Geneva Convention, which would otherwise regulate US treatment of wartime detainees, did not apply to the war on terrorism because al-Qaeda was 'merely a violent political movement or organization and not a nation-state'.[47] Or, as Assistant Attorney

---

[46] Ibid. Emphasis added.

[47] Memo 4, Application of Treaties and Laws to al-Qaeda and Taliban Detainees. Memorandum (Draft) for William J. Haynes II General Counsel Department of Defense, from John Yoo

General Jay Bybee would put it in a memo to Counsel at the White House and the Pentagon

Common article 2, which triggers the Geneva Convention provisions regulating detention conditions and procedures for trial of POWs, is limited only to declared war or armed conflict 'between two or more of the High Contracting Parties'. Al Qaeda is not a High Contracting Party. As a result the U.S. military's treatment of Al Qaeda members is not governed by the bulk of the Geneva Conventions, specifically those provisions concerning POWs.[48]

Following this logic one might have expected a different conclusion with regard to detainees designated as Taliban. Lawyers outside the administration, for instance, argued that the Taliban soldiers automatically qualified as privileged combatants and therefore POWs because the Taliban was the de facto authority in control of Afghanistan, which was a state party to the Geneva Conventions.[49] Anticipating this argument, however, DOJ lawyers argued that Afghanistan was in fact a 'failed state', whose territory had been largely overrun and held by violent militia or faction. 'Accordingly, Afghanistan was without the attributes of statehood necessary to continue as a party to the Geneva Conventions, and the Taliban militia, like al-Qaeda, is therefore not entitled to the protections of the Geneva Conventions.'[50] The implication of this was

Deputy Assistant Attorney General and Robert J. Delahunty, Special Counsel, 9 January 2002, available in Karen J. Greenberg and Joshua L. Dratel (eds.), *The Torture Papers*, 38. This opinion was written, as the reference suggests, as a draft memo to the Department of Defense. The same argument appeared in the actual memo which is now published as Memo 6, Memorandum for Alberto R. Gonzales, Counsel to the President, and William J. Haynes II, General Counsel of the Department of Defense, 22 January 2002, from Jay S. Bybee Assistant Attorney General, 22 January 2002, available in Greenberg and Dratel (eds.), *The Torture Papers*, 81.

[48] Memo 4, Application of Treaties and Laws, 48. Memo 6, Memorandum for Alberto Gonzalez, 207. As noted in Chapter 2, these lawyers also argued that the United States was not bound by the Geneva Convention as an expression of customary international law because 'it would create severe distortions in the structure of the [US] Constitution'.

[49] For example, Marco Sassòli, 'The Status of Persons Held in Guantánamo under International Humanitarian Law', *Journal of International Criminal Justice*, 2 (2004), 102; George H. Aldrich, 'The Taliban, Al Qaeda, and the Determination of Illegal Combatants', *American Journal of International Law*, 96 (2002), 894–5.

[50] Memo 4, Application of Treaties and Laws, 50, 58–9. See also Memo 7. Memorandum for the President, Decision Re Application of the Geneva Convention on Prisoners of War to the Conflict with al-Qaeda and the Taliban, from Alberto R. Gonzales 25 January 2002, available in Greenberg and Dratel, *The Torture Papers*, 118. Even if the Taliban were identified as a militia, some argued that they were still entitled to POW status by virtue of their compliance with Article 4 conditions. For instance, it was argued that the black turbans of the Taliban were enough of a distinguishing feature for them to qualify as lawful combatants. The DOJ noted, however, that they had already been informed by the DOD that 'the Taliban militia failed to confirm its acceptance of the Geneva Conventions, did not fulfil its obligations, and did not act consistently with the most fundamental obligations of the laws of war, such as the prohibition on using civilians to shield military forces.' It also advised them 'that the Taliban militia's command

that no one could claim to be a lawful combatant while resisting the US occupation of Afghan territory because Afghanistan as a state did not exist until the United States had helped to re-establish a sovereign government. A further implication was that the Afghanis were in effect stateless people who as a result lacked those rights that were due others under international law.

These arguments were contested by the State Department. For instance, the State Department's legal adviser William Taft IV argued that

a distinction between our conflict with Al Qaeda and our conflict with the Taliban does not conform to the structure of the [Geneva] Conventions.... The Conventions call for a decision whether they apply to the conflict in Afghanistan. If they do, their provisions are applicable to all persons involved in the conflict—Al Qaeda, Taliban, Northern Alliance, U.S. troops, civilians etc.[51]

This interpretation of the law supported the political arguments of the State Department, which argued that the Conventions *should* apply to the conflict. In a memo sent to the White House on 26 January 2002, for instance, Secretary of State Colin Powell questioned a draft decision made on 18 January not to apply the Geneva Conventions to Taliban and al-Qaeda prisoners. It would, he argued, 'reverse over a century of US policy and practice...and undermine the protections of the law of war for our troops'.[52] Taft made similar political arguments. 'A decision that the Conventions do not apply to the conflict in Afghanistan', he argued, '...deprives our troops there of any claim to the protection of the Convention in the event they are captured and weakens the protections accorded by the Conventions to our troops in future conflicts'.[53]

structure probably did not meet the first of these [Article 4] requirements; that the evidence strongly indicates that the requirement of a distinctive uniform was not met; and that the requirement of conducting operations in accordance with the law and customs of armed conflict was not met' Memo 4, Application of Treaties and Laws, 61–2. See also Memo 12 Memorandum for Alberto R. Gonzales, Counsel to the President, Re: Status of Taliban Forces under Article 4 of the Third Geneva Convention of 1949, from James S. Bybee, Assistant Attorney General, 7 February 2002, available in Greenberg and Dratel, *The Torture Papers*, 136–43.

[51] Memo 10, Comments on Your Paper on the Geneva Convention, from William H. Taft, IV to Counsel to the President, 2 February 2002, available in Greenberg and Dratel, *The Torture Papers*, 129–33.

[52] Memo 8, Draft Decision Memorandum for the President on the Applicability of the Geneva Convention to the Conflict in Afghanistan, Memorandum to Counsel to the President, Assistant to the President for National Security Affairs, from Colin L. Powell, 26 January 2002, available in Greenberg and Dratel, *The Torture Papers*, 122–25. In a memo to the President a day earlier, Alberto Gonzales also noted that the Secretary of State had requested that the President reconsider the decision made on 18 January not to apply the Geneva Conventions to al-Qaeda and the Taliban. The memo also laid out other arguments for applying the Geneva Conventions such as 'undermining military culture'. Ultimately, however, Gonzales noted that 'the arguments for reconsideration and reversal [of the decision] are unpersuasive.' Memo 7. Memorandum for the President, 118–21.

[53] Memo 10, 'Comments on Your Paper', 129–33.

Nonetheless, the President decided on 7 February 2002, to adopt much of the argument presented by the DOJ and to stick by his decision not to apply the Geneva Conventions to al-Qaeda. 'By its terms', the President noted,

Geneva applies to conflicts involving 'High Contacting Parties', which can only be States. Moreover it assumes the existence of 'regular' armed forces fighting on behalf of States. However, the war against terrorism ushers in a new paradigm, one in which groups with broad, international reach commit horrific acts against innocent civilians, sometimes with the direct support of States. Our Nation recognizes that this new paradigm—ushered in not by us, but by terrorists—requires new thinking in the law of war, but thinking that should nevertheless be consistent with the principles of Geneva.[54]

The President went on to accept that 'none of the provisions of Geneva apply to our conflict with al-Qaeda in Afghanistan or elsewhere throughout the world because, among other reasons, al-Qaeda is not a High Contracting Party to Geneva'.[55] As a compromise, the President accepted that the Conventions applied to the Taliban but, based on the facts supplied to him by the Department of Defense (DOD) and the recommendation of the DOJ, *he had determined* that the Taliban detainees were unlawful combatants. He concluded that as '*a matter of policy*, the United States Armed Forces shall continue to treat detainees humanely and, to the extent appropriate and consistent with military necessity, in a manner consistent with the principles of Geneva.'[56]

What made this strategy so controversial of course was the fact that state sovereignty was no longer a constitutional rule of international society. States were expected to respect human rights and IHL. While human rights advocates could agree that al-Qaeda operatives were probably unlawful combatants and that international society should prosecute them as a means of restricting the right to wage war, they further argued that the United States could have achieved these objectives within the framework provided by the Geneva Conventions. Unlawful combatants could be prosecuted for violations of the laws of war under these Conventions, but any decision to deny them POW status and immunity from prosecution had to be confirmed *by a competent tribunal*.[57] From this perspective, in other words, the United States did not

---

[54] Memo 11, 'Humane Treatment of al Qaeda and Taliban Detainees, from President George Bush to the Vice President et al.', 7 February 2002, available in Greenberg and Dratel (eds.), *The Torture Papers*, 134.

[55] Memo 11, 'Humane Treatment'.

[56] Memo 11, 'Humane Treatment', 135. Emphasis added.

[57] Aldrich, 'The Taliban', 897. In anticipation of this argument, DOJ lawyers argued that under Article II of the US Constitution the President had the right to interpret treaties on behalf of the Nation. 'He could' therefore, 'interpret Geneva III, in light of the known facts concerning the operation of Taliban forces during the Afghanistan conflict, to find that all Taliban forces do not fall within the legal definition of prisoner of war as defined by Article 4. A presidential

need to suspend the Geneva Conventions unless it had other objectives, which were to detain individuals at the sole discretion of the President and to engage in interrogation practices that were otherwise prohibited. As we now know, this was indeed part of the reason for not applying the Geneva Conventions to the war on terrorism. In the memo used to dismiss the State Department's concerns, for instance, White House Counsel Alberto Gonzales argued that the 'new war'

places a high premium on . . . the ability to obtain information from captured terrorists and their sponsors in order to avoid further atrocities against American civilians, and the need to try terrorists for war crimes such as wantonly killing civilians. In my judgement, this new paradigm renders obsolete Geneva's strict limitations on questioning of enemy prisoners . . . [58]

This in itself was not an argument that could authorize the use of aggressive interrogation techniques. Read alongside other arguments, however, it con-tributes to a picture of an administration seeking legal authorization for such acts. For instance, DOJ lawyers argued that there was 'a wide range of such techniques that will not rise to the level of torture' and were not therefore proscribed by the law.[59] Likewise, a working group, which was set up to discuss the legal implications of the aggressive interrogation methods being considered by the Commander of Joint Task Force 170 in Cuba, recommended on 4 April 2003 that all the techniques that had been requested be approved.[60] Written to conform to the arguments of the DOJ, it noted that due

determination of this nature would eliminate any legal 'doubt' as to the prisoner's status, as a matter of domestic law, and would therefore obviate the need for Article 5 tribunals. Memo 6, Memorandum for Alberto Gonzales, 110. Bybee followed up this advice in another memo sent to Counsel to the President Alberto Gonzales. 'We believe that based on the facts provided by the Department of Defense . . . the President has reasonable grounds to conclude that the Taliban, as a whole, is not legally entitled to POW status under Articles 4(A)(1) through (3). . . . We therefore conclude that there is no need to establish tribunals to determine POW status under Article 5'. Memo 12, Memorandum for Alberto R. Gonzales, Counsel to the President, Re: Status of Taliban Forces Under Article 4 of the Third Geneva Convention of 1949, from James S. Bybee, Assistant Attorney General, 7 February 2002, in Greenberg and Dratel, *The Torture Papers*, 137.

[58] Memo 7, Memorandum for the President, Decision Re Application of the Geneva Con-vention on Prisoners of War to the Conflict with al-Qaeda and the Taliban, from Alberto R. Gonzales, 25 January 2002, in Greenberg and Dratel, *The Torture Papers*, 119.

[59] Memo 14, Memorandum for Alberto R. Gonzales, Counsel to the President, Standards of Conduct for Interrogation under 18 U.S.C. §§2340–2340A, from James S. Bybee, Assistant Attorney General, 1 August 2002, in Greenberg and Dratel (eds.), *The Torture Papers*, 173.

[60] Memo 26, Working Group Report on Detainee Interrogations in the Global War on Ter-rorism: Assessment of Legal, Historical, Policy and Operational Considerations, 4 April 2003, in Greenberg and Dratel (eds.), *The Torture Papers*, 286–359. On the drafting of this report and the attempts by the General Counsel to the Navy, Alberto Mora to reverse policy, see Jane Mayer, 'The Memo', *The New Yorker*, 20 February 2006. Mayer also reports that in March 2005 the Pentagon declared the working group report a non-operational 'historical' document.

to the unique nature of the war of terrorism in which the enemy covertly attacks innocent civilian populations without warning, and further due to the critical nature of information believed to be known by certain of the al Qaeda and Taliban detainees regarding future terrorist attacks, it may be appropriate for the appropriate approval authority to authorize as a military necessity the interrogation of such unlawful combatants in a manner beyond that which may be applied to a prisoner of war who is subject to the protections of the Geneva Conventions.[61]

The point here is not to cast judgement on the morality of this position. The question of whether torture or aggressive interrogation techniques are justified when faced with the prospect of another attack on the scale of 9/11 is beyond the scope of this chapter. The point, however, is that there were officials in the US government who argued that the threat posed by al-Qaeda was such that aggressive interrogation practices were required and that they were effective. In order to facilitate a policy to that effect, US lawyers advanced a conception of international society that restricted the right to wage war to the state and then stripped individuals of rights if they were to take up arms on behalf of any organization other than a state. For those who opposed US policy this was a strange and self-serving conception of international society. The evidence presented here, however, demonstrates that while it was no doubt self-serving it was a conception of international society that placed the sovereign state rather than the individual at the centre of its normative framework. It was, in other words, a pluralist conception of international society based on sovereign statehood and that enabled the Bush administration to further its idea of America's national interest.

STATE SOVEREIGNTY AND JUDICIAL OVERSIGHT

The concern that US officials could be held accountable for violating the laws of war as they hunted down the al-Qaeda network clearly informed the decision to declare the Geneva Conventions void in the war on terrorism. For instance, Gonzales argued that this decision '[s]ubstantially reduces the threat of domestic criminal prosecution under the War Crimes Act (18 U.S.C.2441)'. Adhering to the President's determination that the Geneva Conventions did not apply 'would guard effectively against misconstruction or misapplication of Section 2441'.[62] Yet the administration was not only concerned with challenges to its policy under the domestic application of IHL.

---

[61] Memo 26, 'Working Group Report on Detainee Interrogations', 287.
[62] Memo 7, Memorandum for the President, 119.

As the documentary evidence demonstrates, it was also very much concerned with possible challenges under US constitutional law, in particular the right of the detainees to challenge their detention in US courts. That evidence also demonstrates how lawyers again advanced a conception of international society based on state sovereignty because it was in this kind of society that the United States could best pursue its interests as defined by the Bush administration.

The question of the detainee's right to habeas corpus relief was dealt with specifically by DOJ lawyers in their memorandum to General Counsel to the Department of Defense, William J. Haynes II. Central to their argument that the detainees did not have the right to contest their detention in US courts was the 1950 Supreme Court decision in *Johnson* v. *Eisentrager*. This case involved German soldiers who had travelled to the Far East to continue the fight against the allies despite the German surrender in 1945. They had been detained by US forces in China and convicted of war crimes by an American military commission in Nanking. Having been transported back to post-war Germany, they contested their detention arguing that the 1929 Geneva Conventions had been violated. The US Supreme Court ruled then that as enemy aliens who had never entered the United States they had no right to appeal against their detention in US courts.[63]

Based on this ruling, the DOJ lawyers argued that the federal courts had no jurisdiction to entertain a petition for a writ of habeas corpus filed on behalf of the detainees because they were not US citizens, nor were they being held on US sovereign territory. The Guantánamo Bay base was in fact leased from Cuba in 1903, and while the lease agreement stated that the United States 'shall exercise complete jurisdiction and control over and within' the leased areas, it further stipulated that Cuba retained 'ultimate sovereignty'. On this basis, it was concluded 'that a district court cannot properly entertain an application for a writ of habeas corpus by an enemy alien detained at Guantánamo Naval Base, Cuba.'[64] This argument was tested before US courts when lawyers acting on behalf of British, Australian, and Kuwaiti detainees filed a complaint seeking to be informed of the charges against them, to be allowed to meet with their families and with counsel, and to have access to the courts or some other impartial tribunal. In decisions that agreed with the US government's argument, a district court and then the Court of Appeals

---

[63] Memo 3, Possible Habeas Jurisdiction over Aliens Held in Guantánamo Bay, Cuba, from Patrick F. Philbin, Deputy Assistant Attorney General and John Yoo, Deputy Assistant Attorney General, to William J. Haynes II, General Counsel, Department of Defense, 28 December 2001, available in Greenberg and Dratel, *The Torture Papers*, 29–37.

[64] Memo 3, Possible Habeas Jurisdiction, 37.

ruled that it had no jurisdiction to entertain claims from aliens held outside the sovereign territory of the United States.[65]

The government's argument, and the initial willingness of the US courts to accept it, again reveals why the United States has a particular interest in defending the society of states. In this case, American lawyers used the principle of sovereignty to help manufacture what Lord Johan Steyn called 'a legal black hole'.[66] Those captured on the Afghan battlefield or elsewhere did not have rights as POWs because they were acting on behalf of a non-state entity that could not consent to the laws of war and could not therefore engage in legitimate acts of violence. Yet, if this made them criminals, they could not claim the civil rights they were entitled to under American law because they were not being held on US sovereign territory. The implication of the US argument was that the detainees had a right to appeal to the Cuban government because it retained 'ultimate sovereignty', but, of course, the Cuban government was in no position to contest the ultimate control that the US military asserted over the base at Guantánamo. To the extent that the detainees had rights as nationals of other states, these merely translated into diplomatic protests, which Washington could easily ignore because no other state had jurisdiction or any real political influence.[67] The US judiciary, in other words, had convinced itself that the President knew how best to respond to al-Qaeda. It was, moreover, happy to acknowledge that the area between sovereign states was anarchical and that the President could legitimately wield US power in this space without fear of legal redress or restraint.

It may be coincidence that the judiciary's willingness to defer to the executive on this point changed after the graphic evidence of abuse in an Iraqi prison was made public in 2004. Regardless of the impact of the scandal, the US Supreme Court overturned prior decisions in its decision on *Rasul* v. *Bush*, which was delivered in the summer of that year. It found that the detainees at Guantánamo differed from those in *Eisentrager* because they

are not nationals of countries at war with the United States, and they deny that they have engaged in or plotted acts of aggression against this country; they have never been afforded access to any tribunal, much less charged with and convicted of wrongdoing;

---

[65] *Rasul* v. *Bush*, 215 F.Supp. 2d 55 (DC Dist. 2002), LEXIS 14031; *Al Odah et al.* v. *United States*, 321 F.3d 1134 (DC Cir. 2003), LEXIS 4250.

[66] Lord Johan Steyn, 'Guantánamo Bay: The Legal Black Hole. 27th F. A. Mann Lecture, 25 November, 2003', reprinted in *International and Comparative Law Quarterly*, 53 (2004), 1–15.

[67] Attempts to seek redress in foreign courts also failed. While expressing surprise that 'the writ of the United States courts does not run in respect of individuals held by the government on the territory that the United States hold as lessee under a long term agreement', a Court of Appeal for England and Wales nonetheless found that it did not have jurisdiction. *R (Abbasi and another)* v. *Secretary of State for Foreign and Commonwealth Affairs* [2002] EWCA Civ. 1598.

and for more than two years they have been imprisoned in territory over which the United States exercises exclusive jurisdiction and control.[68]

Although this decision prompted the DOD to set up Combatant Status Review Tribunals, it did not stop the administration and its supporters in Congress from pursuing a policy of trial by military commission.[69] In the fall of 2004, however, a US District Court Judge James Robertson ruled that the proposed trial of Salim Ahmed Hamdan, Osama bin-Laden's former driver, was unlawful because the DOD had failed to recognize the possibility that the detainee could be a POW protected by the Third Geneva Convention.[70] In reversing this decision, the Court of Appeals for the District of Columbia circuit sided with the government's formulation that because al-Qaeda was not a state Hamdan could not apply for the protections or immunities that were afforded POWs under the Geneva Convention.[71] In an effort to prevent the Supreme Court reversing this decision, Congress then passed the Detainee Treatment Act (DTA), which sought to remove the jurisdiction that the Supreme Court had found to exist in *Rasul*. However, in *Hamdan* v. *Rumsfeld*, which was delivered in June 2006, the Supreme Court denied the government's motion to dismiss the case based on the DTA. In a 5–3 decision (the new Chief Justice John Roberts took no part in the deliberation or decision because of his prior involvement at the Appeals Court stage), it ruled that the military commissions violated the Uniform Code of Military Justice *and* the Geneva Conventions.[72]

There are two aspects to the Supreme Court's intervention worth focusing on here. The first is the decision, despite the arguments of the executive and legislative branches, to extend the jurisdiction of US courts to Guantánamo Bay. In *Rasul*, for instance, the Court in effect stated that US law could fill the void that the executive had manufactured by arguing that IHL did not apply to the war on terrorism. As Justice Kennedy put it in his concurring opinion:

Guantánamo Bay is in every practical respect a United States territory, and it is one far removed from any hostilities.... From a practical perspective, the indefinite lease of Guantánamo Bay has produced a place that belongs to the United States, extending the 'implied protection' of the United States to it.[73]

---

[68]   *Rasul* v. *Bush*, 542 US 466 (2004), LEXIS 4760.
[69]   Department of Defense, 'Combatant Status Review Tribunal Order Issues', News Release No. 651-04, 7 July 2004.
[70]   *Hamdan* v. *Rumsfeld*, 344 F. Supp. 2d 152; 2004 US Dist. LEXIS 22724.
[71]   *Hamdan* v. *Rumsfeld*, 367 US App. D.C. 265; 415 F.3d 33, 2005 US App. LEXIS 14315.
[72]   *Hamdan* v. *Rumsfeld*, No. 05-184, Supreme Court of the United States, 2006, LEXIS 5185.
[73]   Concurring Opinion of Justice Kennedy, *Rasul* v. *Bush* (2004).

This provoked the following dissent from Justice Scalia:

Since 'jurisdiction and control' obtained through a lease is no different in effect from 'jurisdiction and control' acquired by lawful force of arms, parts of Afghanistan and Iraq should logically be regarded as subject to our domestic laws. Indeed, if 'jurisdiction and control' rather than sovereignty were the test, so should the Landsberg prison in Germany, where the United States held the *Eisentrager* detainees.[74]

For Scalia, US courts had no jurisdiction over Guantánamo Bay because Cuba was 'the ultimate sovereign'. This argument, that state sovereignty is a defence against imperialism disguised as extraterritoriality, mirrors the pluralist position against the exercise of universal jurisdiction, which was discussed in Chapter 3. It can be argued, as indeed Chapter 3 concluded, that while the pluralist position articulated by Scalia may be genuinely concerned for international order and for self-determination based on sovereign states, it also suits the particular interests of a US government that seeks to construct anarchical spaces and avoid effective legal restraint. Scalia's intention no doubt was to prevent judicial adventurism and imperialism. The consequence, however, is that he was defending a conception of international society based on state sovereignty where US power is not effectively checked either by international or by domestic law. In this sense, Scalia's concern to prevent the extraterritorial application of US law ends up legitimizing a potentially more pernicious form of neoimperialism. As it turned out the concern over the extraterritorial application of US law was mitigated by the later ruling in *Hamdan* that IHL did govern US actions in Guantánamo.

The eventual application of IHL to the war on terrorism is the second aspect of the Supreme Court's intervention that is significant here. In *Hamdan*, the Supreme Court did not decide the merits of the government's argument that the Geneva Conventions did not apply because al-Qaeda was a non-state actor.[75] This is because, as Justice Stevens stated, 'there is at least one provision in the Geneva Conventions that applies here even if the relevant conflict is not one between signatories.'[76] This provision was Article 3 common to all four Geneva Conventions. It provides that in a 'conflict not of an international character, occurring in the territory of one of the High Contracting Parties, each Party to the conflict shall be bound to apply' certain minimum provisions. These include the humane treatment of detainees and a prohibition

---

[74] Dissenting Opinion of Justice Scalia, in *Rasul* v. *Bush*, 2004.

[75] Although see Dissenting Opinion of Justice Thomas in *Hamdan* v. *Rumsfeld*, 2006, 49, in which he argues that the 'President's findings about the nature of the present conflict ... represents a core exercise of his commander-in-chief authority that this Court is bound to respect.'

[76] Opinion of Justice Stevens, in *Hamdan* v. *Rumsfeld*, 2006, 66.

on 'the passing of sentences...without previous judgment pronounced by a regularly constituted court affording all the judicial guarantees which are recognized as indispensable by civilized peoples'.[77] In the Supreme Court's view, therefore, the Geneva Conventions did govern the war on terror and this latter provision made the military commissions illegal.

DOJ lawyers had anticipated this argument, but had argued that like Article 2, which did not apply because al-Qaeda was not a state, Article 3 was also inapplicable because the war against al-Qaeda was international in scope. As John Yoo and Robert Delahunty argued in their advice to the DOD, Article 3 applied only to civil wars that took place on the territory of state parties. It did not apply to those international conflicts like the war on terrorism, where one of the parties is a transnational actor.[78] This argument was, moreover, accepted by the Court of Appeals, which ruled that while the conflict was not of an 'international character' (thus ruling out application under Article 2), it was nonetheless 'international in scope' (thus ruling out application under Article 3).[79] For Justice Stevens, however, this reasoning was 'erroneous'.[80] He ruled that the scope of Article 3 was much broader and applied to transnational wars as well as to civil wars. His evidence for this was the fact that 'limiting language that would have rendered Common Article 3 applicable "especially [to] cases of civil war, ..." was omitted from the final version of the Article'.[81] Thus, the Supreme Court ruled that the Geneva Conventions were applicable and that the procedures of the government's military commissions did not meet its standards.

CONCLUSION

The decision to apply IHL pertaining to non-international conflict is significant because it closed the anarchical space between sovereign states that the Bush administration first sought to construct and then sought to exploit. While the *Hamdan* judgment said nothing about the government's power to detain enemy combatants for the duration of the war on terror, it did rule that the protections of Common Article 3 of the Geneva Conventions applied to that conflict. This was a blow to the US government's strategy,

[77] Geneva Conventions I–IV, Article 3.
[78] Memo 4 Application of Treaties and Laws, 46.
[79] *Hamdan* v. *Rumsfeld*, 2005, LEXIS 14315. See also Dissenting Opinion of Justice Thomas, in *Hamdan* v. *Rumsfeld*, 2006, 42–3.
[80] Opinion of Justice Stevens, in *Hamdan* v. *Rumsfeld*, 2006, 67.
[81] Opinion of Justice Stevens, in *Hamdan* v. *Rumsfeld*, 2006, 68.

which had sought to tackle a transnational problem (al-Qaeda) through the institutions of the society of sovereign states because it is in that kind of society that the US government can conduct its policy free from any real restraint. The argument that individuals acquired rights only as citizens of states and that these were forfeited by members of transnational armed forces was manufactured to legitimize a policy that involved the abuse of detainees. The Supreme Court's intervention acted as a check on the US government and it did so in part by using an alternative (solidarist) conception of international society. In such a society, individuals have rights because they are human beings and not because they are citizens of particular states or members of particular organizations. It is, at least according to a majority of justices on the Supreme Court, incumbent on the US government to respect those rights. Whether those rights were to be respected merely because the United States was a party to the Geneva Conventions or because they were considered peremptory norms of international society is left unsaid. However, Justice Kennedy's concurring argument that it is 'domestic statutes' that control the case and that Congress has the power to change those statutes if it wishes to do so suggests that sovereign consent remains at the core of American understandings of international society.[82]

At the centre of this debate was the Bush administration's claim that the 9/11 attacks had changed international society by ushering in a new legal paradigm. In fact, some of the arguments used by US lawyers to construct this paradigm are not so new and indeed somewhat familiar to students of international society. As Hedley Bull noted, the doctrine that states 'alone have the right to use force' is a 'fundamental or constitutional principle' of international society.[83] Sovereign states have for a long time 'sought to preserve for themselves a monopoly of the legitimate use of violence'. This, he also noted, came about in two stages:

first the forging of the distinction between public war, or war waged on the authority of a public body, and private war, or war waged without any such authority, and the curtailment of the latter; and second, the emergence of the idea that the state was the only public body competent to confer such authority.[84]

Of course, this process was part of the original 'Grotian moment', when the modern Westphalian conception of international society was struggling to be born. What this chapter has argued is that a similar process is presently

[82] Opinion of Justice Kennedy, concurring in part, in *Hamdan* v. *Rumsfeld*, 2006, 2. See also Justice Alito's Dissenting Opinion that it is domestic law that determines what the Geneva Conventions mean by 'a regularly constituted court'. Dissenting Opinion of Justice Alito, in *Hamdan* v. *Rumsfeld*, 3.

[83] Bull, *The Anarchical Society*, 65–6.   [84] Bull, *The Anarchical Society*, 178–9.

taking place now that the Westphalian conception of international society is being challenged by violent TNAs. The United States, as noted throughout this book, is among the most tenacious defenders of the Westphalian system and the Bush administration's argument that individuals fighting on behalf of transnational entities like al-Qaeda cannot be lawful combatants is very much part of that process. Far from being a 'new' paradigm, the US government recalls a very old conception of international society to wage its war against terrorism.

The reason US policy appeared 'new', even to the Bush administration, was because international society since 1949 has been characterized by the postmodern belief that individuals are protected by international law even in a time of war. International society, in other words, has evolved in a solidarist direction. For the Bush administration, however, this hindered the fight against terrorism. It therefore sought to construct an 'anarchical society', where the rights of states and their nationals were recognized and enforced by states, but where the rights of individuals and members of stateless entities disappeared into a legal void between states. In such a society, the United States was under no obligation to respect the protections that were afforded these persons under the Geneva Conventions. Moreover, in such a society, where states were the only means of enforcing international law, the US government had nothing to fear. It could simply ignore the protestations of other governments and, as Chapter 3 demonstrated, it could coerce any national government that dared launch legal action. As in its opposition to the ICC, the United States defends the society of states because its principles help to discredit postmodern challengers and because it is in this kind of society that the United States can secure its particular interests more easily.

8

Conclusion: International Society and American Empire

There is a tendency to see American foreign policy under the Bush adminis-tration as a threat to international society. In 2003, for instance, Tim Dunne questioned whether 'the dominant rules and institutions of the twentieth century international society remain intelligible today'.[1] The institutions of sovereignty and non-intervention were, he suggested, being threatened by America's offensive security strategy, which involved the use of pre-emptive and preventative military force. This was illustrated clearly by the US invasion of Iraq in March 2003, which according to Dunne was illegitimate 'given the complete absence of consensus that such conduct was appropriate'.[2] The fact that the United States was willing to ignore rules in this manner, and the fact that it was an explicit goal of the Bush administration to maintain the imbal-ance of power that enabled it to act in this way with impunity, suggested that the United States stood 'in opposition to international society as understood by classical English School writers'.[3] In fact, Dunne concludes that US military power and its post-9/11 policy

signal the emergence of an imperial authority that is hostile to many of the norms and values associated with the UN system. This does not mean that the US will oppose the rules and institutions of international society in all respects but it will retain an option to disregard the rights of other members. Like a suzerain power, it sets its own legal and moral standard, and admits to no external sources of authority.[4]

Dunne is right to argue that the United States is in a position to pick-and-choose which international laws it respects. Set against the evidence presented in this book, however, it is apparent that the United States can guarantee certain privileges even when it acts *within* the boundaries of international society. The reason the United States defends the principle that states have an exclusive right to prosecute war criminals is because it is in a position of such

---

[1] Tim Dunne, 'Society and Hierarchy in International Relations', *International Relations*, 17 (2003), 303.
[2] Dunne, 'Society and Hierarchy', 314.   [3] Dunne, 'Society and Hierarchy', 315.
[4] Dunne, 'Society and Hierarchy', 315.

power relative to other states that it is able to guarantee effective immunity for its citizens. Moreover, in this context, the 'UN system', which Dunne sets up in opposition to US imperialism, is nothing of the sort. In fact, the UN system merely codifies the privileges of the suzerain power by notionally legitimizing judicial intervention into the affairs of other communities while shielding the great powers from similar forms of accountability.[5]

Of course, the United States does not present its opposition to the ICC and its defence of the society of states in these terms. As noted in Chapters 5 and 6, the United States claims to be motivated by a concern for democracy and international security. Yet the ICC is not a threat to these values and thus it is difficult to avoid the conclusion that the United States makes these arguments for another purpose. Indeed, its policy on the ICC recalls E. H. Carr's now famous attack on 'the doctrine of the harmony of interests'. Under this heading, Carr argued that powerful members of any society, national or international, often clothed their 'own interest in the guise of a universal interest for the purpose of imposing it on the rest'.[6] Set against the challenge posed by the ICC, it is easy to see how the US defence of an international society of states fits Carr's thesis. This final chapter elaborates on that thesis as a means of summarizing the main points of the book. It has the additional purpose of demonstrating the modified Realist argument that international society exists because it suits the interests of the great powers. This, however, does not mean that the ICC is set to fail. Such a conclusion ignores the fact that certain ideals, especially those of the Court, have a power of their own and that too is something Carr would have recognized. The utopian who ignores the influence of power is, he noted, hopelessly misguided, but 'the realist, who believes that, if you look after the power, the moral authority will look after itself, is equally in error'.[7]

A HARMONY OF INTERESTS?

Jack Goldsmith and Stephen Krasner invoke Carr's realism in order to criticize the idealism of the Court. For them, the Court 'represents a folly reminiscent of the League of Nations' because its aims are unacceptable to the world's

---

[5] Like Dunne, Linklater and Suganami warn of the 'evil of unilateralism masquerading as solidarism', *The English School of International Relations*, 272. It might be said that his argument here is a warning of unilateralism masquerading as pluralism.

[6] E. H. Carr, *The Twenty Years' Crisis 1919–39. An Introduction to the Study of International Relations*, 2nd edn. (Basingstoke, UK: Palgrave, 2001), 71.

[7] Carr, *The Twenty Years' Crisis*, 93.

most powerful nation.[8] However, Goldsmith and Krasner's reading of Carr is incomplete despite their acknowledgement of Carr's own idealism. Carr attacked the utopianism of the 1920s and 1930s not only because it was unrealistic. For Carr, the interwar idealists had been in denial because they also failed to acknowledge how power relations between states were being affected by their plans for peace. The liberal assumption that all states were interested in peace was only allowed to influence policy because it helped the dominant states marshal support for an international order that advanced their particular interests. Yet for Carr that liberal vision was inherently naive because it continued to advance the interests of the 'haves' at the expense of the 'have nots'. When the great powers called for cooperation to enforce the rule of law, therefore, they were not necessarily interested in the common good. Rather, they were more interested in legitimizing and maintaining their own privileged positions in international society.[9]

Had Goldsmith and Krasner applied this reading of Carr, they may have reached a different conclusion on the question of US opposition to the ICC. As noted in Chapter 4, the US government argues that the creation of the ICC is a threat not only to international justice—because the Prosecutor will inevitably pursue politicized prosecutions—it is also a threat to international peace and security—because the Prosecutor will be insensitive to the politics of the conflict he is investigating. It further argues that the common good is best served by keeping the means of referral within the boundaries of international society (i.e. the UN Security Council). Only then can the world be certain of a prudent and impartial pursuit of justice. There is therefore, at least according to the US government, a harmony between its particular interests in maintaining a veto on the judicial process and the universal interest in the responsible exercise of criminal prosecutions. Yet, as Carr would tell us, this kind of argument is usually nothing more than 'an ingenious moral device invoked . . . by privileged groups in order to justify and maintain their dominant position'.[10] As Chapter 4 concluded, the United States opposes the Court not because it is concerned about the common good per se but because it has lost the ability to determine what the common good is.

To be sure, the ICC is a threat to the society of states but the point here is that it is not necessarily contrary to the universal interest. As Chapter 4 argued, the creation of an Independent Prosecutor in fact democratizes how decisions on international criminal justice are made by, in effect, giving a voice to those who are otherwise silenced by national and international society. The United States argues that the Independent Prosecutor is unaccountable and a threat

---

[8] See Jack Goldsmith and Stephen D. Krasner, 'The Limits of Idealism', *Daedalus* (2003), 57.
[9] Carr, *The Twenty Years' Crisis*, 79.   [10] Carr, *The Twenty Years' Crisis*, 75.

to international peace and security but it was argued in Chapter 4 that this is an instrumental rather than a normative argument. The so-called 'Singapore Compromise', codified by Article 16 of the Statute, allows the Security Council to postpone an independent investigation by the Prosecutor if it identifies that investigation to be a genuine threat to international peace and security. What the United States cannot accept, however, is that such an intervention requires the votes of nine members of the Security Council. Thus, the United States alone cannot stop the Prosecutor proceeding with an investigation. Article 16, in other words, may respond to a common interest in the prudent pursuit of international criminal justice, but it does not respond to the US government's need to control when and where justice is done. In this respect, it debunks the claim that a harmony exists between the United States and the universal interest and it exposes an imperial attitude to international criminal justice.

There is, however, an additional twist to this conclusion and again Carr's critical realism alerts us to it. To repeat the above claim, Carr argued that it 'will not be difficult to show that the utopian, when he preaches the doctrine of the harmony of interests, is innocently and unconsciously ... clothing his own interest in the guise of a universal interest for the purpose of imposing it on the rest of the world'.[11] Yet Carr also noted how

[t]he supremacy within the community of the privileged group may be, and often is, so overwhelming that there is, in fact, a sense in which its interests are those of the community, since its well-being necessarily carries with it some measure of well-being for other members of the community as a whole. In so far, therefore, as the alleged natural harmony of interests has any reality, it is created by the overwhelming power of the privileged group, and is an excellent illustration of the Machiavellian maxim that morality is the product of power.[12]

This essentially reflects the outcome of the Security Council debates that were the subject of Chapter 6. Given the American capacity to undermine UN peacekeeping, the UK recognized that it was in the common interest to appease US demands and grant exemptions from the Court's jurisdiction to US personnel serving on UN missions. By changing the legal status of these individuals, Resolutions 1422 (2002) and 1487 (2003) changed the international morality that had been accepted at Rome. Of course, not all states accepted the British argument that power should be allowed to define morality in this way. The German and Canadian delegations led the arguments against these resolutions and in effect challenged Security Council members to call the US's bluff. However, the United States did veto the renewal of the peacekeeping

<hr/>

[11]   Carr, *The Twenty Years' Crisis*, 71.   [12]   Carr, *The Twenty Years' Crisis*, 75.

mandate in Bosnia and that was enough evidence for those on the Security Council to regard the threat to international peace and security as genuine. Such was the imbalance of power that the Security Council was unable to follow its traditional course and impose sanctions on the state posing the threat (i.e. the United States). Instead, it appeased US demands and redefined, at least temporarily, international law.

To accept that the British argument in favour of appeasing US demands was inspired by a genuine concern for the common interest is one thing, but this does not mean that the US demands themselves were inspired by a similar concern. As Chapter 6 makes clear, the US demand grew out of its failure to win the argument at the Rome Conference and at subsequent PrepComs. The United States was unable to guarantee control of the referral process and it was unable, as Ambassador Scheffer put it, to find 'the silver bullet' that would guarantee protection against the prosecution of US service personnel. It eventually gained those exemptions through the institutions of international society (i.e. the UN system) because it is there that US power is more effective. At Rome, the United States had to convince 120 states and hundreds of influential NGOs of its case and it failed, whereas at the UN Security Council in New York it only had to convince 14 other states most of which could be persuaded to sign up to the US–British argument. Had the United States accepted the outcome of the Rome Conference, however, these states would never have faced a dilemma and the compromise that 'justice' made to 'order' would not have been needed. Ultimately, the US stance proves another of Carr's insights.

> The utopian, however eager he may be to establish an absolute standard, does not argue that it is the duty of his country, in conformity with that standard, to put the interest of the world at large before its own interest; for that would be contrary to his theory that the interest of all coincides with the interest of each. He argues that what is best for the world is best for his country, and then reverses the argument to read that what is best for his country is best for the world, the two propositions being, from the utopian standpoint, identical; and this unconscious cynicism of the contemporary utopian has proved [to be an] effective diplomatic weapon.... [13]

In other words, the United States recognized that the continuation of peace-keeping was in the national interest as well as the world's interest. Yet it was not willing to put the world at large and its demand that peacekeepers operate under the jurisdiction of the ICC before its particular interest in immunity for US service personnel. Instead, it argued that what was best for the world was best for the United States and then reversed the argument to read what was best for United States (immunity for peacekeepers) was in fact best for the

---

[13] Carr, *The Twenty Years' Crisis*, 71

UN because only then could it guarantee troop contributions. If this policy was cynical, it could hardly be unconscious. The strategy was exposed by those who opposed it, which included America's traditional allies. As Carr anticipated, however, it was a very effective diplomatic weapon. The United States did convince international society to back its policy of immunities for peacekeepers and it did legitimize that situation in terms of the world's interest in peacekeeping, at least up until the time of the Abu-Ghraib scandal.

EMPIRE OF LIBERTY?

The key point is that the United States is keen to defend the society of states against postmodern challengers like the ICC because the rules and practices of that society offer a means of legitimizing the privileged position that the United States occupies. Because the society of states limits the decision on when to pursue criminal justice either to individual states or to the UN Security Council, it enables the United States, as the most powerful state, to avoid this form of accountability. The defence of the society of states, in other words, is a subtle form of neoimperialism that is designed to maintain the privileges of a suzerain power. Yet, for those who oppose the ICC, US policy is not merely a matter of protecting the national interest. Rather, US policy is also about protecting an international order based on independent, self-governing states because it is only within this kind of order that liberty can truly develop. The United States defends the society of states in other words not merely because it suits America's particular interests, but also because it is at the level of the nation-state that accountability and democracy are strongest. If the society of states is an aspect of America's empire therefore, then it is from this perspective (and to use a phrase that clearly resonates in American history) an 'empire of liberty'.

The first difficulty for defenders of the US position is that the ICC is not a threat to democracy or accountability at the level of the nation-state. As Chapter 4 noted, the Rome Statute recognizes that accountability is often best served at a national level and through the principle of complementarity it encourages nation-states to implement legislation that will lead to appropriate prosecutions. Given this, one might again suggest that the supposed harmony between US interests and 'democracy' is simply another cynical argument designed to disguise the pursuit of particular interests. As Chapter 5 illustrates, however, there is more to US policy than simply the pursuit of interests. The United States is unable to accept the complementarity regime because of a strong image of itself as an independent and exceptional political and legal community. If the United States were truly concerned about the role criminal accountability plays in realizing the enlightenment goal of liberty for all, it would be forced to acknowledge that the society of states has a very poor record in this regard. Yet, unlike other democracies, the United States refuses to recognize that this is a reason to pool its sovereignty and to construct an alternative to the society of states. This is because the idea of a society of states allows American nationalists to construct a particular image of the United States. This is the image of the United States as *the* example of an enlightened political community governed by the rule of law.

To help construct this image, the United States defends those international rules that recognize all states as independent political and legal communities. In this respect, the laws that help to constitute the society of states also help to constitute American exceptionalism. Likewise, the social processes that construct American nationalism will ultimately reaffirm the consciousness that underpins the society of states, that is it will reaffirm the idea that the world is divided into distinct moral and legal communities. As Chapter 5 noted, the exemplarism that is so deeply embedded in American culture existed before 1776. Since that time, however, the sense of destiny, which was a product of religion, became fused with the enlightenment idea that independent communities were based on the consent of the governed. In the nationalist's mindset, therefore, the United States was and still is destined to be the vanguard of the enlightenment. To acknowledge, therefore, that the world needs an alternative to the society of states in order to save the enlightenment idea of universal liberty is to attack the very idea that the United States can be both independent of the world and an example to it.

A second problem for those defending the US position is that it is ultimately very costly. There is much to admire in the US Constitution and the example that American society sets is far from being inappropriate. Yet the question remains whether the example it does set is powerful enough to promote a system of accountability that will guarantee the enlightenment idea of universal liberty. States have proved themselves unwilling or unable to protect people from the most heinous forms of violence and repression. What is perhaps even more damning is that by tolerating impunity the society of states has often failed even to protect *the idea* of humanity. If the society of states allows individuals to portray people as inhuman and to slaughter them without fear of accountability, then the society of states is clearly an obstacle to the goals of justice and liberty. Almost out of frustration with this limitation, US foreign policy has shifted from the exemplarism of what Mead called the 'Jeffersonian tradition' to the interventionism of the Wilsonians. In the context of international criminal justice, this is reflected in America's alternative to the ICC as outlined in Chapter 5. The United States could not support the ICC but in situations where violations are grave and the political will of the sovereign state is weak, we should work, using any influence we have, to strengthen that will. In situations where violations are so grave as to amount to a breach of international peace and security, and the political will to address these violations is non-existent, the international community may, and if necessary should, intercede through the UN Security Council as we did in Bosnia and Rwanda.[14]

All empires have their costs and it is through this aspect of American foreign policy that the costs exacted by the empire of liberty are becoming apparent. As Chapter 6 noted, the US Congress was unwilling to create additional ad hoc courts for Sudan, in part because the Bush administration had previously attacked them for being inefficient. Furthermore, in Iraq the costs of nation building for the purpose of bringing justice to a tyrannical regime have proven extremely costly. Despite these costs, however, the United States continues to try to make the society of states work through its policy of 'democracy promotion' and 'regime change' because its image as the example and the leader of this kind of society is dependent on it.

A third problem for those defending the US position is that it lacks legitimacy. This is especially the case when the United States acts outside the UN system (as in Iraq), but it is also the case when the United States pursues criminal justice through the society of states (as in Yugoslavia and Rwanda). This is because, as noted in Chapters 3 and 6, the United States exploits the way in which the judicial process in this society is vulnerable to the exercise of power. Because individual states exercising universal jurisdiction (e.g. Belgium) are easily influenced by America's relative power and because the Security Council is subject to the great power veto, the international criminal process in the society of states is almost inevitably weakened by the charge of selective justice. Selective justice is better than no justice at all, but clearly there are profound costs to it. Essentially selective justice says to certain victims that their humanity will not be recognized because it is inconvenient for the great power to do so. In this respect, ad hoc justice tends to be self-defeating. An ad hoc court may help reaffirm a common consciousness based on humanity, but it also leaves others wondering why they too are not granted their day in court. It can reaffirm a faith in humanity while simultaneously destroying it.

The hold that American exceptionalism has on US policymakers is such, however, that they are often blind to these costs. The argument that the United States should control the criminal justice process through its position on the Security Council is directly related to the image those policymakers have of America. Because America is seen as an example to, and a leader of the society

---

[14] Marc Grossman, 'American Foreign Policy and the International Criminal Court', Remarks to the Center for Strategic and International Studies, Washington, DC, 6 May 2002.

of states, US policymakers argue that they should be able to determine when and where international criminal justice is done. Far from seeing the costs of ad hoc justice, US policymakers reassure themselves that there is in fact a harmony between the US national interest and the world's interests. This thinking may be sincere, as Carr noted. Indeed, Michael Hunt argues that US diplomats are particularly prone to this way of thinking because of the cultural assumption that US foreign policy is following the enlightenment's script. In this case, however, the assumption that 'by serving themselves Americans would serve the world' is mistaken.[15] The ICC democratizes the process of international criminal justice and does so in a prudent way that does not threaten international peace and security, nor does it threaten democracy based on the nation-state. In this context, and despite its rhetoric, US policy is more about defending the privileges of empire than it is about advancing the cause of liberty.

A 'KANTIAN SOLUTION' IN A 'GROTIAN MOMENT'?[16]

But what about the ICC and those states that support it? Can they claim to be any less self-interested than the United States? For some, the Court is merely an extension of the European impulse to reassert political control over the sovereign states of post-colonial international society; an impulse that was clearly on display in the attempts to prosecute the Senator Pinochet and Foreign Minister Yerodia.[17] The fact that its first investigations involve situations in the Sudan, the DRC, and Uganda only reinforces this impression. Such an impression is, however, mistaken for two reasons. First, European

[15] Michael H. Hunt, *Ideology and US Foreign Policy* (New Haven, CT and London: Yale University Press, 1987), 19.

[16] The term 'Grotian moment' is used by Richard Falk to identify 'a time of potential transition from one type of world order to another'. It draws on Grotius's attempt to understand the break-up of medieval Christendom and the gradual formation of international society. For Falk, the contemporary world is experiencing a Grotian moment in reverse. National loyalty and legitimacy upon which the state and the society of states could previously depend, he argues, is 'relocating' away from the state: upward to a central global authority and downward to the local community. Richard Falk, 'The Grotian Moment: Unfulfilled Promise, Harmless Fantasy, Missed Opportunity?', *International Insights*, 13 (1997), 3–34. In other works, Falk uses the term 'Grotian solution' to identify what this book has referred to as a solidarist conception of international society. Richard Falk, 'The Grotian Quest', in Richard Falk, Friedrich Kratochwil, and Saul H. Mendlovitz (eds.), *International Law. A Contemporary Perspective* (Boulder, CO and London: Westview Press, 1985), 36–42. Given that the Rome Statute offers what is described as a Kantian vision of world society, but keeping in mind that the transition is still incomplete, it is possible to describe the present situation as offering a Kantian solution in Grotian moment.

[17] See e.g. Henry Kissinger 'The Pitfalls of Universal Jurisdiction', *Foreign Affairs*, 80 (2001), 86–96.

governments may have played a decisive role in creating the political momentum behind the ratification campaign that established the ICC, but many post-colonial nations willingly followed the European lead. A post-colonial discourse may help to explain why certain states, notably India, are cautious about sacrificing sovereignty to the ICC, but the fact that other such governments have taken the lead in establishing the Court demonstrates that a post-colonial discourse cannot itself explain state attitudes towards the Court. Second, and more significantly, to argue that the Court is a tool of any state is to misunderstand the manner in which cases are referred to the Court and the processes that lead the Prosecutor to take up a case. The Court is independent of the society of states. A state party can refer a situation to the Court, but it cannot exempt its leaders from any prosecution that results from that referral. Thus, when Uganda referred its conflict with the Lord's Resistance Army to the Court, human rights groups reminded the Prosecutor that he had the power to investigate all allegations of core crimes, regardless of the perpetrator's relationship to the state.[18] This does not mean that power will not influence the Court. Like any Prosecutor, the ICC Prosecutor will inevitably be restricted by time and resources and this will lead to its own form of selectivity. The point is, however, that the Prosecutor's claim that his interests are in harmony with the global common good is much more credible than those of the UN Security Council or those of individual states exercising universal jurisdiction. The Prosecutor's decisions will be influenced by power—that is a reality—but the charges that such decisions are selfish and at the expense of the common good are less likely to stick.

Chapters 1 and 4 argued that the Rome Statute helped to constitute a Kantian conception of world society. Kant did not specifically advocate an independent court like the ICC, but the appearance of such a court should not be unexpected to anyone who has studied Kant's writings on history. For Kant, progress towards a historical point at which justice could be administered universally was the consequence of what he called 'the unsocial sociability of men'. This described the tendency of men 'to come together in society, coupled, however, with a continual resistance which constantly threatens to break this society up'. This propensity, Kant continued,

is obviously rooted in human nature. Man has an inclination to *live in society*, since he feels in this state more like a man, that is, he feels able to develop his natural capacities. But he also has a great tendency to *live as an individual*, to isolate himself, since he also encounters in himself the unsocial characteristic of wanting to direct everything in accordance with his own ideas.[19]

[18] Human Rights Watch, 'ICC: Investigate All Sides in Uganda', 4 February 2004.
[19] Kant, *Idea for a Universal History*, 44.

Without these asocial qualities, 'human talents would remain hidden for ever in a dormant state'. Out of the antagonism and discord that these qualities create, however, the human species discovers the means of liberating itself.

The natural impulses which make this possible, the sources of the very unsociableness and the continual resistance which cause so many evils, at the same time encourage man towards new exertions of his powers and thus towards further development of his natural capacities.[20]

The creation of the ICC fits this view of human progress. It is a response to the failure of the society of states to prevent the 'many evils' of the twentieth century in part because individual states were willing to isolate themselves. Yet, as Kant might expect, the ICC is not an end-point of history because the process continues to be plagued by individual states who 'want to direct everything in accordance with [their] own ideas'.

Kant's warnings against world government are often cited as evidence of his resistance to supranational institution building. They might be read, moreover, as an endorsement of a Wilsonian international society of states based on republican principles. Yet Kant also noted that 'attaining a civil society which can administer justice universally' was the 'greatest problem for the human species';[21] and others have suggested that the inconsistencies in Kant's political philosophy can be resolved in a manner that supports global institutions like the ICC. As Jürgen Habermas argues:

Because Kant believed that the barriers of national sovereignty were insurmountable, he conceived of the cosmopolitan community as a federation of states, not of world citizens. This assumption proved inconsistent insofar as Kant derived every legal order, including that within the state, from a more original law, which gives rights to every person 'qua human being'. Each individual has the right to equal freedom under universal law... This founding law in human rights designates individuals as bearers of rights and gives to all modern legal orders an inviolable individualistic character. If Kant holds that this guarantee of freedom... is precisely the essential purpose of perpetual peace, 'indeed for all three variants of public law, civil, international and cosmopolitan law', then he ought not allow the autonomy of citizens to be mediated through the sovereignty of their states.[22]

The significance of this interpretation is more than academic. The state-centric reading of Kant restricts the liberal imagination and could

---

[20] Kant, *Idea for a Universal History*, 45.   [21] Kant, *Idea for a Universal History*, 45.

[22] Jürgen Habermas, 'Kant's Idea of Perpetual Peace, with the Benefit of Two Hundred Years' Hindsight', in James Bohman and Matthias Lutz-Bachman (eds.), *Perpetual Peace. Essays on Kant's Cosmopolitan Ideal* (Cambridge and London: MIT Press, 1997), 128. Quoting *Perpetual Peace*.

conceivably (although incorrectly) provide the philosophical depth to policies of 'democracy promotion' and even 'regime change', which, because they are dependent on the will of the particular, inevitably corrupt the original appeal of the universal.[23] A cosmopolitan reading of Kant, however, would indicate a path of *national* self-sacrifice that is not as costly as the *human* sacrifices accompanying the policy of regime change and is ultimately more effective in advancing the goal of universal liberty without prompting the charge of imperialism.

Again, Habermas is helpful in clarifying the point and expanding on its implication. 'The politics of human rights undertaken by a world organiza-tion', he writes,

turns into a fundamentalism of human rights only when it undertakes an intervention that is really nothing more than a struggle of one party against the other and thus uses a moral legitimation as a cover for a false juridical justification.... The correct solution to the problem of the moralization of power politics is therefore 'not the demoralization of politics, but rather the democratic transformation of morality into a positive system of law with legal procedures of application and implementation.' Fundamentalism about human rights is to be avoided not by giving up on the politics of human rights, but rather only through the cosmopolitan transformation of the state of nature among states into a legal order.[24]

In other words, just as Wilsonians recognize that a Hobbesian analysis of IR is insufficient to advance the liberal ideals of the enlightenment, so Kantians argue that a Wilsonian analysis is equally insufficient and in many ways coun-terproductive. A Kantian approach would recognize the achievements of the Rome Conference in codifying a consensus on what constitutes IHL and in creating legal procedures for its application and implementation. It would call upon states to support the Court by making the small national sacrifice of renegotiating the social contract that constituted their particular identities. Kant's gradualist approach to progressive change suggests as much. 'It must still be possible', he wrote in *The Metaphysics of Morals,*

---

[23] For example, see John Macmillan, 'A Kantian Protest Against the Peculiar Discourse of InterLiberal State Peace', *Millennium, Journal of International Studies*, 24 (1994), 549–62. As noted in Chapter 1, Kant explicitly ruled out 'regime change' because 'there would be an interval of time during which the condition of right would be nullified'. Kant, *The Metaphysics of Morals*, reprinted in Reiss (ed.), *Kant*, 175.

[24] Habermas, 'Kant's Idea of Perpetual Peace', 147–9, quoting and translating Klaus Günther, 'Kampf gegen das Böse? Wider die ethische Aufrüstung der Kriminalpolitik', *Kritische Justiz*, 17 (1994), 144. For similar views in American academia, see Jean L. Cohen, 'Whose Sovereignty? Empire versus International Law', *Ethics and International Affairs*, 18 (2004), 1–24.

for the sovereign to alter the existing constitution if it cannot readily be reconciled with the idea of the original contract, and yet in so doing to leave untouched that basic form which is essential if the people are to constitute a state.[25]

By amending the constitution of international society, the complementarity principle of the Rome Statute allows states to do just that. It allows state parties to contribute to the original enlightenment idea of universal justice, while leaving untouched the essence of the nation-state. Those post-Westphalian states that support the ICC are, after all, still states.

As Chapter 5 noted, however, it is America's need to be seen as exceptional, rather than the original idea of universal justice, that is driving its opposition to the ICC. It clings to the idea of a society of Westphalian states in order to reconstitute this exceptional identity and it prefers policies of 'regime change' and 'nation building' in order to make that society work. As the US occupation of Iraq shows, however, the human sacrifices demanded by this course of action are immense. Furthermore, these sacrifices are possibly counterproductive. As Carr noted, the course most detrimental to international morality

is surely to pretend that the German people are the bearers of a higher ethic, or that American principles are the principles of humanity, or that the security of Great Britain is the supreme good of the world, so that no sacrifices at all by one's own nation are in fact necessary.[26]

Thus, like Kant, Carr argued that it is only by compromising one's national identity and indeed national interests that an impartial notion of the global common good can emerge. Carr was not hopeful that the far-reaching and virtuous sacrifices of this kind would be forthcoming. Yet Carr's realism was not fatalistic. National societies had saved themselves from conflict by virtuous acts of self-sacrifice among the powerful and 'even in international relations, self-sacrifice is not altogether unknown'. Indeed, Carr concluded that any

international moral order must rest on some hegemony of power. But this hegemony, like the supremacy of a ruling class within the state, is in itself a challenge to those who do not share it; and it must, if it is to survive, contain an element of give and take, of self-sacrifice on the part of those who have, which will render it tolerable to other members of the world community.[27]

The point here is not that American hegemony is threatened by its failure to sign up to the ICC. The point instead is that the task of global leadership

---

[25] Kant, *The Metaphysics of Morals*, reprinted in Reiss (ed.), *Kant*, 162.
[26] Carr, *The Twenty Years' Crisis*, 152.   [27] Carr, *The Twenty Years' Crisis*, 151–2.

can be made easier (as the New Deal liberals of a previous age well knew) by relatively small national sacrifices.[28] Supporting the ICC, in other words, requires the United States to surrender control of the process of international criminal justice and to amend the image of itself as somehow separate from the world. This might be asking a lot, but it is ultimately a smaller price to pay than that being exacted by a policy designed to defend the society of states.

THE ROLE OF PHILOSOPHERS?

Kant was perhaps more optimistic than Carr about the progress of human history. They did, however, share the view that education played a significant role. Carr is best known for his warning that international law was a product of power. Yet, as noted at the outset of this chapter, he also argued that there were limits to the influence that power had over the production of morality. The first limitation was 'the inherent utopianism of human nature'. Military and economic power, he wrote, 'always tend to reach a point where it defeats its own end by inciting the mind to revolt against that power'. The second limitation was education. The danger that 'the truth will out' he suggested was a serious limitation on the influence that power had over opinion. In this respect, education, 'which is one of the strongest instruments of . . . power, tends at the same time to promote a spirit of independent inquiry which is also one of the strongest antidotes against it'.[29] This echoed Kant's view of the role philosophers played in the moral progress of humankind. 'Popular enlightenment', he wrote,

is the public instruction of the people upon their duties and rights towards the state to which they belong. Since this concerns only natural rights and rights which are derived from ordinary common sense, their obvious exponents and interpreters among the people, *will not be officials appointed by the state, but free teachers of right, i.e. philosophers.*[30]

And elsewhere,

It is not to be expected that kings will philosophize or that philosophers will become kings; nor is it to be desired, however, since the possession of power inevitably corrupts

[28] See the author's 'High Stakes and Low-Intensity Democracy. Understanding America's Policy of Promoting Democracy', in Michael Cox, Takashi Inoguchi, and G. John Ikenberry (eds.), *American Democracy Promotion. Impulses, Strategies and Impacts* (Oxford: Oxford University Press, 2000).

[29] Carr, *The Twenty Years' Crisis*, 129.

[30] Immanuel Kant, *The Contest of Faculties*, reprinted in Reiss (ed.), *Kant*, 186.

the free judgement of reason. Kings and sovereign peoples who are to govern them-selves by egalitarian law should not, however, force the class of philosophers to disap-pear or to remain silent, but should allow them to speak publicly. This is essential in both cases in order that light may be thrown on their affairs. And since the class of philosophers is by nature incapable of forming seditious factions or clubs, they cannot incur suspicion of disseminating propaganda.[31]

Evidence presented in this book, mainly in Chapters 2 and 7, suggests that there is no shortage of philosophers who are willing to 'remain silent' so that they can speak to power. Where critical theorists like Carr and Kant call upon the academic community to hold politicians true to their word when they claim to be acting in the common interest, certain international lawyers in the United States work hard to interpret international law in a way that suits America's and indeed the US President's particular interests. Indeed Goldsmith and Krasner's choice to read Carr (see above) through the 'Realist' rather than 'Critical' lens must be understood against the background of their service to the Bush administration.[32] This may be unconscious. For instance, those, including Goldsmith, who argue for a strictly positivist understanding of the sources of international law, may have been genuinely concerned that any other standard would undermine democracy based on the social contract between the state and its people. The implication of the arguments of what Kant would have called 'these sorry comforters', however, is that the great powers can more or less determine the law that binds them.[33] As Carr noted, this view turns law into 'the weapon of the stronger'.[34]

What Dratel has called the 'corporatization' of government lawyering has it seems taken hold in Washington. This is

a wholly result-oriented system in which policy-makers start with an objective and work backward, in the process enlisting the aid of intelligent and well-credentialed lawyers who, for whatever reason—the attractions of power, careerism, ideology, or just plain judgement—all too willingly failed to act as a constitutional or moral

---

[31] Immanuel Kant, *Perpetual Peace*, reprinted in Reiss (ed.), *Kant*, 115.

[32] Goldsmith served as Special Counsel to the Department of Defense in 2002–3, before moving to the Department of Justice as Assistant Attorney General and Krasner was appointed as the State Department's director for Policy Planning on 4 February 2005.

[33] 'Although it is largely concealed by governmental constraints in law-governed civil society, the depravity of human nature is displayed without disguise in the unrestricted relations which obtain between various nations. It is therefore to be wondered at that the word right has not been completely banished from military politics as superfluous pedantry, and that no state has been bold enough to declare itself publicly in favour of doing so. For Hugo Grotius, Pufendorf, Vattel and the rest (sorry comforters as they are) are still dutifully quoted in justification of military aggression, although their philosophically or diplomatically formulated codes do not and cannot have the slightest legal force, since states as such are not subject to a common external constraint.' Kant, *Perpetual Peace*, 103.

[34] Carr, *The Twenty Years' Crisis*, 163.

compass that could brake their client's descent into unconscionable behaviour constituting torture by any definition, legal or colloquial. The slavish dedication to a superior's imperatives does not serve the client well in the end and reduces the lawyer's function to that of a gold-plated rubber stamp.[35]

Carr's hope in 'education' and the Kantian idea of 'publicity', or what Habermas calls the public sphere, is only effective if it is occupied by publicly spirited intellectuals. The corruption of this spirit has always been a threat to the American Republic, but now it threatens to maintain an empire that requires enormous national sacrifice and does not benefit universal liberty. This realization will create political pressure for alternatives that philosophers are duty bound to provide. A starting point would be a rereading of what the critical theories of Kant and Carr had to say about the relationship of power to law and about the possibility that both these concepts can respond to the demands for just change.

[35] Joshua L. Dratel, 'The Legal Narrative', in Karen J. Greenberg and Joshua L. Dratel (eds.), *The Torture Papers. The Road to Abu-Ghraib*, Cambridge University Press, 2005, xxii.

Bibliography

Ackerman, B., 'Constitutional Politics/Constitutional Law', *The Yale Law Journal* 99 (1989), 453–547.

Adler, E., Buzan, B., and Dunne, T., 'Forum Afterword', *Millennium, Journal of International Studies*, 34 (2005), 195–9.

Akande, D., 'International Law Immunities and the International Criminal Court', *American Journal of International Law*, 98 (2004), 407–33.

Albert, M., Brock, L., and Wolf, K. D. (eds.), *Civilizing World Politics. Society and Community Beyond the State* (Lanham, MD, Boulder, CO, New York, and London: Rowman and Littlefield, 2000).

Aldrich, G. H., 'New Life for the Laws of War', *American Journal of International Law*, 75 (1981), 764–83.

—— 'Progressive Development of the Laws of War: A Reply to Criticisms of the 1977 Geneva Protocol I', *Virginia Journal of International Law*, 26 (1986), 693–720.

—— 'The Taliban, Al Qaeda, and the Determination of Illegal Combatants', *American Journal of International Law*, 96 (2002), 891–8.

Anderson, K., 'The Ottawa Convention Banning Landmines, the Role of International Non-Governmental Organizations and the Idea of International Civil Society', *European Journal of International Law*, 11 (2000), 91–120.

Arbour, L., 'Will the ICC Have an Impact on Universal Jurisdiction?', *Journal of International Criminal Justice*, 1 (2003), 585–8.

Archibugi, D., 'Immanuel Kant, Cosmopolitan Law and Peace', *European Journal of International Relations*, 1 (1995), 425–56.

—— 'From the United Nations to Cosmopolitan Democracy', in D. Archibugi and D. Held (eds.), *Cosmopolitan Democracy. An Agenda for a New World Order* (Cambridge: Polity Press, 1995).

Arend, A. C., 'International Law, Terrorism, and U.S. Courts', paper presented at International Studies Association Annual Conference, Montreal, 20 March 2004.

Arsanjani, M. H., 'Financing', in A. Cassese, P. Gaeta, and J. R. W. D. Jones (eds.), *The Rome Statute of the International Criminal Court. A Commentary Vol. I and II* (Oxford: Oxford University Press, 2002).

Bailyn, B., *The Ideological Origins of the American Revolution* (Cambridge and London: Harvard University Press, 1992).

Barker, Sir E., 'Natural Law and the American Revolution', in *Traditions of Civility. Eight Essays* (Cambridge: Cambridge University Press, 1948).

Bass, G. J., *Stay the Hand of Vengeance. The Politics of War Crimes Tribunals* (Princeton, NJ and Oxford: Princeton University Press, 2000).

Bassiouni, M. C., 'International Crimes: *Jus Cogens* and *Obligatio Erga Omnes*', *Law and Contemporary Problems*, 59 (1996), 63–74.

Bassiouni, M. C., 'From Versailles to Rwanda in Seventy-Five Years: The Need to Establish a Permanent International Criminal Court', *Harvard Human Rights Journal*, 10
(1997), 11–62.

_____ and Wise, Edward M. (eds.), *Aut Dedere, Aut Judicare. The Duty to Extradite
or Prosecute in International Law* (Dordrecht, the Netherlands, Boston, MA, and
London: Martinus Nijhoff, 1995).

Baxter, R. R., 'So-Called "Unprivileged Belligerency": Spies, Guerrillas and Saboteurs',
The British Yearbook of International Law, 28 (1951), 323–45.

Becker, E., 'US Issues Warning to Europeans in Dispute Over New Court', *The New
York Times*, August 26 (2002).

Bellamy, A. J. and Hanson, M., 'Justice Beyond Borders? Australia and the International Criminal Court', *Australian Journal of International Affairs*, 56 (2002), 417–
33.

_____ 'Conclusion: Whither International Society?', in Alex J. Bellamy (ed.), *International Society and Its Critics* (Oxford: Oxford University Press, 2005).

Benvenuti, P., 'The ICTY Prosecutor and the Review of the NATO Bombing Campaign
against the Federal Republic of Yugoslavia', *European Journal of International Law*,
12 (2001), 503–29.

Bianchi, A., 'Globalization of Human Rights: The Role of Non-State Actors', in
G. Teubner (ed.), *Global Law Without a State* (Dartmouth, MA, 1997), 179–212.

_____ 'International Law and US Courts: The Myth of Lohengrin Revisited', *European
Journal of International Law*, 15 (2004), 751–81.

Black, C., 'The International Criminal Tribunal for the Former Yugoslavia: Impartial?',
Mediterranean Quarterly, 11 (2000), 29–40.

Black-Branch, J., 'Sovereign Immunity Under International Law: The Case of
Pinochet', in D. Woodhouse (ed.), *The Pinochet Case: A Legal and Constitutional
Analysis* (Oxford: Hart, 2000).

Bloomfield, L. P., 'U.S. Government and the International Criminal Court', Remarks by
Assistant Secretary for Political-Military Affairs to the Parliamentarians for Global
Action, Consultative Assembly of Parliamentarians for the International Criminal
Court and the Rule of Law, United Nations, New York, 12 September 2003.

Boister, N., 'The ICJ in the Belgian Arrest Warrant Case: Arresting the Development
of International Criminal Law', *Journal of Conflict and Security Law*, 7 (2002), 293–
314.

Bolton, J. R., 'Should We Take Global Governance Seriously?', *Chicago Journal of
International Law*, 1 (2000), 205–21.

_____ 'Unsign That Treaty', *Washington Post*, 4 January 2001.

_____ Remarks to the Federalist Society, Washington, DC, 14 November 2002.

Booth, K., 'Military Intervention: Duty and Prudence', in Lawrence Freedman (ed.),
Military Intervention in European Conflicts (Oxford: Blackwell, 1994).

_____ and Williams, H., 'Kant: Theorist Beyond Limits', in Ian Clark and Iver B. Neumann (eds.), *Classical Theories of International Relations* (London: Macmillan and
St. Martin's Press, 1996).

Bork, R. H., 'Judicial Imperialism', *Wall Street Journal*, 17 June 2003.

Bradley, C. A., 'U.S. Announces Intent Not to Ratify International Criminal Court Treaty', *ASIL Insights*, (2002) 87.

___ and Goldsmith, J. L., 'Customary International Law as Federal Common Law: A Critique of the Modern Position', *Harvard Law Review*, 110 (1997), 815–76.

___ ___ 'Commentary: Federal Courts and the Incorporation of International Law', *Harvard Law Review*, 111 (1998), 2250–75.

Brands, H. W., *What America Owes the World. The Struggle for the Soul of Foreign Policy* (Cambridge: Cambridge University Press, 1998).

Bravin, J., 'U.S. Fails to Solve ICC Dispute Over Peacekeeping Forces', *Wall Street Journal*, 5 July 2002.

___ 'US Warms to Hague Tribunal', *Wall Street Journal*, 14 June 2006.

Brierly, J. L., *The Law of Nations: An Introduction to the International Law of Peace*, 6th edn. (Oxford: Oxford University Press, 1963).

Bring, O., 'The Westphalian Peace Tradition in International Law. From *Jus ad* Bellum to *Jus Contra* Bellum', in Michael N. Schmitt (ed.), *International Law Across the Spectrum of Conflict: Essays in Honour of Professor L. C. Green* (US Naval War College: International Law Studies Volume 75, 2000).

Brody, R. and Duffy, H., 'Prosecuting Torture Universally: Hissène Habré, Africa's Pinochet?', in H. Fischer and C. Kress, and S. R. Lüder (eds.), *International and National Prosecutions of Crimes under International Law. Current Developments* (Berlin: Berlin Verlag Arno Spitz, 2001).

Broomhall, B., *International Criminal Justice and the International Criminal Court. Between State Consent and the Rule of Law* (Oxford: Oxford University Press, 2003).

Brown, B. S., 'The Statute of the ICC: Past, Present and Future', in Sarah B. Sewall and Carl Kaysen (eds.), *The United States and the International Criminal Court* (London: Rowman and Littlefield, 2000).

___ 'Unilateralism, Multilateralism, and the International Criminal Court', in Stewart Patrick and Shepard Forman (eds.), *Multilateralism and US Foreign Policy. Ambivalent Engagement* (Boulder, CO, and London: Lynne Reinner, 2002), 323–44.

Brown, C., 'Ethics of Co-Existence: The International Theory of Terry Nardin', *Review of International Studies*, 14 (1998).

___ Nardin, T., and Rengger, N., *International Relations in Political Thought. Texts from the Ancient Greeks to the First World War* (Cambridge: Cambridge University Press, 2002).

___ 'International Theory and International Society: the Viability of the Middle Way?', *Review of International Studies*, 21 (1995), 183–96.

___ *International Relations Theory: New Normative Approaches* (Hemel Hempstead, 1992).

___ 'The "English School": International Theory and International Society', in Mathias Albert, Lothar Brock, and Klaus Dieter Wolf (eds.), *Civilizing World Politics. Society and Community Beyond the State* (Lanham, MD, Boulder, CO, New York, and London: Rowman and Littlefield, 2000).

___ 'World Society and the English School: An "International Society" Perspective on World Society', *European Journal of International Relations*, 7 (2000), 423–41.

Brown, G. W., 'State Sovereignty, Federation, and Kantian Cosmopolitanism', *European Journal of International Relations*, 11 (2005), 495–522.

Bull, H., 'International Theory: The Case for a Classical Approach', *World Politics*, 42 (1966), 361–77.

—— 'The Grotian Conception of International Society', in H. Butterfield and M. Wight (eds.), *Diplomatic Investigations* (London: Allen and Unwin, 1966).

—— 'International Theory: The Case for a Classical Approach', in K. Knorr and J. N. Rosenau (eds.), *Contending Approaches to International Politics,* (Princeton, NJ: Princeton University Press, 1969).

—— *The Anarchical Society: A Study of Order in World Politics,* 2nd edn. (London: Macmillan, 1977).

—— 'The Great Irresponsibles? The United States, the Soviet Union and World Order,' *International Journal*, 35 (1979–80), 437–447.

—— 'The Importance of Grotius in the Study of International Relations', in Hedley Bull, Benedict Kingsbury, and Adam Roberts (eds.), *Hugo Grotius and International Relations* (Oxford: Clarendon Press, 1990).

Burke-White, W. W., 'Complementarity in Practice: The International Criminal Court as Part of a System of Multi-Level Global Governance in the Democratic Republic of Congo', *Leiden Journal of International Law*, 18 (2005), 557–90.

Burley, A. M., 'The Alien Tort Statute and the Judiciary Act of 1789: A Badge of Honor', *American Journal of International Law*, 83 (1989), 461–93.

Butler, A. H., 'The Growing Support for Universal Jurisdiction in National Legislation', in Stephen Macedo (ed.), *Universal Jurisdiction. National Courts and the Prosecution of Serious Crimes Under International Law* (Philadelphia, PA: University of Pennsylvania Press, 2004).

Buzan, B., 'From the International System to International Society: Structural Realism and Regime Theory Meet the English School', *International Organization*, 47 (1993), 327–52.

—— 'The English School: An Underexploited Resource in IR', *Review of International Studies*, 27 (2001), 471–88.

—— *From International to World Society? English School Theory and the Social Structure of Globalisation* (Cambridge: Cambridge University Press, 2004).

Byers, M., *Custom, Power and the Power of Rules. International Relations and Customary International Law* (Cambridge: Cambridge University Press, 1999).

—— 'The Law and Politics of the Pinochet Case', *Duke Journal of Comparative and International Law*, 10 (2000), 415–42.

—— 'The Shifting Foundations of International Law: A Decade of Forceful Measures against Iraq', *European Journal of International Law*, 13 (2002), 21–41.

Campbell, D., *Writing Security: United States Foreign Policy and the Politics of Identity* (Manchester, UK: Manchester University Press, 1998).

Carr, E. H., *The Twenty Years' Crisis 1919–1939. An Introduction to the Study of International Relations,* 2nd edn. (Basingstoke, UK: Palgrave, 2001).

Casey, L. A., Prepared Statement to the Hearing Before the Subcommittee on International Operations, 23 July 1998.

_____ 'The Case Against the International Criminal Court', *Fordham International Law Journal*, 25 (2002), 840–72.

Cassese, A., 'The Status of Rebels under the 1977 Geneva Protocol on Non-International Armed Conflict', *The International and Comparative Law Quarterly*, 30 (1981), 416–39.

_____ 'The Martens Clause: Half a Loaf or Simply Pie in the Sky?', *European Journal of International Law*, 11 (2000), 187–216.

_____ Cassese, A., 'From Nuremberg to Rome: International Military Tribunals to the International Criminal Court', in Antonio Paolo Cassese, Paolo Gaeta, and John R. W. D. Jones (eds.), *The Rome Statute of the International Criminal Court. A Commentary Vol. I and II* (Oxford: Oxford University Press, 2002).

_____ 'When May Senior State Officials Be Tried for International Crimes? Some Comments of the *Congo* v. *Belgium* Case', *European Journal of International Law*, 13 (2002), 853–75.

_____ Gaeta, P., and Jones, J. R. W. D. (eds.), *The Rome Statute of the International Criminal Court. A Commentary Vol. I and II* (Oxford: Oxford University Press, 2002).

_____ 'Is the Bell Tolling for Universality? A Plea for a Sensible Notion of Universal Jurisdiction', *Journal of International Criminal Justice*, 1 (2003), 589–95.

Chandler, D., 'International Justice', *New Left Review*, 6 (2000), 55–66.

Chigara, B., 'Pinochet and the Administration of International Criminal Justice', in Diana Woodhouse (ed.), *The Pinochet Case: A Legal and Constitutional Analysis* (Oxford: Hart, 2000).

Clapham, A., 'Issues of Complexity, Complicity and Complementarity: From the Nuremberg Trials to the Dawn of the International Criminal Court', in Phillipe Sands (ed.), *From Nuremberg to The Hague. The Future of International Criminal Justice* (Cambridge: Cambridge University Press, 2003).

Clark, I., 'Traditions of Thought and Classical Theories of International Relations', in Ian Clark and Iver B. Neumann (eds.), *Classical Theories of International Relations* (London: Macmillan, 1996).

Cohen, J. L., 'Whose Sovereignty? Empire versus International Law', *Ethics and International Affairs*, 18 (2004), 1–24.

Committee of International Relations, 'Hyde Praises Decision by Bush Administration to Unsign Treaty Establishing International Criminal Court', Committee of International Relations, US House of Representatives, 6 May 2002, at: http://www.house.gov/international_relations

Condorelli, L. and Ciampi, A. 'Comments on the Security Council Referral of the Situation in Darfur to the ICC', *Journal of International Criminal Justice*, 3 (2005), 590–9.

Conso, G., 'The Basic Reasons for US Hostility to the ICC in Light of the Negotiating History of the Rome Statute', *Journal of International Criminal Justice*, 3 (2005), 314–22.

Crawford SC, J., Sands, P., QC, and Wilde, R., 'Joint Opinion, In the Matter of the Statute of the International Criminal Court and in the Matter of Bilateral

Agreements Sought by the United States under Article 98 (2) of the Statute', 5 June 2003, at http://www.amicc.org/docs/Art98-14une03FINAL.pdf

Cronin, B., *Community Under Anarchy. Transnational Identity and the Evolution of Cooperation* (New York: Columbia University Press, 1999).

Cuellar, M. F., 'The International Criminal Court and the Political Economy of Antitreaty Discourse', *Stanford Law Review*, 55 (2003), 1597–632.

Cutler, C., 'The "Grotian Tradition" in International Relations', *Review of International Studies*, 17 (1991), 41–56.

D'Amato, A., 'Trashing Customary International Law', *American Journal of International Law*, 81 (1987), 101–5.

Danilenko, G. M., 'International Jus Cogens: Issues of Law-Making', *European Journal of International Law*, 2 (1991), 42–61.

Danner, A. M., 'Navigating Law and Politics: The Prosecutor of the International Criminal Court and Independent Counsel', *Stanford Law Review*, 55 (2003), 1633–65.

De Greiff, P., 'Comment: Universal Jurisdiction and Transitions to Democracy', in Stephen Macedo (ed.), *Universal Jurisdiction: National Courts and the Prosecution of Serious Crimes Under International Law* (Philadelphia, PA: University of Pennsylvannia Press, 2006).

Deen-Racsmány, Z., '*Prosecutor v. Taylor*: The Status of the Special Court for Sierra Leone and Its Implications for Immunity', *Leiden Journal of International Law*, 18 (2005), 299–322.

Dempsey, J., 'Little Applause on Criminal Court Deal', *Financial Times*, 15 July 2002.

Doyle, M., 'Kant, Liberal Legacies, and Foreign Affairs', *Philosophy and Public Affairs*, 12(1983), 205–35.

Doyle, M. W., 'Liberalism and World Politics', *The American Political Science Review*, 80 (1986), 1151–69.

Draper, G. I. A. D., 'Wars of National Liberation and War Criminality', in Michael Howard (ed.), *Restraints on War. Studies in the Limitation of Armed Conflict* (Oxford: Oxford University Press, 1979).

Drezner, D., 'On the Balance between International Law and Democratic Sovereignty', *Chicago Journal of International Law*, 2 (2001), 321–36.

Dunne, T., *Inventing International Society: A History of the English School* (London: Macmillan, 1998).

——— 'Sociological Investigations: Instrumental, Legitimist and Coercive Interpretations of International Society', *Millennium: Journal of International Studies*, 30 (2001), 67–91.

——— 'System, State and Society: How Does it All Hang Together', *Millennium: Journal of International Studies*, 34 (2005), 157–70.

——— 'A New Agenda', in A. J. Bellamy (ed.), *International Society and Its Critics* (Oxford: Oxford University Press, 2005).

——— and Wheeler, N. J., 'Hedley Bull's Pluralism of the Intellect Solidarism of the Will', *International Affairs*, 72 (1996), 91–107.

_____ _____ 'Good International Citizenship: A Third Way for British Foreign Policy', *International Affairs*, 74 (1998), 847–70.

Durkheim, E., *The Division of Labour in Society* (Glencoe, IL.: Free Press, 1933).

Economides, S., 'The International Criminal Court', in K. E. Smith and M. Light (eds.), *Ethics and Foreign Policy* (Cambridge: Cambridge University Press, 2001).

Edgar, A. D., 'Peace, Justice and Politics: The International Criminal Court, "New Diplomacy", and the UN System', in A. F. Cooper, J. English, and R. Thakur (eds.), *Enhancing Global Governance: Towards a New Diplomacy?* (United Nations University Press, 2002).

Elsea, J., *US Policy Regarding the International Criminal Court*, Congressional Research Service Report RL31495, 2002.

Falk, R. A., 'On the Quasi-Legislative Competence of the General Assembly', *American Journal of International Law*, 60 (1966), 782–91.

_____ *The Status of Law in International Society* (Princeton, NJ: Princeton University Press, 1970).

_____ 'The Grotian Quest', in Richard Falk, Friedrich Kratochwil, and Saul H. Mendlovitz (eds.), *International Law. A Contemporary Perspective* (Boulder, CO and London: Westview Press, 1985).

_____ 'The Grotian Moment: Unfulfilled Promise, Harmless Fantasy, Missed Opportunity?', *International Insights*, 13 (1997), 3–34.

_____ *Law in an Emerging Global Village. A Post-Westphalian Perspective* (New York: Transnational, 1998).

_____ 'Assessing the Pinochet Litigation: Wither Universal Jurisdiction?', in S. Macedo (ed.), *Universal Jurisdiction. National Courts and the Prosecution of Serious Crimes Under International Law* (Philadelphia, PA: University of Pennsylvania Press, 2004).

Fassbender, B., 'The United Nations Charter as Constitution of the International Community', *Columbia Journal of Transnational Law*, 36 (1998), 529–619.

Feith, D., 'Law in the Service of Terror—The Strange Case of the Additional Protocol', *National Interest*, 1 (1985), 36–47.

Feith, D. J., 'Protocol I: Moving Humanitarian Law Backwards', *Akron Law Review*, 19 (1986), 531–5.

_____ 'International Responses', in Uri Ra'anan et al. (eds.), *Hydra of Carnage. International Linkages of Terrorism. The Witnesses Speak* (Lexington, KY: Lexington Books, 1986), 265–86.

Fletcher, G. P., 'Against Universal Jurisdiction', *Journal of International Criminal Justice*, 1 (2003), 580–4.

_____ 'Black Hole in Guantánamo Bay', *Journal of International Criminal Justice*, 2 (2004), 121–32.

Foley, M., *American Political Ideas. Tradition and Usages* (Manchester, UK and New York: Manchester University Press, 1991).

_____ 'The Democratic Imperative', in Anthony McGrew (ed.), *Empire. The United States in the Twentieth Century* (London: Hodder and Stoughton in association with Open University Press, 1994).

Forsythe, D. P., 'The United States and International Criminal Justice', *Human Rights Quarterly*, 24 (2002), 974–91.

Fourmy, O., 'Powers of the Pre-Trial Chambers', in Antonio Paolo Cassese, Paolo Gaeta, and John R. W. D. Jones (eds.), *The Rome Statute of the International Criminal Court. A Commentary Vol. I and II* (Oxford: Oxford University Press, 2002), 1207–30.

Gaeta, P., 'Is the Practice of "Self-Referrals" a Sound Start for the ICC?', *Journal of International Criminal Justice*, 2 (2004), 949–52.

Gasser, H., 'Agora: Protocol I to the Geneva Convention. An Appeal for Ratification by the United States', *American Journal of International Law*, 81 (1987), 912–25.

Goldsmith, J. and Krasner, S., 'The Limits of Idealism', *Daedulus*, 132 (2003), 47–63.

_____ 'Support War Crimes Trials for Darfur', *Washington Post*, 23 January 2005.

Greenberg, K. J. and Dratel, J. L. (eds.), *The Torture Papers. The Road to Abu Ghraib* (Cambridge: Cambridge University Press, 2005).

Grossman, M., 'American Foreign Policy and the International Criminal Court', Remarks to the Center for Strategic and International Studies, Washington, DC, 6 May 2002, at: www.state.gov/p/9949.htm

Grotius, H., *De Jure Belli Ac Pacis. Libri Tres* (Washington, DC: Carnegie Institution of Washington, [1646] 1925).

Habermas, J., 'Kant's Idea of Perpetual Peace, with the Benefit of Two Hundred Years' Hindsight', in J. Bohman and M. Lutz-Bachman (eds.), *Perpetual Peace. Essays on Kant's Cosmopolitan Ideal* (Cambridge and London: MIT Press, 1997).

Hall, S., 'The Persistent Spectre: Natural Law, International Order and the Limits of Legal Positivism', *European Journal of International Law*, 12 (2001), 269–307.

Hampsher-Monk, I., *A History of Modern Political Thought. Major Political Thinkers from Hobbes to Marx* (Oxford: Blackwell, 1992).

Hartz, L., *The Liberal Tradition in America: An Interpretation of American Political Thought since the Revolution*, 2nd edn. (San Diego, CA: Harcourt Brace Jovanovich, 1991).

Hathaway, J. C., 'America, Defender of Democratic Legitimacy?', *European Journal of International Law*, 11 (2000), 121–34.

Helms, J. and Miller, Z., 'No Court Dates for America', *Washington Times*, 11 April 2002.

Henckaerts, J. M. and Doswald-Beck, L., *Customary International Humanitarian Law, Volume I, Rules* (Cambridge: Cambridge University Press, 2005).

Higgins, R., *The Development of International Law Through the Political Organs of the United Nations* (Oxford: Oxford University Press, 1963).

Hoge, W., 'UN Votes to Send Any Sudan War Crime Suspects to World Court', *New York Times*, 1 April 2005.

Holmes, J. T., 'The Principle of Complementarity', in R. Lee (ed.), *The International Criminal Court. The Making of the Rome Statute. Issues, Negotiations, Results* (The Hague: Kluwer Law International, 1999).

Holt, V. K. and Dallas, E. W., *On Trial: The US Military and the International Criminal Court*, Report No. 55, The Henry L. Stimson Center, March 2006.

Human Rights Watch, 'The Case Against Hissène Habré, an "African Pinochet" ', www.hrw.org/justice/habre

—— 'ICC: Investigate All Sides in Uganda', 4 February 2004, http://hrw.org/english/docs/2004/02/04/uganda7264.htm

Hunt, M. H., *Ideology and U.S. Foreign Policy* (New Haven, CT and London: Yale University Press, 1987).

Huntington, S., *Who Are We? America's Great Debate* (Free Press, 2004).

Hurrell, A., 'Kant and the Kantian Paradigm in International Relations', *Review of International Studies*, 16 (1990), 183–206.

—— 'Vattel: Pluralism and Its Limits', in I. Clark and I. B. Neumann (eds.), *Classical Theories of International Relations* (London: Macmillan, 1996).

—— 'Conclusion: International Law and the Changing Constitution of International Society', in Michael Byers (ed.), *The Role of Law in International Politics. Essays in International Relations and International Law* (Oxford: Oxford University Press, 2000).

—— 'Keeping History, Law and Political Philosophy Firmly within the English School', *Review of International Studies*, 27 (2001), 489–94.

Ignatieff, M. (ed.), *American Exceptionalism and Human Rights* (Princeton, NJ and Oxford: Princeton University Press, 2005).

Jackson, R., *The Global Covenant. Human Conduct in a World of States* (Oxford: Oxford University Press, 2000).

—— *Classical and Modern Thought on International Relations. From Anarchy to Cosmopolis* (New York: Palgrave Macmillan, 2005).

James, A., 'System or Society?', *Review of International Studies*, 19 (1993), 269–88.

Jenks, C. W., *Law, Freedom, and Welfare* (London: Stevens and Sons, 1963).

Jones, C. A., 'War in the Twenty-First Century: An Institution in Crisis', in Richard Little and John Williams (eds.), *The Anarchical Society in a Globalized World* (Basingstoke, UK: Palgrave Macmillan, 2006).

Kagan, R., *Paradise and Power. American and European in the New World Order* (London: Atlantic Books, 2003).

Kahn, P. W., 'American Exceptionalism, Popular Sovereignty, and the Rule of Law', in M. Ignatieff (ed.), *American Exceptionalism and Human Rights* (Princeton, NJ and Oxford: Princeton University Press, 2005).

Kamminga, M. T., 'Lessons Learned From the Exercise of Universal Jurisdiction in Respect of Gross Human Rights Offenses', *Human Rights Quarterly*, 23 (2001), 940–74.

Kant, I., *Idea for a Universal History with a Cosmopolitan Purpose*, reprinted in Hans Reiss (ed.), (translated by H. B. Nisbet), *Kant. Political Writings*, 2nd edn. (Cambridge: Cambridge University Press, 1991).

—— *Perpetual Peace. A Philosophical Sketch*, reprinted in Hans Reiss (ed.), (translated by H. B. Nisbet), *Kant. Political Writings*, 2nd edn. (Cambridge: Cambridge University Press, 1991).

Kant, I., *The Metaphysics of Morals*, reprinted in Hans Reiss (ed.), (translated by H. B. Nisbet), *Kant. Political Writings*, 2nd edn. (Cambridge: Cambridge University Press, 1991), 131–75.

――― *The Contest of Faculties*, reprinted in Hans Reiss (ed.), (translated by H. B. Nisbet), *Kant. Political Writings*, 2nd edn. (Cambridge: Cambridge University Press, 1991).

Kaul, H., 'Preconditions to the Exercise of Jurisdiction', in Cassese et al. (eds.), *The Rome Statute of the International Criminal Court. A Commentary* (Oxford: Oxford University Press, 2002).

Kelly, J. P., 'The Twilight of Customary International Law', *Virginia Journal of International Law*, 40 (2000), 449–543.

Khan, I., 'Terrorists Should be Tried in Court', *The Guardian*, 12 October 2001.

Kirsch, QC, P. and Robinson, D., 'Reaching Agreement at the Rome Conference', in Antonio Cassese et al. (eds.), *The Rome Statute of the International Criminal Court. A Commentary Volume 1* (Oxford: Oxford University Press, 2002).

Kissinger, H., 'The Pitfalls of Universal Jurisdiction', *Foreign Affairs*, 80 (2001), 86–96.

Koh, H. H., 'Commentary: Is International Law Really State Law?', *Harvard Law Review*, 111 (1998), 1824–59.

Koskenniemi, M., *The Gentle Civilizer of Nations: The Rise and Fall of International Law, 1870–1960* (Cambridge: Cambridge University Press, 2001).

Kralev, N., 'NATO Hopeful Vows to Aid U.S. on World Court', *Washington Times*, 26 July 2002.

――― 'US Balks at Global Court Use for Darfur', *Washington Times*, 21 January 2005.

Kress, C., ' "Self-Referrals" and "Waivers of Complementarity" Some Considerations in Law and Policy', *Journal of International Criminal Justice*, 2 (2004), 944–8.

Lagos, R. and Muñoz, H., 'The Pinochet Dilemma', *Foreign Policy*, 114 (1999), 26–39.

Lang, D. G., *Foreign Policy in the Early Republic. The Law of Nations and the Balance of Power* (Baton Rouge and London: Louisiana University Press, 1985).

Lauterpacht, H., 'The Grotian Tradition in International Law', *The British Yearbook of International Law*, 23 (1946), 1–55.

――― *International Law and Human Rights* (London: Stevens and Sons, 1950).

Lavalle, R., 'A Vicious Storm in a Teacup: The Action by the United Nations Security Council to Narrow the Jurisdiction of the International Criminal Court', *Criminal Law Forum*, 14 (2003), 195–220.

Laville, S., 'UK Court Convicts Afghan Warlord', *The Guardian*, 19 July 2005.

Lee, R. (ed.), *The International Criminal Court. The Making of the Rome Statute. Issues, Negotiations, Results* (The Hague: Kluwer Law International, 1999).

――― 'An Assessment of the ICC Statute', *Fordham International Law Journal*, 25 (2002), 750–66.

Leigh, M., 'The United States and the Rome Statute', *American Journal of International Law*, 95 (2001), 124–31.

Leonard, E. K., *The Onset of Global Governance. International Relations Theory and the International Criminal Court* (Aldershot, UK: Ashgate, 2004).

——— 'Discovering the New Face of Sovereignty. Complementarity and the International Criminal Court', *New Political Science*, 27 (2005), 87–104.

Lessig, L., 'Erie-Effects of Volume 110: An Essay on Context in Interpretive Theory', *Harvard Law Review*, 110 (1997), 1785–1812.

Lieven, A., *America Right or Wrong. An Anatomy of American Nationalism* (London: HarperCollins, 2004).

Lind, M., *The Next American Nation. The New Nationalism and the Fourth American Revolution* (London: Free Press, 1995).

Linklater, A., 'What Is a Good International Citizen?', in Paul Keal (ed.), *Ethics and Foreign Policy* (London: Allen and Unwin, 1992), 21–41.

——— 'Citizenship and Sovereignty in the Post-Westphalian State', *European Journal of International Relations*, 2 (1996), 77–103.

——— *The Transformation of Political Community. Ethical Foundation of the Post-Westphalian Era* (Oxford: Polity Press, 1998).

——— 'Citizenship and Sovereignty in the Post-Westphalian European State', in D. Archibugi, D. Held, and M. Kohler (eds.), *Re-Imagining Political Community. Studies in Cosmopolitan Democracy* (Oxford: Polity Press, 1998).

——— 'Cosmopolitan Citizenship', in K. Hutchings and R. Dannreuther (eds.), *Cosmopolitan Citizenship* (Basingstoke, UK: Macmillan, 1999).

——— 'The Good International Citizen and the Crisis in Kosovo', in A. Schnabel and R. Thakur (eds.), *Kosovo and the Challenge of Humanitarian Intervention. Selective Indignation, Collective Action, and International Citizenship* (Tokyo, New York, and Paris: United Nations University Press, 2000).

——— and Suganami, Hidemi, *The English School of International Relations. A Contemporary Reassessment* (Cambridge: Cambridge University Press, 2006).

Little, R., 'International System, International Society and World Society: A Re-Evaluation of the English School', in B. A. Roberson (ed.), *International Society and the Development of International Relations Theory* (London: Pinter, 1998).

——— 'The English School's Contribution to the Study of International Relations', *European Journal of International Relations*, 6 (2000), 395–422.

——— 'The English School vs. American Realism: A Meeting of Minds Divided by a Common Language?', *Review of International Studies*, 29 (2003), 443–60.

Lowe, A. V., 'Do General Rules of International Law Exist?', *Review of International Studies*, 9 (1983), 207–13.

Lynch, C., 'European Countries Cut Deal to Protect Afghan Peacekeepers', *Washington Post*, 20 June 2002.

——— 'U.S. Seeks Court Immunity for E. Timor Peacekeepers', *Washington Post*, 16 May 2002.

——— 'Bush Promises to Try To Save Bosnia Mission. U.S. Immunity to War Court Is Key', *Washington Post*, 3 July 2002.

——— 'US, Europe Debate Venue for Darfur Trials', *Washington Post*, 20 January 2005.

Lynch, C., 'UN Council's Resolution on Atrocities in Sudan is Passed', *Washington Post*, 1 April 2005.

Macedo, S. (ed.), *Universal Jurisdiction: National Courts and the Prosecution of Serious Crimes Under International Law* (Philadelphia, PA: University of Pennsylvannia Press, 2006).

Macmillan, J., 'A Kantian Protest Against the Peculiar Discourse of Inter-Liberal State Peace', *Millennium Journal of International Studies*, 24 (1994), 549–62.

MacPherson, B., 'Authority of the Security Council to Exempt Peacekeepers from the International Criminal Court Proceedings', *ASIL Insights*, (2002), 89.

Magliveras, K. and Bourantonis, D., 'Rescinding the Signature of an International Treaty: The United States and the Rome Statute Establishing the International Criminal Court', *Diplomacy and Statecraft*, 14 (2003), 21–49.

MaGuire, P., *Law and War. An American Story* (New York: Columbia University Press, 2001).

Malanczuk, P., *Akehurst's Modern Introduction to International Law*, 7th edn. (London and New York: Routledge, 2003).

Marschik, A., 'The Politics of Prosecution: European National Approaches to War Crimes', in T. L. H. McCormack and G. J. Simpson (eds.), *The Law of War Crimes. National and International Approaches* (The Hague: Kluwer, 1997).

Mayall, J., 'Introduction', in James Mayall (ed.), *The Community of States* (London: Allen and Unwin, 1982).

McDougall, W. A., *Promised Land, Crusader State: The American Encounter with the World since 1776* (Boston, MA: Houghton Mifflin, 1997).

McGoldrick, D., 'Political and Legal Responses to the ICC', in D. McGoldrick, P. Rowe, and E. Donnelly (eds.), *The Permanent International Criminal Court. Legal and Policy Issues* (Oxford and Portland, OR: Hart, 2004).

Mead, W. R., *Special Providence: American Foreign Policy and How It Changed the World* (New York: Knopf, 2001).

Mégret, F., 'Epilogue to an Endless Debate: The International Criminal Court's Third Party Jurisdiction and the Looming Revolution in International Law', *European Journal of International Law*, 12 (2001), 247–68.

Mendelsohn B., 'Sovereignty under Attack: The International Society Meets Al Qaeda Network', *Review of International Studies*, 31 (2005), 45–68.

Meron, T., 'The Time Has Come for the United States to Ratify Geneva Protocol I', *The American Journal of International Law*, 88 (1994), 678–86.

_____ *Human Rights and Humanitarian Norms as Customary Law* (Oxford: Clarendon Press, 1989).

Miller, D., 'Bounded Citizenship', in K. Hutchings and R. Dannreuther (eds.), *Cosmopolitan Citizenship* (Basingstoke, UK: Macmillan, 1999).

Morris, M., 'High Crimes and Misconceptions: The ICC and Non-Party States', *Law and Contemporary Problems*, 64 (2001), 13–66.

_____ 'Universal Jurisdiction in a Divided World', *New England Law Review*, 35 (2001), 337–61.

Mosler, H., *The International Community as a Legal Community* (Alphen aan den Rijn, the Netherlands: Sijthoff and Noordhoff, 1980).

Murphy, J., *The United States and the Rule of Law in International Affairs* (Cambridge: Cambridge University Press, 2004).

Myrdal, G., *An American Dilemma: The Negro Problem and Modern Democracy* (New York: HarperCollins, 1962).

Nardin, T., *Law, Morality, and the Relations of Nations* (Princeton, NJ: Princeton University Press, 1983).

_____ 'Legal Positivism as a Theory of International Society', in D. R. Mapel and T. Nardin (eds.), *International Society: Diverse Ethical Perspectives* (Princeton, NJ: Princeton University Press, 1998).

Neha, J., 'A Separate Law for Peacekeepers: The Clash between the Security Council and the International Criminal Court', *European Journal of International Law*, 16 (2005), 239–54.

Nel, P., 'Between Counter-Hegemony and Post-Hegemony: The Rome Statute and Normative Innovation in World Politics', in A. F. Cooper, J. English, and R. Thakur (eds.), *Enhancing Global Governance: Towards a New Diplomacy?* (United Nations University Press, 2002).

Neuman, G. L., 'Sense and Nonsense about Customary International Law: A Response to Professors Bradley and Goldsmith', *Fordham Law Review*, 66 (1997), 371–92.

Neumann, I. B., 'The English School and the Practices of World Society', *Review of International Studies*, 27 (2001), 503–7.

Noortmann, M., 'Non-State Actors in International Law', in M. Noortmann, B. Arts, and B. Reinalda (eds.), *Non-State Actors in International Relations* (Aldershot, UK: Ashgate, 2001).

Onuf, N., 'The Constitution of International Society', *European Journal of International Law*, 5 (1994), 1–19.

Paulus, A. L., 'The Influence of the United States on the Concept of the "International Community"', in Ambers and G. Nolte (eds.), *United States Hegemony and the Foundations of International Law* (Cambridge: Cambridge University Press, 2003).

_____ and Simma, B., 'The "International Community": Facing the Challenge of Globalization. General Conclusions', *European Journal of International Law*, 9 (1998), 266–77.

Perkins, J. A., 'The Changing Foundations of International Law: From State Consent to State Responsibility', *Boston University International Law Journal*, 15 (1997), 433–510.

Popovski, V., 'International Criminal Court. A Necessary Step Towards Global Justice', *Security Dialogue*, 31 (2000), 405–19.

Prosper, P., Remarks on Darfur, War Crimes, The ICC and the Quest for Justice, The Brookings Institute, 22 February 2005, at www.brookings.edu/comm/events/20050225.pdf

Rabkin, J., 'Is EU Policy Eroding the Sovereignty of Non-Member States?', *Chicago Journal of International Law*, 1 (2000), 273–90.

Rabkin, J., 'The Politics of the Geneva Conventions: Disturbing Background to the ICC Debate', *Virginia Journal of International Law*, 44 (2003), 169–205.

Ratner, S. R. and Abrams, J. S., *Accountability for Human Rights Atrocities in International Law. Beyond the Nuremberg Legacy* (Oxford: Oxford University Press, 2001).

Ralph, J., 'High Stakes and Low-Intensity Democracy. Understanding America's Policy of Promoting Democracy', in M. Cox, T. Inoguchi, and G. J. Ikenberry (eds.), *American Democracy Promotion. Impulses, Strategies, and Impacts* (Oxford: Oxford University Press, 2000).

Ramanathan, U., 'India and the ICC', *Journal of International Criminal Justice*, 3 (2005), 627–34.

Reagan, R., Letter of Transmittal, The White House, 29 January 1987. Reprinted in 'Agora: The US Decision Not to Ratify Protocol I to the Geneva Conventions on the Protection of War Victims', *American Journal of International Law*, 81 (1987), 910–2.

Remec, P., *The Position of the Individual in International Law According to Grotius and Vattel* (The Hague: Martinus Nijhoff, 1960).

Reus-Smit, C., 'The Constitutional Structure of International Society and the Nature of Fundamental Institutions', *International Organization*, 51 (1997), 555–89.

—— (ed.), *The Politics of International Law* (Cambridge: Cambridge University Press, 2004).

Reydams, L., 'Universal Criminal Jurisdiction: The Belgian State of Affairs', *Criminal Law Forum*, 11 (2000), 183–216.

—— 'Belgium Reneges on Universality: The 5 August 2003 Act on Grave Breaches of International Humanitarian Law', *Journal of International Criminal Justice*, 1 (2003), 679–89.

Rice, C., 'Promoting the National Interest', *Foreign Affairs*, 79 (2000), 45–62.

Rivkin Jr., D. B. and Casey, L. A., 'Crimes Outside the World's Jurisdiction', *New York Times*, 22 July 2003.

Roach, S. C., *Politicizing the International Criminal Court. The Convergence of Politics, Ethics and Law* (Lanham, MD: Rowman and Littlefield, 2006).

—— 'US Foreign Policy and the International Criminal Court: Towards a Third Way of Strategic Accommodation', *International Politics*, 43 (2006), 53–70.

Roberts, A., 'Counter-Terrorism, Armed Force and the Laws of War', *Survival*, 44 (2002), 7–32.

—— and Guelff, R. (eds.), *Documents on the Laws of War* (Oxford: Oxford University Press, 2003).

Roberts, G. B., 'The New Rules for Waging War: The Case against Ratification of Additional Protocol I', *Virginia Journal of International Law*, 26 (1985), 109–70.

Robertson, G., 'There Is a Legal Way Out of This', *The Guardian*, 14 September 2001.

—— 'Lynch Mob Justice or a Proper Trial', *The Guardian*, 5 October 2001.

Ruggie, J. G., 'American Exceptionalism, Exceptionalism, and Global Governance', in Michael Ignatieff (ed.), *American Exceptionalism and Human Rights* (Princeton, NJ and Oxford: Princeton University Press, 2005), 304–8.

Sadat, L. N., *The International Criminal Court and the Transformation of International Law. Justice for the New Millennium* (Ardsley, NY: Transnational, 2002).

_____ and Carden, S. R., 'The New International Criminal Court. An Uneasy Revolution', *Georgetown Law Journal*, 88 (2000), 381–474.

Sandoz, Y., Christophe, S., and Zimmerman, B. (eds.), *Commentary on the Additional Protocols of 8 June 1977 to the Geneva Conventions of 12 August 1949* (Geneva: Martinus Nijhoff Publishers for the International Committee of the Red Cross, 1987).

Sands, P., *Lawless World. America and the Making and Breaking of Global Rules* (London: Allen Lane, 2005).

_____ 'International Law: Alive and Kicking', *The Guardian*, 17 May 2005.

Sarooshi, D., 'The Peace and Justice Paradox: The International Criminal Court and the UN Security Council', in D. McGoldrick, P. Rowe, and E. Donnelly (eds.), *The Permanent International Criminal Court. Legal and Policy Issues* (Oxford and Portland, OR: Hart, 2004).

Schabas, W. A., *An Introduction to the International Criminal Court* (Cambridge: Cambridge University Press, 2004).

_____ 'United States Hostility to the International Criminal Court: It's All about the Security Council', *European Journal of International Law*, 15 (2004), 701–20.

_____ 'The Unfinished Work of Defining Aggression: How Many Times Must the Cannonballs Fly, before They Are Forever Banned?', in D. McGoldrick, P. Rowe, and E. Donnelly (eds.), *The Permanent Court International Criminal Court. Legal and Policy Issues* (Oxford and Portland, OR: Hart, 2004).

_____ First Report of the International Law Association, Berlin Conference (2004), International Criminal Court, at www.ila-hq.org/

_____ 'Darfur and the "Odious Scourge": The Commission of Inquiry's Findings on Genocide', *Leiden Journal of International Law*, 18 (2005), 871–85.

Scharf, M., 'The ICC's Jurisdiction over the Nationals of Non-Party States', in S. B. Sewall and C. Kaysen (eds.), *The United States and the International Criminal Court* (London: Rowman and Littlefield, 2000), 213–36.

_____ 'The ICC's Jurisdiction over the Nationals of Non-Party States: A Critique of the US Position', *Law and Contemporary Problems*, 64 (2001), 67–117.

Scheffer, D. J., 'International Criminal Court: The Challenge of Jurisdiction', Address to Annual Meeting of the American Society of International Law, Washington, DC, 26 March 1999, at: www.state.gov/documents/organization/6552.doc

_____ Head of the US Delegation to the UN Diplomatic Conference on the Establishment of a Permanent International Criminal Court, Testimony Before the Senate Foreign Relations Committee, 23 July 1998.

_____ 'The United States and the International Criminal Court', *American Journal of International Law*, 93 (1999), 12–22.

_____ 'Staying the Course with the International Criminal Court', *Cornell International Law Journal*, 47 (2002), 47–100.

_____ 'Original Intent at the Global Criminal Court', *Wall Street Journal* [Europe], 20 September 2002.

_____ 'Article 98 (2) of the Rome Statute: America's Original Intent', *Journal of International Criminal Justice*, 3 (2005), 333–53.

Schmidt, H. and Take, I., 'Democratization without Representation', in M. Albert, L. Brock, and K. D. Wolf, (eds.), *Civilizing World Politics. Society and Community Beyond the State* (Lanham, MD, Boulder, CO, New York, and London: Rowman and Littlefield, 2000).

Sewall, S. B. and Kaysen, C. (eds.), *The United States and the International Criminal Court* (Lanham, MD, Boulder, CO, New York, and Oxford: Rowman and Littlefield, 2000).

Simma, B. and Paulus, A. L., 'The "International Community": Facing the Challenge of Globalization. General Conclusions', *European Journal of International Law*, 9 (1998), 266–77.

Simons, M., 'Dutch Court Puts Former Congo Officer on Trial in Torture Case', *New York Times*, 25 March 2004.

Skordas, A., 'Hegemonic Custom?', in Michael Byers and Georg Nolte (eds.), *United States Hegemony and the Foundations of International Law* (Cambridge: Cambridge University Press, 2003).

Smith, T. W., 'The New Law of War: Legitimizing Hi-Tech and Infrastructural Violence', *International Studies Quarterly*, 46 (2002).

Sofaer, A., 'Terrorism and the Law', *Foreign Affairs*, 64 (1986), 901–22.

——— 'Agora: The US Decision Not to Ratify Protocol I to the Geneva Conventions on the Protection of War Victims (cont'd)', *American Journal of International Law*, 82 (1988), 784–7.

Spees, P., 'Women's Advocacy in the Creation of the International Criminal Court: Changing Landscapes of Justice and Power', *Signs: Journal of Women in Culture and Society*, 28 (2003), 1233–54.

Spiro, P. J., 'The New Sovereigntists. American Exceptionalism and Its False Prophets', *Foreign Affairs*, 79 (2000), 9–15.

Sriram, C. L., 'Review Article. New Mechanisms, Old Problems? Recent Books on Universal Jurisdiction and Mixed Tribunals', *International Affairs*, 80 (2004), 971–9.

Stahn, C., 'The Ambiguities of Security Council Resolution 1422 (2002)', *European Journal of International Law*, 14 (2003), 85–104.

Stephan, P. B., 'International Governance and American Democracy', *Chicago Journal of International Law*, 1 (2000), 237–56.

Steyn, Lord J., 'Guantánamo Bay: The Legal Black Hole. 27th F. A. Mann Lecture, 25 November 2003', reprinted in *International and Comparative Law Quarterly*, 53 (2004), 1–15.

Sylvester, D. J., 'International Law as Sword or Shield? Early American Foreign Policy and the Law of Nations', *International Law and Politics*, 32 (1999), 1–87.

Thiessen, M. A., 'When Worlds Collide', *Foreign Policy*, 123 (2001), 64–74.

Toope, S., 'Powerful but unpersuasive? The Role of the United States in the Evolution of Customary International Law', in M. Byers and G. Nolte (eds.), *United States Hegemony and the Foundations of International Law* (Cambridge: Cambridge University Press, 2003).

Turns, D., 'Aspects of National Implementation of the Rome Statute: The United Kingdom and Selected Other States', in D. McGoldrick, P. Rowe, and E. Donnelly (eds.), *The Permanent International Criminal Court. Legal and Policy Issues* (Oxford and Portland, OR: Hart, 2004).

United Nations, *Report of the Secretary-General Pursuant to General-Assembly Resolution 53/35. The Fall of Srebrenica,* (1999), at: www.un.org/peace/srebrenica.pdf

____ *Report of the Independent Inquiry into the Actions of the United Nations During the 1994 Genocide in Rwanda,* (1999), at: www.un.org/News/dh/latest/rwanda.htm

Van Der Vyver, J. D., 'Civil Society and the International Criminal Court', *Journal of Human Rights,* 2 (2003), 425–39.

Van Der Wilt, H., 'Bilateral Agreements between the United States and States Parties to the Rome Statute: Are They Compatible with the Object and Purpose of the Statute?', *Leiden Journal of International Law,* 18 (2005), 93–111.

Van Elst, R., 'Implementing Universal Jurisdiction over Grave Breaches of the Geneva Convention', *Leiden Journal of International Law,* 13 (2000), 815–54.

Vattel, E. de, *The Law of Nations or the Principles of Natural Law Applied to the Conduct and to the Affairs of Nations and of Sovereigns* (Washington, DC: Carnegie Institution of Washington, [1758] 1916).

Vigezzi, B., *The British Committee on the Theory of International Politics (1954–1985)* (Milan, Italy: Edzioni Unicopli, 2005).

Vincent, J., *Human Rights and International Relations* (Cambridge: Cambridge University Press, 1986).

____ 'Western Conceptions of a Universal Moral Order', *British Journal of International Studies,* 4 (1978), 20–46.

von Bogdandy, A., 'Constitutionalism in International Law. Comment on a Proposal from Germany', *Harvard International Law Journal,* 47 (2006), 223–42.

Waltz, K., *Theory of International Politics* (New York, London: McGraw-Hill, 1979).

Wedgwood, R., 'The International Criminal Court: An American View', *European Journal of International Law,* 10 (1999), 93–107.

____ 'The Constitution and the ICC', in S. B. Sewall and C. Kaysen (eds.), *The United States and the International Criminal Court* (London: Rowman and Littlefield, 2000), 119–36.

____ 'The Law of War: How Osama Slipped Away', *National Interest,* 66 (2001/2), 69–73.

____ 'Al Qaeda, Terrorism and Military Commissions', *American Journal of International Law,* 96 (2002), 328–37.

Weisburd, A. M., 'State Courts, Federal Courts and International Cases', *Yale Journal of International Law,* 20 (1995), 1–64.

____ 'American Judges and International Law', *Vanderbilt Journal of Transnational Law,* 36 (2003), 1475–1532.

Weller, M., 'Undoing the Global Constitution: UN Security Council Action on the International Criminal Court', *International Affairs,* 78 (2002), 693–712.

Wenig, J. M., 'Enforcing the Lessons of History: Israel Judges the Holocaust', in T. L. H. McCormack and G. J. Simpson (eds.), *The Law of War Crimes. National and International Approaches* (The Hague: Kluwer, 1997), 103–22.

Weschler, L., 'Exceptional Cases in Rome: The United States and the Struggle for an ICC', in Sarah B. Sewall and Carl Kaysen (eds.), *The United States and the*

International Criminal Court (Lanham, MD, Boulder, CO, New York, and Oxford: Rowman and Littlefield, 2000).

Wheeler, N. J., 'Pluralist or Solidarist Conceptions of International Society—Bull and Vincent on Humanitarian Intervention', *Millennium Journal of International Studies*, 21 (1992), 463–87.

—— *Saving Strangers. Humanitarian Intervention in International Society* (Oxford: Oxford University Press, 2000).

Whelan, F. G., 'Legal Positivism and International Society', in D. R. Mapel and T. Nardin (eds.), *International Society: Diverse Ethical Perspectives* (Princeton, NJ: Princeton University Press, 1998).

White, R. A., *Breaking Silence: The Case That Changed the Face of Human Rights* (Washington, DC: Georgetown University Press, 2004).

Wight, M., *International Theory. The Three Traditions*, Gabriele Wight and Brian Porter (eds.) (Leicester, UK and London: RIIA, 1991).

Wilkinson, B., 'Princeton Principles', in Stephen Macedo (ed.), *Universal Jurisdiction: National Courts and the Prosecution of Serious Crimes under International Law* (Philadelphia, PA: University of Pennsylvannia Press, 2006).

Williams, J., 'Pluralism, Solidarism, and the Emergence of World Society in English School Theory', *International Relations*, 19 (2005), 19–38.

Williams, S., 'Laudable Principles Lacking Application: The Prosecution of War Criminals in Canada', in T. L. H. McCormack and G. J. Simpson (eds.), *The Law of War Crimes. National and International Approaches* (The Hague: Kluwer, 1997).

Wippman, D., 'The International Criminal Court', in Christian Reus-Smit (ed.), *The Politics of International Law* (Cambridge: Cambridge University Press, 2004), 151–188.

Wirth, S., 'Immunity for Core Crimes? The ICJ's Judgement in the *Congo* v. *Belgium* Case', *European Journal of International Law*, 13 (2002), 877–93.

Woodhouse, D. (ed.), *The Pinochet Case. A Legal and Constitutional Analysis* (Oxford and Portland, OR: Hart, 2000).

Zappalà, S., 'Do Heads of State in Office Enjoy Immunity from Jurisdiction for International Crimes? The *Ghaddafi* Case before the French *Cour de Cassation*', *European Journal of Law*, 12 (2001), 595–612.

—— 'The Reaction of the US to the Entry into Force of the ICC Statute: Comments on the UN SC Resolution 1422 (2002) and Article 98 Agreements', *International Journal of Criminal Justice*, 1 (2003), 114–34.

Zwanenburg, M., 'The Statute of an International Criminal Court and the United States: Peacekeepers under Fire?', *European Journal of International Law*, 10 (1999), 124–43.

Cases

The Case of the S.S. "Lotus", Permanent Court of International Justice, 7 September 1927, at: www.worldcourts.com/pcij/eng/decisions/1927.09.07_lotus/

The Paquete Habana, 175 U.S. 677 (1900)

Filártiga v. *Peña-Irala*, 630 F.2d. 30 June 1980.

Tel-Oren v. *Libyan Arab Republic*, 726 F.2d 774 (DC Cir. 1984).

Regina v. *Bartle and the Commissioner of Police for the Metropolis and Others EX Parte Pinochet (on appeal from a Divisional Court of the Queen's Bench)*, 24 March 1999, at: www.publications.parliament.uk/pa/ld199899/ldjudgmt/jd990324/pino1.htm

Regina v. *Bartle and the Commissioner of Police for the Metropolis and Others EX Parte Pinochet (on appeal from a Divisional Court of the Queen's Bench)*, 28 November 1998, at: www.publications.parliament.uk/pa/ld199697/ldjudgmt/ldjudgmt.htm

Case Concerning the Arrest Warrant of 11 April 2000 (*Congo* v. *Belgium*) 14 February 2002, at: www.icj-cij.org/icjwww/idocket/iCOBE/iCOBEframe.htm

Case concerning the Military and Paramilitary Activities in and against Nicaragua (*Nicaragua* v. *United States of America*), Judgment of June 1986.

R (Abbasi and another) v. *Secretary of State for Foreign and Commonwealth Affairs* [2002] EWCA Civ. 1598.

Rasul v. *Bush*, 215 F.Supp. 2d 55 (DC Dist. 2002), LEXIS 14031

Al Odah et al. v. *United States*, 321 F.3d 1134 (DC Cir. 2003), LEXIS 4250.

Rasul v. *Bush*, 542 U.S. 466 (2004), LEXIS 4760.

Hamden v. *Rumsfeld*, 344 F.Supp. 2d 152; 2004 US Dist. LEXIS 22724.

Hamden v. *Rumsfeld*, 367 US App. D.C. 265; 415 F.3d 33, 2005 US App. LEXIS 14315.

Hamden v. *Rumsfeld*, No. 05–184, Supreme Court of the United States, 2006, LEXIS 5185.

Sosa v. *Alvarez-Machain*, No. 03–339, Supreme Court of the United States, 2004.

Treaties

Vienna Convention on Diplomatic Relations (1961) April 18, U.N. Doc. at: untreaty.un.org/ilc/texts/instruments/English/conventions/9_1_1961.pdf

Vienna Convention on the Law of Treaties (1969) May 23, U.N. Doc. A/Conf. 39/27, at: www.un.org/law/ilc/texts/treaties.htm

Protocol Additional to the Geneva Conventions of 12 August 1949, and relating to the Protection of Victims of International Armed Conflicts (Protocol I), 8 June 1977, at:

Protocol Additional to the Geneva Conventions of 12 August 1949, and relating to the Protection of Victims of Non-International Armed Conflicts (Protocol II), 8 June 1977, at: www.icrc.org/

The Rome Statute of the International Criminal Court, U.N. Doc. A/CONF.183/9*, at: www.un.org/law/icc/statute/romefra.htm

Documents

Brief for the United States as Respondent Supporting the Petitioner *Sosa* v. *Alvarez-Machain* (2004).

Common Position 2001/443/CFSP of 11 June 2001, Official Journal of the European Communities, L 155/19.

Common Position 2002/474/CFSP of 20 June 2002, Official Journal of the European Communities, L 164/1.

CICC, Proposed Text of Article 98 Agreements with the United States, July 2002, emphasis added, www.iccnow.org

EU Guiding Principles concerning arrangements between a State Party to the Rome Statute of the International Criminal Court and the United States regarding the conditions to Surrender of Persons to the Court, 30 September 2002, www.iccnow.org

Counsel of Europe, Parliamentary Assembly Resolution 1300 adopted 25 September 2002 and Report of the Committee on Legal Affairs and Human Rights of the Council of Europe, Threats to the International Criminal Court, 24 June 2003, assembly.coe.int

Department of Defense, *Quadrennial Defense Review Report*, February 6, 2006.

Index